Complex Adaptive Leadership

I dedicate this Second Edition of my book to my family, loyal friends and to all those who take these ideas out and across the world.

Complex Adaptive Leadership

Embracing Paradox and Uncertainty

SECOND EDITION

NICK OBOLENSKY

LONDON AND NEW YORK

First published 2014 by Gower Publishing

Published 2016 by Taylor & Francis

2 Park Square, Milton Park, Abingdon, Oxon OX14 4RN

711 Third Avenue, New York, NY 10017, USA

Routledge is an imprint of the Taylor & Francis Group, an informa business

Gower Applied Business Research
Our programme provides leaders, practitioners, scholars and researchers with thought provoking, cutting edge books that combine conceptual insights, interdisciplinary rigour and practical relevance in key areas of business and management.

British Library Cataloguing in Publication Data
A catalogue record for this book is available from the British Library.

The Library of Congress has cataloged the printed edition as follows:
Obolensky, Nick.
  Complex adaptive leadership : embracing paradox and uncertainty / by Nick Obolensky.
     pages cm.
  Revised edition of the author's Complex adaptive leadership published in 2010.
  Includes bibliographical references and index.
  ISBN 978-1-4724-4791-3 (hardback) -- ISBN 978-1-4724-4793-7 (ebook) --
ISBN 978-1-4724-4792-0 (epub) 1. Leadership--Philosophy. 2. Organizational behavior.
3. Management--Employee participation. I. Title.
  HD57.7.O265 2014
  658.4'092--dc23

                                                                            2014016621

ISBN: 978-1-4724-4791-3 (pbk)

Contents

List of Figures

Acknowledgements

Many helped in creating the first edition of this book. I would particularly like to thank Professor Jonathan Gosling at the Centre for Leadership, Exeter University for his advice and support when many others had given up; Mike Williams, author of many books on leadership; Professor Julian Birkinshaw at London Business School for his support, advice and friendship; Dr Mark Dennis at Bristol University for his help with matters scientific and mathematic; and Jerry Cowhig at the Institute of Physics Publishing for helping arrange a review.

With regards to the updated Second Edition in paperback, I would like to thank all the associates of Complex Adaptive Leadership Ltd around the world who have played a role in taking the ideas out into business to good effect, and to our multi-national clients and their thousands of managers who have had the courage to take a new approach to leadership, better attuned to the twenty-first century, and apply it to good effect.

Reviews of
Complex Adaptive Leadership

'...a startlingly worthwhile read for a business manager keen to develop a practical understanding of different strategies with which to engage subordinates...a clever integration of ideas about leadership as well as a practical guide...of most use to managers making the transition from middle to more senior management levels, as well as to leadership coaches...an entertaining, highly readable, well set out and informative book.'

Integral Leadership Review, 2012

'We love Nick Obolensky's writing. He is erudite, enthusiastic and fascinating in equal measure, and offers perspectives on leading in a complex environment that may bring a "eureka" moment for a number of readers.'

Project Management Institute UK, 2012

'Obolensky's work is a marvellous resource that connects adaptive leadership with complexity science. I would recommend (the) book to those graduate-level students of leadership who are seeking to gain a deeper understanding of the ways in which macro and micro currents of chaos and complexity are inviting continued organizational evolution and adaptive leadership. This book will also be a strong support to researchers and scholars.'

Leadership and Organizational Development Journal, 2011

'...provides an excellent conceptual framework that permits a comprehensive analysis of every aspect of leadership...'

First Trust Bank Economic Outlook and Business Review, 2010

'Drawing upon a wide range of wisdom and ideas, from Lao Tzu to Lorenz and modern chaos theory, Obolensky brilliantly argues the case for organisations and their leaders to adapt to the complex, uncertain world of today and tomorrow. He also proffers excellent practical advice on how to do so.'

Philip Sadler CBE, Vice-president, Ashridge Business School, Senior Fellow, Tomorrow's Company, 2010

'A true tour de force, in a class of its own from being well-grounded both in the science and in practical experiences.'

Margaret J. Wheatley, author of *Leadership and the New Science* and other books, 2010

'*Chaos and order: the perpetual tension that drives and binds any organisation. What should leadership do – conserve order or inspire creativity and change? In this wonderfully clear, thorough and provocative book Obolensky describes leadership as a fusion of anarchy and oligarchy, and shows how things really get done – through polyarchy. This book is a must-read for anyone seriously interested in understanding what is happening to authority, initiative and influence in contemporary organizations; leaders who value conceptual clarity about their predicament will find it invaluable.*'
Professor Jonathan Gosling, Centre for Leadership Studies, Exeter University, UK, 2009

'*This book provides a novel, provocative and useful approach to leadership, which I have seen put to good use by Professor Obolensky with senior executives in London Business School's Centre for Management Development. Today, leaders have to be able to work in a complex and fast-changing environment, and to do this effectively means challenging a lot of the traditional assumptions about the nature of leadership. This book does a terrific job of introducing some new thinking about leadership, while also keeping the reader's feet firmly on the ground. You will enjoy the mind-stretching concepts, the witty anecdotes, and the practical advice Professor Obolensky offers up in this book.*'
Julian Birkinshaw, Professor of Strategic & International Management,
London Business School, UK, 2009

'*So much of the research into leadership is old wine in new bottles. Obolensky's work, without doubt, represents ground-breaking thinking and offers significant new perspectives.*'
Mike Williams, author of *Mastering Leadership*, 2009

From Amazon.com readers' reviews:

'*...an essential contribution to knowledge management.*'

'*...a very comprehensive and helpful review of thinking around complex adaptive thinking.*'

'*...a great book with a lot of great visuals and information from research findings and I found it intellectually stimulating.*'

'*...accessible, relevant, easily applicable and fabulously well referenced with lots of interesting and illuminating stories and anecdotes...an invaluable resource which deserves to be highly influential.*'

'*Time will show, I believe, that these theories and practices allow individuals to grow faster, contribute more, ensure greater stability, and, most importantly, allow individual autonomy.*'

Since the publication of the First Edition the approach in this book has been tried and tested by over 1,000 managers and executives in over 30 countries and 20 industries around the world. Below are some quotations from those who have been trained in the Complex Adaptive Leadership approach, mostly taken several weeks after their programme. Identities have been withheld for client confidentiality (available on request):

Munich, Germany, 2014:
'Complex Adaptive Leadership (CAL), has delivered powerful leadership development to hundreds of our senior managers in our MNC around the world. The programmes are innovative, engaging and ensure specific actions which help move our organisation forward. This leading edge approach is changing the management DNA of our company...'

Beijing, China, 2013:
'I have seen many leadership models in my time as an HR Leadership and Talent Development professional. However, I recently saw the CAL (Complex Adaptive Leadership) approach delivered here in Beijing and I believe it is the best western model that suits the Chinese culture and psyche. The feedback from the participants has been very positive and they all gained great insights in how to manage themselves, their teams and their managers better.'

Munich, Germany, 2013:
'Complex Adaptive Leadership helped me as a leader to focus on what matters, setting in place the framework for the team to work, and identified techniques to use in interpersonal / leadership situations. I would highly recommend it.'

Texas, USA, 2013:
"It was really an enlightening experience – definitely exceeded my expectations."

Gurgaon, India, 2013:
'Complex Adaptive Leadership guided me to overcome the general assumptions we carry during our leadership which need to be overcome and adapted as per the situations. Complexity science is a true way of understanding multiple transitions and make better decisions in complex situations.'

Singapore, 2013:
'One of the most inspiring business programs I have ever had. Hands-on experience mixed with deep theoretical knowledge, but applied with a well balanced mix of tutorials, discussions, and theoretical and practical exercises.'

Helsinki, Finland, 2013
'I am now regularly leaving complex tasks to my team, and let them solve it themselves. I am also now exposing them to greater extent to management, which is a great learning for the guys and it enables me to focus on productive things.'

Athens, Greece, 2013:
'In the past I participated in several "Leadership" workshops with various theories. Complex Adaptive Leadership was the most important, useful and "down to the Earth".'

Shanghai, China, 2013:
'Highly valuable for any leaders to ensure the right focus on tasks that really create an impact (and not waste time on others). Highly recommended!'

Paris, France, 2013:
'Great, fresh approach to leadership. Positive message of empowerment with useful strategies and tactics to improve organisational performance.'

Moscow, Russia, 2013:
'Excellent – a really useful seminar. All the participants were actively involved. Good at helping to set priorities and it was really interesting.'

Birmingham, UK, 2012:
'The Complex Adaptive Leadership approach successfully challenged all the traditional learning about leadership.'

Jakarta, Indonesia, 2012:
'Excellent learning! Lots of valuable management working tools and mind opening experiences and radical ideas to change the mindset.'

Riga, Latvia, 2012:
'What I liked most was learning that for more complex systems there is no necessity to have big direct leadership.'

MBA programme, USA:
'I found it fascinating to the point that I couldn't wait for the next module to keep going. The text book by Obolensky was excellent – and definitely a keeper...'

London, UK, 2011:
'Having attended many such courses over quite some number of years, I would (even a year on) consider Complex Adaptive Leadership to be at the very top for engagement & content.'

Netherlands, 2011:
'Before I was critical given the length of the program, but now I can say: worth every minute!'

Hong Kong, 2011:
'Our Firm's Managing Director promotion event entailed a half day piece around Complex Adaptive Leadership. The journey getting there was fantastic throughout.'

Portugal, 2011:
'Good approach breaking down problems. Lots of practical examples and exercises.'

Preface to the Second Edition

This preface will not repeat nor replace the preface to the First Edition which follows, but rather gives a quick summary to what has been changed for the Second Edition, and why.

Since its publication in mid 2010 'Complex Adpative Leadership – Embracing Paradox and Uncertainty' has become a bestseller in Gower's lists and this Second Edition is in paperback form. The success of the book owes much to the fact the subject of 'Complexity' is gaining much more attention, as is the relatively new area of Complexity Science.[1] The reason is clear – growing complexity in the world. Complexity is generally seen as a problem. However, this book shows that complexity is not so much a value destroying problem as a value creating opportunity. If understood, complexity can be leveraged for organisational and individual advantage. The Second Edition adds the following to the First Edition:

1. New research: Since its publication in 2010 wider research into complexity and its effect on organisations has been published in various papers and this edition takes some of that into account. Of special mention should be:

   a) An IBM Study[2] which interviewed over 1,500 CEOs around the world in 2009/2010 to find out what their pressing issues were. The #1 issue identified was growing complexity and 70 per cent of CEOs considered most executives were poorly placed to handle it.

   b) Harvard Business Review's series of three articles under the heading 'Spotlight on Managing Complex Organisations'[3] was published in September 2011. These furthered the links between the area of complexity research with leadership of organisations, adding some good models and suggestions.

2. New books: A range of new books, based on research by leading academics was published around the same time as the publication of the First Edition. These included work by those who subsequently became associates of Complex Adaptive Leadership Ltd (see http://www.complexadaptiveleadership.com/global-team) including work by Mary Uhl Bien,[4] Julian Birkinshaw,[5] and Jules Goddard.[6] Other books and articles which add to this edition includes work by Ronald Heifitz et al.[7] (who coined the phrase 'Adaptive Leadership' around the same time as the first edition) and continued work

---

1   Many have not heard of this new area of scientific endeavour but it is increasingly growing and Stephen Hawking is often quoted as saying the twenty-first century will be one of complexity.

2   IBM Global CEO report (2010) 'Capitalising on Complexity'.

3   *Harvard Business Review* (September 2011) 'Focus on managing complex organisations': Sullivan, T. 'Embracing Complexity – An interview with Michael J. Mauboussin'; Morieux Y. 'Smart Rules – Six ways to get people to solve problems without you'; Sargut, G. and Gunter McGrath, R. 'Learning to live with complexity – how to make sense of the unpredictable and the undefinable in todays's hyperconnected business world'.

4   Uhl-Bein M. and Marion, R. (Eds) (2007) *Complexity Leadership: Part 1: Conceptual Foundations (Leadership Horizons)*, Information Age Publishing.

5   Birkinshaw, J. (2010) *Reinventing Management: Smarter Choices for Getting Work Done*, Josey-Bass.

6   Goddard, J. and Eccles, T. (2013) *Uncommon Sense, Common Nonsense – Why Some Organisations Consistently Outperform Others*, Profile Books.

7   Heifitz, R., Linksy, M. and Grashow, A. (2009) *The Practice of Adaptive Leadership: Tools and Tactics for Changing Your Organization and the World*, Harvard Business Press.

by David Snowden who invented, with Mary Boone, the Cynefin model.[8] This simple model is a very useful way of understanding complexity compared to, for example, the complicated. Other authors which have informed this Second Edition and deserve special mention include Ralph Stacey,[9] Alan Moore,[10] and William Duggan.[11]

3. New experience. Since the publication of the First Edition, Complex Adaptive Leadership Ltd has been formed and seeks to enable a diverse, highly experienced and talented world class group of associates around the globe. The company has delivered in the past two years the CAL approach to over 1,000 executives of over 40 nationalities, in over 30 countries from over 20 diverse industries (see http://www.complexadaptiveleadership.com/clientsandservices/). This has shown:

   a) The CAL approach has wide appeal and applicability across cultures and industries.
   b) A variety of applications has demonstrated the effectiveness of this approach and some of the stories of those who have (and continue) to use CAL are included in this edition.

We are told by many that the CAL approach is not old wine in new bottles (as in so many leadership approaches) but a genuinely new, innovative and effective way of looking at, and practicing, leadership attuned to the twenty-first century. Over the past few years of taking Complex Adaptive Leadership into many companies it is clear that this leadership approach is unique as it covers three interlinked levels – Contextual, Organisational and Individual as shown in Figure P.1 below:

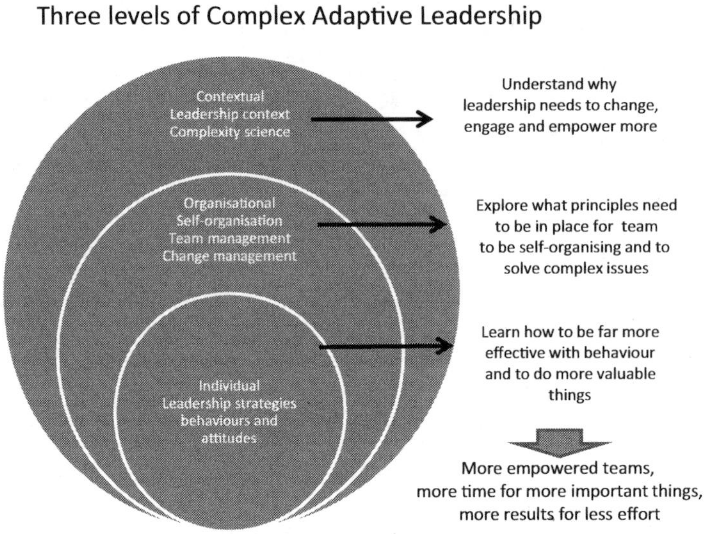

Three levels of Complex Adaptive Leadership

Figure P.1   **The levels of Complex Adaptive Leadership**

The preface to the First Edition now follows which gives an overview of the book.

8   Snowden, D. and Boone, M. (2007) 'A leaders framework for decision making', *Harvard Business Review*.

9   Stacey, R.D. (2010) *Complexity and Organisational Reality – Uncertainty and the need to rethink management after the collapse of capitalism*, 2nd Edition', Routledge.

10   Moore, A. (2011) *No Straight Lines – Making sense of our non-linerar world*, Bloodstone Books.

11   Duggan, W. (2007) *Strategic Intuition: The Creative Spark in Human Achievement*, Columbia Business School.

Preface to the First Edition: What's This All About?

'Complex Adaptive Leadership – Embracing paradox and uncertainty' is an intriguing title. This book may well change your view of what leadership is, and what to do about uncertainty.

If you've just picked the book up for a quick look, perhaps it would be best if each of the five key concepts of 'Complex' 'Adaptive', 'Leadership', 'Paradox' and 'Uncertainty', as treated in this book, are afforded a brief introduction.

'Complex'. Complexity science and chaos theory are two sides of the same coin – sadly the coin itself lacks a name and many argue whether chaos is a subset of complexity or vice versa. For many the two are synonymous. Complexity suggests many interconnecting parts each affecting each other in an open interactive and iterative process which cannot be controlled or fully predicted. Complexity science shows that under seemingly simple things there is a complex dynamical system at play. So the cup of coffee on your desk may seem simple, but for it even to be there, with the myriad of interconnected events and people at play to bring it all together, is complex. At the same time complex dynamics can have some simple underlying rules. The human genome is very complex but is just four strands of DNA repeated many times. So simplicity and complexity, order and chaos, are interconnected in a dynamic rather than being two different and contradictory states a paradox. Complexity is not necessarily complicated. Indeed, in trying to deal with complexity many leaders make things unnecessarily complicated. This book will show that some simple rules and understanding can help manage complexity, and get more for less.

'Adaptive'. This suggests something which can make itself more suitable to a changing environment. It assumes a process which can measure and use feedback to change and be fit for the environment which is changing around it. So linking the first two concepts, 'Complex Adaptive' means a dynamic involving an organisation or organism of many interconnecting parts which improves to meet changing circumstance, and which has complicated underlying dynamics to produce visible simple results.

'Leadership'. This book treats leadership in an unusual way. When one says 'Leadership' the usual automatic sense more often than not is that leadership is something done by leaders.[1] When we talk about 'strong leadership', role models such as Churchill spring to mind. When we talk about a 'lack of leadership', what we seem to bemoan is the need for a person to take control in a decisive way. In other words, the underlying assumption is usually oligarchic (that is, 'a small group of people having control').[2]

---

1   *The Oxford English Dictionary* defines the term 'leadership' as a derivative of the word leader which it defines as 'the person who leads, commands or precedes a group, organisation or country'.

2   Oligarchy as defined by *The Oxford English Dictionary*; the word comes from the Greek *oligio* 'few' and *arkhein* 'to rule'. '-archy' words such as oligarchy, anarchy (itself another form of oligarchy) monarchy (frequently an expression of oligarchy), hierarchy (frequently an expression of oligarchy), anarchy (no ruler – hence chaos), polyarchy (rule by the many), and others share the same Greek root. 'To rule' is not a term used much nowadays and is thus replaced by 'To lead' for the purpose of this book.

We mostly assume that leadership is something done by the (hopefully talented) few, exercised over the many. Such an assumption is not unreasonable and indeed has been fairly constant for thousands of years. However, this assumption is becoming increasingly strained. This book is about seeing leadership differently – it does not see leadership as something done solely by leaders but proposes a form of leadership which is an adaptive, complex and seemingly chaotic dynamic involving all. This is a more polyarchic view (leadership of the many by the many – a seeming paradox). This viewpoint will probably challenge some of your comfortably held beliefs about leadership and give you something to think about. Hopefully it will encourage you to enhance your current skills and do what you do in a more effective way.

'Paradox'. Paradox is a self-contradiction which exists contrary to expectation. It is when two opposite states co-exist in seeming harmony. We like to have things black and white, and cling to the concept of 'either/or' as a child might cling to a blanket for comfort. It is easier to consider right vs. wrong – right vs. right is much harder. Yet the world we live in is full of paradox and to embrace this means having a different mind-set. It is not so much 'either/or' thinking but 'both/and', and realising within most paradoxes a deeper truth exists. In this book the key paradox is that leaders need to be able to follow well, and enable others to take the lead, rather than just provide the lead themselves, expecting others to follow. The paradox is that in enabling others to lead, and being able to follow, one can best lead. Paradox, as treated in this book, is when two opposites co-exist, indicating a deeper, less obvious, hard to define yet powerful truth.

'Uncertainty'. This seems to be a dirty word, and one which most MBA courses work hard to dispel! We try hard to eradicate uncertainty and many tools and techniques are geared to do just that – reduce uncertainty and enable a more predictable and managed outcome. Project management techniques and forecasting tools are good examples. This book does not in any way intend to denigrate such tools and techniques – they are useful and often vital.[3] However, reality is often more complex than many predictive tools can cope with. It is only relatively recently in science that the paradox between deterministic outcome and deeper uncertainty has become apparent. This book is intended to complement the more predictive and deterministic tools that exist, by enabling a deeper appreciation for the dynamics of uncertainty and complexity. Uncertainty is treated in this book as a necessary part of life, and a natural part of dynamic improvement and progress.

Let's make it clear at the very beginning – Complex Adaptive Leadership is not about throwing away traditional leadership wisdom, and getting rid of oligarchic assumption completely. It is, however, about challenging the underlying assumptions of leadership and seeing leadership in a different way, which means letting go (but not necessarily abandoning) some long held beliefs. The paradox is that although both oligarchic and polyarchic approaches may seem contradictory, they are in fact complementary. And as a polyarchic approach is more ambiguous, an ability to understand and embrace uncertainty is key.

---

3   My last book, *Practical Business Re-engineering – Tools and Techniques for Achieving Effective Change*, was full of such models – and they can be very useful. But they are not the whole story!

So, this book will appeal to you if:

1. You think that something fundamental is changing in the world and there is a deeper shift that you cannot yet quite explain – this book won't give many ultimate answers, but it will offer some insight.
2. You wish to understand why leaders often struggle, and why organisations are often sub-optimal. This will give some ideas at an organisational level to improve sustainable performance.
3. You are interested in leadership, and wish to understand how to lead better – this book will give some everyday actions which can be used to good effect, to gain better results for less effort.

The book is in four main parts, and is designed to encourage action by the end. The first three parts look at:

- **Why** is there a need for Complex Adaptive Leadership (CAL), and why it has evolved in the context of polyarchy (leadership of the many by the many).[4]
- **What** it (CAL) looks like at the organisational level.
- **How** can it be applied day to day by individual leaders at the personal level.

The final part gives a suggested template for you to put into practice what you have learnt. There are also appendices of additional interest.

Part I (Chapters 1–4) is about *why* Complex Adaptive Leadership has emerged. It is about the *context* and how the flow of change is creating opportunities for leadership to be practised in a new and dynamic way:

- Chapter 1 explains that polyarchy is really a fusion, or natural evolution, of anarchy and oligarchy, and that Complex Adaptive Leadership does not mean that traditional approaches have to be thrown out. It may *seem* a revolutionary approach to leadership, but in fact it is an evolutionary phenomenon. The paradox is that two contradictory views of leadership co-exist and can operate at the same time.
- Chapter 2 explains the emergence of polyarchy and that the need for Complex Adaptive Leadership is due to the massive pace of technological change. It highlights the natural discontinuity which has occurred because our assumptions about leadership have not changed as fast as the context within which it is practised.
- Chapter 3 shows the organisational context, and explains the need to evolve or die. It explores how organisations which survive are successfully evolving from traditional 'functional silos' through 'matrix' towards 'complex adaptive system' structures.
- Chapter 4 exposes the leadership charade played by many, with leaders pretending to know solutions to the problems of the organisations they lead, and followers

---

4   Polyarchy is a Greek word, and hitherto has been limited to the more esoteric regions of political science. In that field polyarchy is often seen as similar and even interchangeable with democracy. This book sees democracy as an expression of polyarchy (not the other way around as is normally viewed in political science). Polyarchy challenges traditional assumptions and, for some, deeply held beliefs about what leadership is. It defines leadership as a dynamic rather than just an attribute, or an 'art', practised by leaders alone.

expecting them to know. This state of affairs persists despite the fact that most of the time followers know that the leaders know that they do not know!

Part II (Chapters 5–7) is about *what* the underlying features of Complex Adaptive Leadership are. This part takes a more strategic view and shows that the underlying organisational principles to manage *complexity* and *chaos* are, in fact, simple:

- Chapter 5 considers how chaos theory and complexity science has emerged, and is aimed at enabling you to be more comfortable with chaos and complexity, and underlying paradoxes and uncertainties.
- Chapter 6 should help you connect with complexity on an emotional and experiential level and introduces the simple Four + Four principles which can help govern organisational complexity.
- Chapter 7 shows examples of the Four + Four principles in action, and how they can operate within an organisation.

Part III (Chapters 8–10) is about *how*, in a practical day-to-day sense, one can exercise Complex Adaptive Leadership. This part takes a more tactical view. It looks at *leadership* and suggests a dynamic approach using a new and simple model.

- Chapter 8 suggests that the so-called difference between 'Management' and 'Leadership' exists mainly due to oligarchic and hierarchic assumptions. However, such a distinction can lay some useful foundation of 'complementary opposites' to build on. A new model (which is inspired by the older Situational Leadership model) is used to show the dangers and pitfalls and how leaders can often end up working/ trying too hard.
- Chapter 9 looks at the flipside of leadership and shows various ways of looking at followership. It suggests leaders get the followers they deserve, and vice-versa.
- Chapter 10 indicates how one can combine the leadership roadmap and the followership viewpoint in a powerful and simple way for both individuals and organisations.

Part IV (Chapter 11 and Appendices) looks at the *future* and the wider significance of Complex Adaptive Leadership and polyarchy.

- Chapter 11 suggests a template to follow for further reflection, and to put some of the lessons you take from this book into action.
- Appendix A looks at Taoism and how a basic appreciation of this Eastern philosophy can help understand the underlying dynamics of Complex Adaptive Leadership. It looks at some of the aspects in the book and applies the Taoist Yin/Yang model to show how the natural paradoxes of Complex Adaptive Leadership can co-exist in a powerful way. The Yin/Yang symbol occurs in some parts of the book to enable a deeper understanding of paradox and shows how 'both/and' thinking can be applied to leadership, and how complementary opposites can exist at many levels.
- Appendix B looks at how polyarchy can be applied to traditional leadership models. By considering one such model in detail (John Adair's), the appendix shows that polyarchy is not another leadership model but a fundamentally different leadership

assumption that can be *applied* to traditional models to gain further insight. In other words it can add to the usefulness of traditional leadership models.

- Appendix C looks at the implications of polyarchy for politics. In mature democracies the turn-out of voters is in steady decline – whilst many put this down to 'voter apathy' there might be other more significant reasons, which may call for a new approach to government itself.
- Appendix D suggests some leadership development paths that could be taken in order to thrive in a polyarchic environment. These skills are needed by leaders *and* followers, many of whom are stuck in an oligarchic assumptive organisation but surrounded by fast emerging polyarchic realities.

The book is laid out in a classical way but in front of most chapters there is a suggested exercise that you can do. Some involve thinking, some involve action, and some involve both. The exercises are designed to warm you up to what follows in the chapter, and open the mind a little bit more. Some of these exercises are vital for those who would journey the road, others are more for fun – all are recommended.

At the end of each chapter there is a brief summary of the main points. These summaries are aggregated as 'quick breathers' at the end of each section.

The Context

1 *A Journey of Discovery*

A REFLECTIVE EXERCISE TO OPEN UP YOUR MIND AND GET A VIEW OF LEADERSHIP GENERALLY

We are surrounded by issues of leadership. Leadership books and courses are more numerous now than ever before. Leaders are under more scrutiny than they ever have been. We seem fascinated by leaders in all spheres of life – and we also seem to have a different attitude from our forbears.

Here are some questions to ponder:

- Has your own attitude to leaders changed in your life, and if so how?
- If we take as a starting point the attitude to those in authority/leaders as held by your grandparents, and then look at those attitudes held by your parents, and then by you, and then by the younger generation, is there a changing trend? If so, what is it?
- Why do you think that this has occurred?

Spend a few minutes reflecting on your answers to these three questions.

To begin the journey of discovery into the world of Complex Adaptive Leadership and complexity, one needs to get an idea of the context. Chaos and complexity science studies have many roots. In his map[1] showing the history of Complexity Science, Brian Castellani from Kent State University identifies two main roots: Cybernetics and systems thinking[2] Systems thinking is the opposite to analytical thinking. Whilst analytical thinking seeks to get an understanding of the whole by breaking it up and analysing the parts, systems thinking does the opposite. It looks at the whole and from that, one can gain an understanding of the parts[3]. Paradoxes are easier to grasp with a systemic view. So let's start by getting an overview of how we typically view leadership.

The exercise at the start of this chapter may well have raised some interesting thoughts and reflections. Each of us will have had our own experience of leadership and witnessed changing attitudes. Many bemoan the fact that the 'younger generation' seem to have less respect towards authority than the older (although such a complaint is hardly new).[4]

---

1   http://en.wikipedia.org/wiki/File:Complexity-map-overview.png, accessed: February 2014.

2   Systems thinking was pioneered by biologists who emphasised a living organism as an integrated whole, and was further enriched by gestalt psychologists and quantum physics. Alexander Bogdanov was the first to publish a general systems theory in 1912. His work, *Tektology: Universal Organisational Science*, published in Imperial Russia between 1912 and 1917, preceded many of the ideas that were written about later.

3   There are a variety of tools one can used from systems thinking and these are well explained by my colleague with whom I have been lucky enough to work recently, Prof. Mike Jackson in his book *Systems Thinking – Creative Wholism for Managers*.

4   For example, note what Socrates is reputed to have said: 'The children now love luxury; they have bad manners, contempt for authority; they show disrespect for elders and love chatter in place of exercise. Children are now tyrants,

'The death of deference', however, seems to be sharper today than ever before. We hold our leaders to account more now than we have done. In the past we assumed they were more capable than us and we were therefore happy to follow. However, with the fast pace of change that we look at later in Chapter 2, the older generation has been left behind more than ever before. The upshot is that the 'art' of leadership seems to be harder to practice today than in the past. This may explain the explosion of leadership development courses, seminars and books. There is something deeper going on, and it is hard to pinpoint.

Let's take a very wide view. *Homo Sapiens* have not been on this planet for very long. In fact if the history of the planet was compressed into 24 hours, we have been around for just over a second. The Earth is around 4,500 million years old. We began to emerge as a species about 100,000 years ago.[5] Civilisation and written history emerged around 6,000 years ago. So at first we had anarchy (which means no leader, chaos). Then as we became more civilised we needed to organise. Elites grew and oligarchy became prevalent. Leadership was hierarchic and done by the few over the many. As we will see in Chapters 2–4, the oligarchic assumption upon which we rest our views of leadership is becoming rather shaky. But the point here is that polyarchy has come out of oligarchy and anarchy – it can be seen like cogs in the machine, and is the third cog driven by the other two.

Figure 1.1   Underlying dynamics of polyarchy

So those who see Complex Adaptive Leadership and polyarchy as a revolutionary idea designed to overthrow completely the assumptions of oligarchy, will be sadly

not the servants of their households. They no longer rise when elders enter the room. They contradict their parents, chatter before company, gobble up dainties at the table, cross their legs, and tyrannize their teachers.' Attributed to Socrates by Plato, according to W.L. Patty and L.S. Johnson, *Personality and Adjustment*.

5   Apes appeared around 20 million years ago, upright apes around four million years ago, 'Homo Erectus' first appeared in Asia around 1.5 million years ago, becoming extinct about 250,000 years ago, 'Homo Neanderthal' first appeared 125,000 years ago becoming extinct 35,000 years ago leaving Homo Sapiens to continue (having first appeared in Africa and Asia around 100,000 years ago, and in Europe 40,000 years ago). F. Capra gives a good timeline in his book *The Web of Life – A New Synthesis of Mind and Matter*, as well as a good insight into the history of systemic thinking.

disappointed. One can take the view that this is a Darwinian type of evolution, and only those leaders who understand polyarchy will survive – the survival of the fittest.[6] One could also see it as a Hegelian dialectic with polyarchy as the natural synthesis of anarchy ('thesis') and its opposite oligarchy ('antithesis'). Worth noting here is that one of the fundamentals of Tao is to be able to understand the dynamic of opposites and paradox. One could even see polyarchy in terms of dialectic materialism (although Engels and Marx are hardly the vogue any more). Whatever metaphorical or theoretical viewpoint one may choose, polyarchy is fast emerging and represents a deeper and hitherto hidden shift of change in the world. Leadership in a polyarchy is more complex than in an oligarchy.

To understand how polyarchy can best be exploited, there needs to be an understanding of three key and interrelated points:

- The context within which leadership exists, both globally and locally, is the starting point. Leadership in any form cannot produce results without a context within which to exist. And the context within which we live today is in many ways unique to the history of our species. The changes in technology and knock-on social changes are the most dramatic ever seen. Yet our leadership assumptions are still relatively stuck. This is looked at in more detail in Chapter 2.

- After understanding the wider context, one needs to understand the limitations of oligarchy as it exists today. These limitations are due both to the fast changing times and also result from the organisational contextual factors. We all intuitively have a healthy suspicion of the heroic charismatic leaders in a way we never seemed to have before.[7] Whether we like it or not, oligarchy and its sister hierarchy exist all around us and will continue to do so for some time, despite the stresses and strains. However, structures are becoming more fluid and traditional boundaries are becoming more dynamic. Knowledge and wisdom are becoming wider spread, and this means leadership needs to be more dynamic and honest. This is looked at in more detail in Chapters 3 and 4.

- And finally, one needs to understand the dynamics of anarchy – not the philosophical nihilistic revolutionary 'off-with-all-their-heads' anarchy, but the anarchy of chaos and complexity. It is only recently in the area of science and mathematics that non-deterministic approaches are making their usefulness known. The development of chaos mathematics and quantum mechanics seems to go against traditional deterministic scientific theories hundreds of years old, and yet they have reaped great results. For example we would not have solid state electronics, lasers, semi-conductors, remote controls or DVDs without such advances in these relatively new 'non-deterministic' sciences. So perhaps it is no surprise that in the field of leadership the need for a more non-deterministic 'complex' approach is emerging. Complex Adaptive Leadership combines both deterministic and non-deterministic approaches to a powerful effect. This is looked at in more detail in Chapters 5, 6 and 7.

---

6   Darwin's survival of the fittest was not about the strongest or physically 'fittest'. It was about 'fit for purpose' or the best 'fit' to the situation. He published his theories in *The Origin of Species* in 1859, having worked on the theory for 20 years. His main argument was that species evolved through a gradual and opportunistic process of natural selection.

7   In his study *Good to Great*, which looked at great and enduring companies, Collins concluded that: *'A charismatic visionary leader is absolutely not required for a visionary company and, in fact, can be detrimental...'*

Once these three points are understood then the way of using a more polyarchic approach becomes clearer. And so the approaches in Chapters 8–11 will make more sense and be more useful.

Throughout the book the theme of Taoism crops up. This is because it is a useful philosophy which can help a deeper understanding of paradox and complexity. And in the true spirit of Tao, here is a paradoxical caveat: Tao cannot be fully explained in words. According to Lau Tzu, '*He who knows cannot speak and he who speaks cannot know.*' According to Chuang Tzu, '*If a man asks "What is Tao?" and another answers, neither knows.*'[8] Now that sounds like a bunch of mystical bunkum, but stay with it! Taoism is a very old philosophy. It was first codified by Li Ehr Tan, more commonly known as Lau Tzu (which means 'Old Master'). The exact identity of Lau Tzu is still in question. He wrote in China around the fifth century BC. In China his work is simply known as Lau Tzu, although his book later became called *Tao Te Ching*[9] and this is the title more commonly used in the West. The writings of Lau Tzu are more a collection of wisdoms some of which can be dated back to Shamanism from Siberia, a faith a few thousand years older than Lau Tzu's time. The other book within which Taoist beliefs are explored is called *I Ching (The Book of Changes)*, written a few hundred years later by Chuang Tzu. There are many leadership references in the *Tao Te Ching*, and some are explored further in Appendix A.

Perhaps the key quotation from Lau Tzu about Leadership is:

The worst leader is one that lies and is despised; not much better is one that leads using oppression and fear; a little better is the leader who is visible, loved and respected; however, the best leader is one whom the people hardly knows exists, leaving them happy to say, once the aim is achieved, 'We did it ourselves'.[10]

Such a quotation is often used and few seem to disagree – but many think: 'That sounds all fine and dandy – but how does one go about it?' This book intends to provide the answer, not only how, but also why. This book connects with Taoism in four ways, or at four levels.

1. Tao literally means 'the way'. So at the very basic level this book proposes a new 'way' of leadership. However, there are some very deep precepts in Taoism which, if you 'get', will enable you better to understand and put into practice the powerful approaches in this book. The precepts will enable you to embrace paradox and uncertainty. This book is not just about the way of leadership generally, but a particular way which enables polyarchy to flow enabled by a type of leadership which is very dynamic, and enables Lau Tzu's words above to become a reality.

2. At the second level, this new approach to leadership expresses the dynamics of opposites and paradoxes. So far we have uncovered some paradoxes. For example we said polyarchy is about anarchy *and* oligarchy (two opposites at once). Perhaps

---

8   The two central texts to Taosims are the *Tao-te Ching* by L. Tzu, and *Zhuangzi* (the latter is named after the author). Much debate rages about exactly who these men were and when these texts were written, but whatever the historical details, the texts have influenced many over thousands of years and contain much wisdom.

9   Tao means the way, Te means virtue and Ching means classical. A possible translation would be 'The classical way of virtue'. The book is made up of 81 chapters or verses of sayings. The first 37 are about the Tao (the way) and verses 38–81 are about Te (virtue). Appendix A explores the *Tao-Te Ching* and its reflections on leadership in more detail.

10   Verse 17, *Tao Te Ching* by L. Tzu, trans. M. Kwok, M. Palmer and J. Ramsay.

the most important precept of Taoism to 'get' is the concept of 'both/and' rather than 'either/or'.[11] Within polyarchy leaders need to know how to follow those they lead as well as lead those who follow. The key symbol of Tao is the Yin/Yang symbol (the 'T'ai C'hi Tu').

Yin means the dark side of mountain, and Yang means the light side. The Yin/Yang symbolises a basic precept of Taoism that opposites exist to complement and support each other. Opposites are a complementary dynamic rather than two antagonistic and static positions facing each other. Each has an element of each other's opposite within themselves – the smaller circle. The Yin/Yang symbolises 'Both/And' rather than 'Either/Or'. It is about going beyond opposites and realising that opposites combine to create something powerful. For example Yin is aligned to the female, and Yang to the male – without each of those opposites there would not be much to write about (nor anyone to write about it). Other powerful opposites exist as shown in Figure 1.2.

3. At the third level the emergence of polyarchy, and the need for a more Yin type of leadership to balance better the traditional Yang approach, is just an *extension* of a deeper change occurring throughout the world. The world has been traditionally more Yang orientated – action, competition and achievement are traditionally valued more than contemplation, co-operation and sustainability. The male has traditionally dominated the female in society. However, that is changing. There is a swing towards Yin. These changes

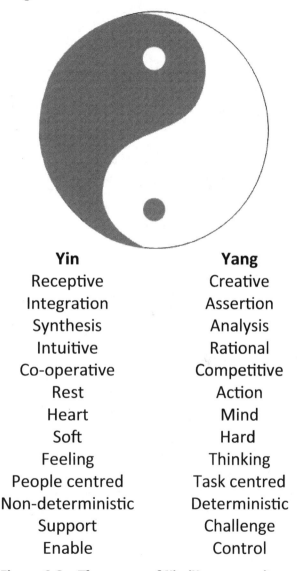

Yin	Yang
Receptive	Creative
Integration	Assertion
Synthesis	Analysis
Intuitive	Rational
Co-operative	Competitive
Rest	Action
Heart	Mind
Soft	Hard
Feeling	Thinking
People centred	Task centred
Non-deterministic	Deterministic
Support	Challenge
Enable	Control

Figure 1.2   The power of Yin/Yang opposites

---

11   This is not the first management book to make open use of Taoist thinking. For example Collins and Porras use the Taoist Yin/Yang symbol repeatedly in their book *Built to Last* and even have a chapter devoted exclusively to the concept of Both/And ('The genius of the And' as they call it vs. Either/Or thinking – 'The tyranny of the OR').

from Yang to Yin, and more balance, are apparent in many ways. For example in modern physics the advent of quantum mechanics is a sign of this deeper change. This is matched by more non-traditional approaches in mathematics, such as chaos mathematics. It is also matched by the move from consumption to conservation, and the growth of interest in the ecology. So whilst the ideas in this book may seem 'radical' or 'fringe', they are merely another expression of a deeper and emerging paradoxical reality which is happening all around us. Lau Tzu said a master is one who knows the Yang but operates within the Yin.

4. At the fourth level, Complex Adaptive Leadership is aimed towards achieving the Taoist state of 'wu-wei' (無為), a concept which can best be described as the art of inaction, acting without effort (such as going with the flow) or refraining from any action which is contrary to the underlying natural flow. Inaction does not necessarily mean switching off and doing nothing, it means holding back and being watchful, ready to act when needed. It is the conscious act of not acting, or holding oneself back. This is often expressed by the paradoxical statement 'wei wu wei' – action through inaction,or effortless doing.[12] Although this sounds very philosophical it has practical application, not least in Chinese history where 'wu wei' was a central tenet of Emperor Kangxi of the Qing dynasty, one of the most successful Chinese Emperors. Although hard working, he had the characters 'wu wei' inscribed above his throne, and this can still be seen in the Inner Court of the Forbidden City in Beijing. In more modern times, 'wu-wei' has been seen as the very foundation of modern market dynamics[13] and the resultant need for governments not to interfere. The aim of Complex Adaptive Leadership is to establish a dynamic 'far from equilibrium', and a context where requisite and effective action can flow naturally in a highly complex and adaptive way *without* the need for action from the assigned leader. This is especially important for complex situations. As we will see, the rules of complexity are quite clear and easy to understand. The underlying dynamics of complexity are in fact simple. This paradoxical conclusion has been made by, amongst many others, the Santa Fe Institute founded in 1984 to specialise in complexity studies. And there is a clear link to the principles of Taoism. The Principal of the Santa Fe Institute, Brian Arthur, once said: *'The complex approach is totally Taoist. In Taoism there is no inherent order... The world is a matter of patterns that change, that partly repeat but never quite repeat, that are always new and different.'*[14]

So the theme of Tao flows through the book with relevance depending on which section is being discussed:

*   The first section of the book looks at the context and describes the underlying flow around us that is relevant to leadership. The art of Taoism is to act within the flow in an entirely natural and almost intuitive way. The flow in this part is looked at from various angles, including historic and organisational, as well as the resultant stresses for leaders.

---

12   For a good explanation of 'wu wei' see R. Kirkland's *Taoism: The Enduring Tradition*.

13   See for example, Gerlach, C. (2005) *Wu-Wei in Europe. A study of Eurasian economic thought*. Working Papers of the Global Economic History Network (GEHN), 12/05.

14   *Introducing Chaos* quoted by Sardar and Abrams.

- The second section of the book looks at complexity and the surprising conclusion that the *more* complex things are, the *less* action is needed from leaders providing they have put in place the necessary environment, processes and culture. The eight key principles which enable this to happen are described, paired in four opposites.
- The third section of the book looks at a model that can be used to improve leadership at all levels, and how the interchange between Yang and Yin is vital. The ultimate goal is to have a Yin-based leadership with the ability to use Yang-based processes to support it.

Chapter Summary

1. The scientific view of complexity and chaos is not the normal view – there are underlying patterns and principles which can be applied. These are paradoxical in nature.
2. Polyarchy is an extension, evolution and synthesis of anarchy (chaos and no leadership) with oligarchy (order and traditional leadership). It sees leadership as a complex dynamic system rather than just an attribute or something only assigned leaders do, and is based on the dynamics and features underscoring complexity science, chaos mathematics and a subset of complexity science – Complex Adaptive Systems theory – hence the term 'Complex Adaptive Leadership'.
3. A basic understanding of Taoism can help grasp the paradoxes which arise and enable a leader to use polyarchy as well as to be more effective within an oligarchic assumption.
4. Complex Adaptive Leadership links modern Western complexity science with ancient Chinese wisdom to offer a new and powerful approach to leadership which can get better results for less effort.

In the next chapter we look at some of the reasons *why* polyarchy is emerging so quickly, and the astonishing pace and extent of change in relatively recent times.

2 The World Wide Context – A Flow Towards Polyarchy

A THOUGHT EXPERIMENT TO OPEN UP YOUR MIND AND GET A VIEW OF THE PLANETARY/SPECIES CONTEXT

This is a brief exercise to get you in the mood for this chapter. It is one that has been done with hundreds of executives all around the world and certainly engenders much debate when the results are considered.

Imagine that you are from another planet – for some that may not be too hard to do…. Anyway, your current employment is with the Inter-Galactic Reference House and your job is to update the inter-galactic report on the state of a variety of planets. Earth is one of the many planets that you report on within your portfolio. You visit every 200 years or so of Earth time, and send an updated report to inter-galactic headquarters of the changes that you see. You have visited Earth for around 4,000 years of Earth time.

Imagine that you have just visited Earth, with your last visit 300 years ago, and now need to write the report on what has changed since your last visit. What are the main headings that you would write regarding the changes you would report on? Looking back over your last half-a-dozen visits, how extensive are these changes compared to the changes you have seen before on this planet?

You may wish to scribble your headings on a piece of paper, or simply reflect for a few minutes.

Having done this exercise with thousands of executives around the world some common headings and trends are often identified, and may well have been identified by you too:[1]

1. Technological changes:
   a) military;

---

[1]   These changes are those considered by some 2,500 international executives/managers working in groups when asked *'What are the areas of main change that you consider significant in the last 100–150 years?'*. The changes considered significant were remarkably similar across the groups. The responses were taken over a 10-year period between 1995–2014. Over 50 nationalities were represented from hundreds of different global companies, and as such the data represents a broadly international view. The groups typically numbered 20 to 30, usually organised in round table format to enable discussion and feedback. These executives/managers were drawn from groups on executive education courses at INSEAD in France, Nyenrode in the Netherlands, London Business School, Henley Business School in the UK, EHL in Switzerland and the Centre for Leadership Studies at Exeter University in the UK. In addition to working with executives in 'open courses' at these academic institutions, data was also gathered from executives of companies in the following countries: Australia, China, Denmark, Estonia, Finland, France, Ghana, Germany, Greece, Hungary, India, Indonesia, Ireland, Italy, Kenya, Kuwait, Latvia, Lithuania, Netherlands, Nigeria, Poland, Russia, Saudi Arabia, Singapore, South Africa, Switzerland, UAE, UK, Uruguay, USA and Zimbabwe.

    b) communication;
    c) transportation.
2. Demographic changes:
    a) numbers;
    b) age/life expectancy;
    c) education/ general awareness.
3. Social/political changes:
    a) globalisation and interdependency;
    b) transparency;
    c) power diffused from traditional establishments (for example, church, state organs) to market and consumers.
4. Environmental changes:
    a) urbanisation;
    b) global warming and environmental damage.
5. Pace of change:
    a) faster;
    b) extensive;
    c) questions of sustainability.

You may well have come up with some other additional headings, and may also not have included some of the headings above. There is no definitive right or wrong here, but hopefully you are beginning to realise the age within which we live is unique from the point of view of change. You may well have noticed that the *scale* of change is remarkable – the difference between the start of the early eighteenth century (your 'last alien visit') and today is *much* larger than the difference between the eighteenth century and sixteenth century (your visit previous to the last one). And the *pace* of change is also remarkable – most of the major differences and new changes over the 4,000 years you have been 'visiting' are relatively recent (achieved in the last 100 years).

To get a better idea of the scale and pace of change, let's consider some of the headings above under technology and general human awareness. If we plot the picture on a graph with the x axis being time, and the y axis being pace of change, a picture emerges (see Figure 2.1 opposite). For ease of reference I have included a 'whistle stop' every 1,000 years – so 4,000 years ago the key civilisation (from a Western point of view) was the Egyptians, followed every 1,000 years later by the Greeks, Romans, Normans and then the present day. This is a very Western point of view, but it helps paint an overall picture and the basic technologies studied are similar in other civilisations (such as the Chinese).

Military technology. It could be said that the main aim of military technology is to kill your foe at a distance whilst remaining safe yourself. The best way to do that in Egyptian time was the bow and arrow, and the use of kinetic energy. There were some innovations along the way with the Greeks and Romans, but the basic technology stayed pretty much the same for a few thousand years. The advent of the musket and canon was the start of big changes, but even that took time to become fully effective. In fact if Napoleon had armed his soldiers with longbows instead of muskets, he might have fared a lot better.[2] The gradual use of gunpowder, and its slowly increasing effectiveness with

---

2   A. Zamoyski describes in his *1812 – Napoleon's Fatal March on Moscow* how it would take an infantry man 1 and a half minutes to reload his musket which had limited range, accuracy and penetrative power. This compares poorly to

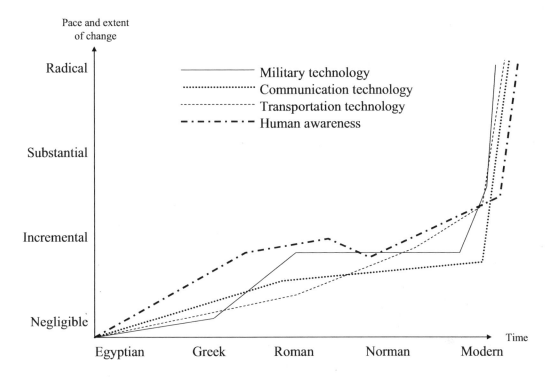

Figure 2.1   Unprecedented pace of changing times

additions such as rifled barrels in the 1880s, compares little to more recent advances. In fact military technology has exploded (forgive the pun) in a very short period of time relative to the scale of time we are looking at (4,000 years). The development of Weapons of Mass Destruction (WMD), coupled with inter-continental delivery capabilities, is a quantum leap in military technology. This pace of change continues, even at the turn of the twenty-first century. For example, in the first Gulf War the number of smart munitions/bombs delivered by air relative to the total was 7–8 per cent, with the rest being 'dumb' (that is, not guided by any special technology). By the second Gulf War only a few years later, that ratio had increased dramatically with 67 per cent being smart.[3]

Communication technology. The same rate of change can be witnessed in communication technology. The Egyptians would communicate over a distance by writing on papyrus and sending a messenger. This basic approach stayed pretty much the same for 95 per cent of the 4,000 years. Whilst some innovative changes were made (paper, printing, stamps, straight roads, use of staged riding posts, and so on), the basic underlying technology did not really change. The advent of the telegraph and use of Morse code is relatively recent.[4] Today we are spoilt by the communication choices

---

a Longbow man a few hundred years earlier who could 'reload' in 10 seconds, shoot with superb accuracy, achieve 300 metres range and could penetrate 10cm of oak (R. Hardy, *Longbow*).

3   N. Childs, 'America's Air War on Iraq', *BBC News* [website], (updated 15 April 2003), http://news.bbc.co.uk/1/hi/2950837.stm, accessed: 16 April 2010.

4   Marconi first sent his telegraph message between France and England in 1899, and then more famously from Poldhu in Cornwall to St John's in Newfoundland in 1901 a distance of over 3,200 km. However, it was Bell who sent the first message electronically in 1876 and formed his Bell Telephone Company in 1877. The next major step in

available. Communicating over a distance using traditional 'snail mail' technology is mostly confined to junk mail nowadays. The reliance on snail mail has been largely replaced by land line phone, fax (itself all but replaced by email), mobile phone, SMS text, video phone, and so on. Consider the changes in your lifetime alone. Whilst the internet may not have fully lived up to the early hype, it certainly has enabled a faster pace and more extensive flow of business and information. This communication technology enables individuals to become networked together, both through IT and also mobile communications. This has huge implications. We can interact more than ever before, and also keep abreast of what is happening across the world through real time instant reporting. Even the boundary between those that 'report' the news and those that 'consume' is becoming blurred, as video mobile phone has enabled anyone to send in news to TV stations for wider distribution, and web enabled technology has widened the scope even further.

Transportation technology. Again the changes here are astonishing. In the Egyptian era a box on wheels pulled by a horse best covered distance over land, and sea was best covered by a floating box with a sail. This stayed pretty much the same for 95 per cent of the time we are considering. Some innovation was achieved – bigger boxes, better wheels, suspension, better sails, bigger masts and so on, but the basic technology stayed static. The twentieth century saw dramatic changes.[5] For example the time between man first flying and landing on the moon was achieved within just over 50 years, under 1 per cent of the time period considered. They say the world is becoming a smaller place – no it isn't, as it is pretty much the same size it has been for a few billion years. What has happened is that transportation technology has enabled distance to be covered far faster by more people than ever before.

Education/General level of human awareness. This is more about how aware we are of the planet we live on, rather than the level of formal education we receive. The two are linked but are not totally inclusive to each other. For example we learn probably more about the world within which we live in our lifetime via TV than we do in the classroom. The explosion of information and communication technology has fuelled this. People have a point of view on issues wider than ever before. If you had asked the average man on the street 150 years ago what he thought of his government's economic and foreign policies, he might have been hard pushed to express a coherent view. Today just about everyone will have a point of view. One might be concerned that the point of view is not as well informed as one would have hoped, but compared to 150 years ago it will be far more formed. One might also be concerned that the media has too much power to shape such points of view. In fact the media's power is limited compared to the power of the people – all the media does is to tap into that power rather than exercise it. So, general human awareness of the issues facing the planet has radically increased. There is still a long way to go, with the literacy level still well below 50 per cent in some parts of the world.[6] Knowledge is also still focused on relatively 'hard' factors such as facts,

---

communication came when Baird gave a display to the Royal Institute on 27 January 1926 of TV. These three major inventions were delivered in the space of 50 years, just over 1 per cent of the timeline shown in Figure 2.1.

5   The steam engine and train was invented in 1804 by an engineer Richard Trevithick first for use in mining, with Stephenson's Rocket being the first passenger train in 1825. The internal combustion engine arrived via Rudolf Diesel in 1897, powered flight by the Wright brothers in 1903, all within just under 100 years, 2 per cent of the timeline shown.

6   The last major study on literacy around the world was the United Nations Development Programme Report 2007/2008 which calculated the total number of illiterate adults globally as being some 862 million. Overall the level

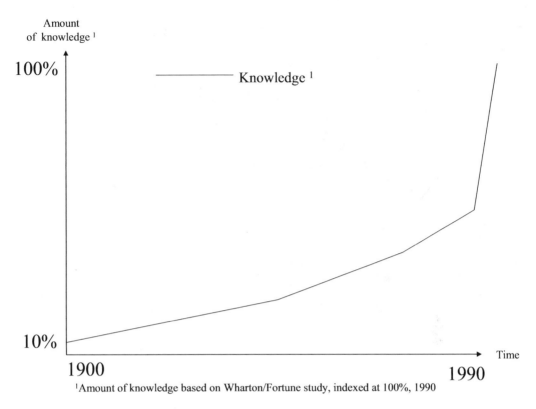

Figure 2.2   **An explosion of knowledge**

figures and technical/utilitarian subjects, with softer areas such as human understanding still lagging. There are some changes here though – witness, for example, the increasing use of psychological tools such as MBTI[7] to help personal understanding. And, sadly, although awareness has grown, wisdom seems still to be lacking. This may in part explain the discontinuity between the rapid changes and relatively stuck oligarchic assumptions. It may also, if one were optimistic, give a hint at the area where the next explosion of growth will be – if the twentieth century saw a growth of knowledge, one can only hope that the twenty-first will see a growth of wisdom.[8]

New knowledge and resultant technology continues to expand. Of 100 per cent of all the people who ever existed throughout history working in Research and Development, the majority are alive today. That either means that the researchers finally discovered

---

of illiterate adults in the world is around 20 per cent. Literacy rates differ largely between developed (for example, USA 98 per cent) and under-developed countries (for example, Chad 25 per cent). 'Education: Literacy', UNESCO [website], http://www.unesco.org/en/literacy, accessed: 16 April 2010 and United National Development Programme (UNDP) Human Development Report 2009, 'Overcoming Barriers: Human Mobility and Development'.

7   MBTI – Myers Briggs Type Indicator – comes from Isabel Brigs-Myers and her mother Katherine Briggs. They took Carl Jung's psychological types, fine-tuned them and created a psychometric questionnaire to enable people to discover an indication of their personality type. It is the most widely used and robust of its type, and has been put to good effect by millions of people around the world. It is a very good tool for enabling people to understand differing types of individuals and how to improve communication. More recently, David Kiersey linked MBTI in an asymmetric way to the four Greek temperaments (see www. Kiersey.com)

8   There is a lot of literature about the move from the 'Information Age' to the 'Wisdom Age' – perhaps the most prophetic is the book by D. Pinchbeck, *2012: The Return of Quetzalcoatl*.

the elixir of life, or that an awful lot of innovation is going on and we are just at the beginning of some more radical change. In fact the curves of the 4,000-year graph look like the bottom of S curves. If the pace of technological change continues, we 'ain't seen nothing yet'.

The age we live in has often been described as the information age. Themes such as 'knowledge management' are frequently discussed. Indeed there has been a rapid increase of knowledge, with another radical curve similar to the 4,000 year curves above. A study in the early 1990s by Wharton, in association with *Fortune* magazine, looked at the amount of knowledge existing today and backtracked that as a percentage to the turn of the century.[9] This was done *before* the explosion of the internet in the mid- to late 1990s. Knowledge was defined as information available which could be put to use.

The study concluded that of 100 per cent of knowledge existing in the early 1990s, only 10 per cent existed in the 1900s.

It is interesting to plot the rate of volatility against the level of knowledge. Volatility can be defined as the level of uncertainty in the equity markets measured by the extent of price changes and swing.[10] A similar curve evolves, as seen in Figure 2.3. In other words the more knowledge there is, the more uncertain times seem to be. Or, put in another slightly controversial way, the more we know, the less certain we are! The paradox is that uncertainty has evolved through a rapid increase of knowledge.

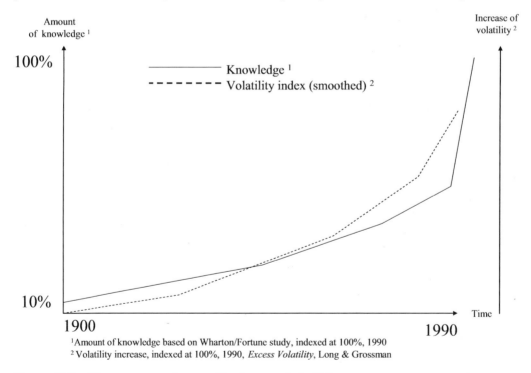

[1] Amount of knowledge based on Wharton/Fortune study, indexed at 100%, 1990
[2] Volatility increase, indexed at 100%, 1990, *Excess Volatility*, Long & Grossman

Figure 2.3   The more we know, the less certain things are

---

9   T. Stewart, 'Brainpower' series, *Fortune* magazine 1991. See also his book *Intellectual Capital*.

10   In *False Dawn*, J. Grey wrote 'The volatility at the core of deregulated financial institutions makes a world economy that is organised as a system of free markets essentially unstable.' This seems to echo the 'far from equilibrium' explored later in Chapter 6.

This should give pause to leaders who feel that one way to keep up is to 'know' more. It seems that knowledge is not perhaps all that it is hyped up to be. Perhaps intuition is also as important, if not more so. And perhaps what you know is not as important as what you actually *do*. The strategies you employ as a leader are more important than what you know – this is not to say knowledge is unimportant, but it is not enough.

The themes of changes above are looked at in isolation but in reality they are linked. There is an underlying flow of change here. For example most of the advances in communication and transportation technology comes from the spend on military technology.[11] We had two devastating wars in the last century which drove a quest for knowledge. Aeronautics really took off (forgive the pun) when the military realised what the plane could offer. Rocket technology had more to do with the need for nuclear weapons delivery than wanting to land a man on the moon – the man on the moon was a great way to convince the US taxpayer to spend rather than panic about the threat from the USSR. The internet and mobile phone came out of the need for redundancy in case of strategic (in the case of the internet) or tactical (in the case of the mobile phone) nuclear interdiction. The military spend in technology still sadly outweighs spends in other areas – but without it we would not be as advanced as we could be. Once the spin offs into other technologies occurred, other advances also took off. For example, the internet now has advanced far beyond the old military back-up system it was designed for, mainly aided by the invention of HTML.[12] The internet continues to evolve with web 2.0, a more interactive experience. And the beneficial knock-on effects go further, with a clear impact on the ability to enable a wider general awareness. In other words, the changes are not isolated but interconnected and in themselves are dynamic. They follow the rules of complexity as will be seen in Chapter 5.

One wonders *why* such a rapid pace of technology has occurred. Part of the reason, as has been indicated, is two horrific World Wars, and huge expenditure on military technology (which fuels many spin-offs). But there are other reasons, including the emergence of new scientific approaches, mostly non-deterministic. The twentieth century saw three main scientific revolutions. First, Einstein's relativity theory eliminated the Newtonian illusion of space and time being independent absolutes. Second, quantum mechanics eliminated the Newtonian dream of a deterministic and objective universe which can be independently observed and measured in a controlled way. Third, chaos theory and its sibling complexity science eliminated the Laplacian fantasy of a clockwork universe and deterministic predictability. These new sciences have enabled huge technological advances, even though some of the science is not yet fully fathomed and understood.[13]

---

11   In OECD countries military spend on technological R&D during the cold war hovered around 40 per cent, although this has dropped to around 30 per cent according to H. Zhang at Harvard and F.N. von Hippel at Princeton University. Military technological spend represents still the largest spending on a single area by mankind. In the US the military budget in 2004 was $455Bn of which $61.8Bn was R&D – this compares to the total renewable energy budget of $2.17Bn in 2006, http://www.treas.gov/offices/management/budget/budgetinbrief/fy2004, accessed: 19 April 2010. This compares to $264Bn spend in the USA in 2000 over all the private sector, and $25Bn in Medical R&D over all sectors. One should remember that the large amount spent on military technology leads to many spin-offs which enable other spend (an example is mobile phone technology).

12   HTML (Hyper Text Mark-up Language) was invented in 1989 at CERN (the nuclear research facility outside Geneva) by Timothy Berners-Lee, a British computer scientist. It brought the World Wide Web a few years later to the internet (itself invented by Vinton Cerf and Robert Kahn in 1973 whilst working for the Advanced Research Project Agency of the US Defense Department).

13   They are considered in more detail in Chapter 5.

So what? Well, let us consider the implications of all of this for the poor people who are called leaders. The world is far more complex, faster changing and uncertain than ever before. People have higher expectations and faster access to what is going on around them, and thus in many cases know more than the leaders do (especially as knowledge and skills have shorter 'shelf lives'). And yet, if we look at the key current underlying assumption of leadership, it is still mainly oligarchic – leadership is mainly seen as something 'done' by the few to the many. Most organisations are structured like a pyramid with one person at the top ('the buck stops here'). There was only one pharaoh, emperor or king typically at any one time. Most organisations today typically have only one CEO. We still have the assumption of leadership that is thousands of years old. A traditional, and perhaps now cynical, point of view is that leadership is as an 'art' or an attribute (often inherited as it cannot be taught, so many would lead us to believe) practised by leaders who are typically the gifted, charismatic, articulate, ambitious, knowledgeable and well-educated few who 'lead' the ungifted, dull, inarticulate, pedestrian, ignorant and ill-educated many...

There are two problems here. First, no matter how gifted the leaders are, if the organisation is actually full of the ungifted, dull, inarticulate, pedestrian, ignorant and ill-educated many, it will not last long nowadays, even if Moses himself were in charge. This is linked to a second issue: the scale and pace of change means that those who are led are now more aware, more informed and have higher expectations than ever before. The old way of leading by command, control, direction and charisma through superior knowledge and personality does not really stack up any more, as increasingly better educated followers know faster than leaders what is happening and often what needs to be done. The harder leaders try to keep up, the less credibility they get. For some leaders

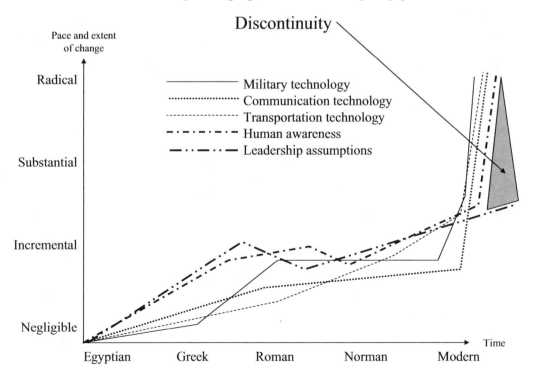

Figure 2.4   The greatest discontinuity of leadership assumption

it must be like the Red Queen in *Alice in Wonderland* – running hard just to keep up, and getting nowhere fast.[14]

From a context point of view then, the pace of change has outstripped by far the leadership assumptions we have. This means we are living in a large period of discontinuity: we have changed the context within which we lead faster than we can change our assumptions about what leadership is.

If one looks around, one can feel the tensions that this discontinuity causes. There has been a slow death of deference; we do not hold leaders in the high regard we used to (witness the change to authority figures from our grandparents to the younger generation today). Leaders seem more cornered, confused and defensive than ever before – no wonder the leadership development industry is thriving!

What is also relevant, and harder to graph, is the change in *power* concentration over the last 1,000 years. One thousand years ago the most powerful institution in Europe was the Church. Over the years power shifted to the state and in more recent times to big business. In fact, if we believe the anti-capitalist factions, power is now vested in the multi-national and big businesses of the world. But if you talk to the top executives of these big companies, most of them do not feel very powerful. Indeed they feel themselves held in the power of the markets, both consumer and capital.

Power has really shifted and diffused more than ever before, even though there are many who feel disenfranchised. Power has not only shifted but atomised – there is no one large group of people that has absolute power. Governments still have power. The church, to a more limited degree, has power. And big business has power. But all the power of these intuitions is small compared to the collective power of the markets (the consumers and those who represent their savings). Once mobilised, such power can be decisive. So no single segment has the kind of concentration of power that we have typically seen over the last few thousand years.

The flow of power – European example

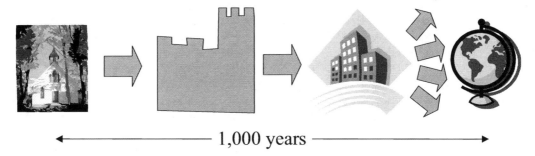

$\longleftarrow$ 1,000 years $\longrightarrow$

Figure 2.5   The flow and atomisation of power

---

14   The 'Red Queen effect' is a term used in complexity science. It originally comes from L. Carroll's story *Through the Looking Glass* where Alice joins the Red Queen running very fast but not getting anywhere – she realises this is due to the scenery moving and the Queen needing to run just to stay still. The term originated in evolutionary studies and is the nickname for Cope's Rule, which states that body size tends to increase in a species to keep up with its changing environment. It was first used in Complexity Science by palaeontologist Lee Van Valen to describe persistent co-evolution.

Power is now more a dynamic than something to be exercised by a single entity.[15] This is another reason why the reality of polyarchy is emerging, and adds to the complexity within which leaders try to lead.

Chapter Summary

1. We have changed the *context* of leadership faster than we have changed our assumptions about *what* leadership actually is.
2. The increase of knowledge in the world is matched by an increase of uncertainty. Knowing more does not necessarily help increase certainty.
3. Oligarchic assumptions are increasingly colliding with fast emerging polyarchic realities.
4. Power has become atomised.
5. The context within which leaders lead is more complex.

In the next chapter we look at the organisational context. This flows directly from the world wide context as the changing world forces organisations to evolve – or die.

---

15   Much has been written about such long term shifts in power – see, for example, *The Economy as a System of Power*, edited by W.J. Samuels and M.R. Tool.

3 The Organisational Context – Evolve or Die

A REFLECTIVE EXERCISE TO OPEN UP YOUR MIND AND GET A VIEW OF THE ORGANISATIONAL CONTEXT

'Organisational Change' is beyond the stage of being a buzzword, so common is the practice. To get in the mood for this chapter here are a few questions for you to reflect on:

What was your organisation like 20 years ago (if indeed it existed – if not, take its earlier times, or choose a former organisation you know well)? How was it actually organised? Ask around if you were not there!

What is the organisation like now and how is it actually 'organised'?

Look forward 20 years and continue the evolution (if any!) – what will the organisation be like and how do you think it will actually be organised?

Is there an underlying trend as far as organisational structure and practice are concerned?

The way we organise is changing, and there are many ways of looking at this evolution. This is being enabled by the changes identified in Chapter 2. Like the technology curves, the pace and extent of change is relatively new as organisational structures have stayed pretty flat for some time. For example, Ricardo Semler describes a company in the North of England in his book *Maverick*.[1] The manufacturing lines are laid out by product lines with a mezzanine floor on which overlook the marketing, finance/admin and leadership teams. In this way the central teams can quickly support and communicate with the product line teams. This may sound fairly modern, but in fact Semler describes a company from the mid-1600s.

Most organisations are traditionally organised on two fundamental themes – specialisms/function (for example, what we do) and hierarchy/rank (for example, how we do it).[2] Indeed a typical organisation chart shows who reports to who doing what, and where. Corporate/organisational culture is an important element as well (for example, formal vs. informal,

---

1   *Maverick* is an instructive read – Semler describes just about all the evolutions an organisation can go through. The last job in the book that he makes redundant in his company Semco is the role of CEO. A similar story is told by R. Stayer in his article 'How I Learned to Let My Workers Lead', where he made himself redundant as their leader. This aspect of creating one's own apparent redundancy is also another barrier for oligarchical leaders to overcome.

2   Earliest evidence of mass organisation in a non-military sense would be the construction of the Egyptian pyramids of 5,000 years ago. It was not until the early twentieth century that organisational theory began to emerge as an area of serious and intense study. The three key early thinkers here would be the American Frederick Taylor (and the scientific management approach of breaking up a process into closely defined jobs and rules), the German Max Weber (and his four principles of specialism, hierarchy, rules and decision making based on objective criteria), and the Frenchman Henri Faylo (who added clear role of management within such a system). These approaches evolved into the quantitative approaches typified by MacNamara. These soon gave rise to the more humanist approach including those of Harvard psychologist Ekton Mayo, leading to organisational behaviour theories such as those of Abraham Maslow (hierarchies of needs), Douglas McGreggor (Theory X and Theory Y) and David McClelland (motivation theory of affiliation, power and achievement).

structured and controlling vs. unstructured and enabling and so on). The trend is towards more cross-functionality and flatter hierarchies, with more informality and enablement.

A simple way of seeing this evolution is shown in Figure 3.1. This evolution is not a 'nice to do' – it is key to survival. In other words, those which do not evolve this way will most likely die, sooner or later. The speed of evolution will be dictated by, amongst other things, the national and market context within which the organisation lives. And the success of the organisation in such an evolution will depend on how well it grapples with underlying polyarchic realities, paradox and uncertainty. This is not always a linear evolution. For example, some companies who do implement the matrix without clarity often end up going backwards to a more silo approach before then evolving, a little more wiser, back towards a matrix.[3] The evolution can sometimes be seen as a helix which, although advances in its shape, goes backwards in order to advance.

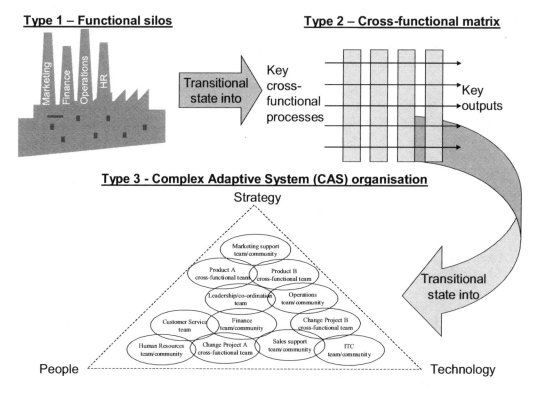

Figure 3.1   From chimneys to Complex Adaptive System via the matrix

So let's look at these states in a little more detail. We will also include the 'transitional states' as these have some unique characteristics. It should be noted that these states are indicative and are used to show an underlying evolution, rather than define a specific and

---

3   It was some time ago in 1978 that the HBR article 'Problems of matrix organisations' identified them as a 'complex, difficult and sometimes frustrating form of organisation to live with. It's also , however, a bellwether of things to come.' Some organisations rush into the matrix to see it as a quick fix to manage complexity. Such was the situation when Nokia and Siemens decided to merge their network companies into Nokia Siemens Networks (NSN). The NSN matrix structure could not deliver and so they retrenched to a more centralised structure before then moving back towards the matrix on a more measured and managed way.

exact 'step by step' manifestation. The evolutionary 'stages' are not so much in steps but are a flow – and the types are just snapshots of how the journey might look, rather than specific states where organisations 'rest' for a breather between the changes.

Most organisations are either somewhere in the first transition (from Type 1 'functional' to Type 2 'matrix') or are indeed grappling with being a Type 2. Not many Type 1 organisations are still out there (those that stuck soon died) and there are not many Type 3 'Complex Adaptive Systems' organisations (as polyarchy is still a relatively new manifestation).

Type 1 – Functional Silo

In this organisation, work is strictly organised along functional specialisms. These specialisms would typically include finance, marketing, operations and so on. Within each department there are levels of hierarchy. The specialisms do not really talk to each other as this is left for higher leadership – indeed that is their role.

Let us briefly, irreverently and for fun, take a cynical view which, unfortunately, some may still recognise. The highest level for marketing would be the Marketing Director. How would things look from such a dizzy height?

She would have to spend some of her time at Board Meetings (which she sees as bored meetings, as all internal focused meetings tend to be). In preparing for these she 'fights her corner' (which is what she thinks she is paid to do after all, so she expects people not to take it personally). She defends her budget against her other so called co-Directors (who she sees as rivals as well as colleagues). She spends time with the CEO both to lobby for what she needs and to ensure that the CEO actually understands what customers want (which is what the organisation should be focused on, after all). She also spends time with the Manufacturing Director fighting off the seemingly endless 'We can't do that … machine set-up times … etc. etc.' that she gets whenever marketing spots an opportunity to actually make some money. She also spends a lot of time with the Finance Director explaining that marketing and communication is not a simple 1+1 exercise, and advertising and sales needs subtlety, not mathematics. Marketing for her, as she often explains to her less imaginative colleagues, is an art not a science…

That may seem a little cynical. But it is all too typical. Consider the frustrations that such a functional approach can lead to in other areas, for example management development. There we get confusing messages. Partly this is due to our oligarchic view of life and that there must be a 'king' – and for marketing, it's the customer! If we go to the marketing seminars we are told that the customer is king.[4] The argument briefly goes something like

---

4   It may be of interest that, according to Google searches, the following score:

'Shareholder is king': 637 results
'Customer is king': 87,200
'Employee is king': 4,400
'Supplier is king': 8
'Community is king': 37,700

So on Google hits alone (if one can judge importance from such a 'tongue-in-cheek' measure) it seems that 'the customer is king' results win. What is of interest is the low score for 'shareholder is king' and high score for 'community is king'.

this: no customers means no revenue – no revenue means no money and thus no business! Hard to argue against that. But then we go to the finance seminar and we are told that the business is there to serve the shareholder – the shareholder is king![5] The argument briefly goes something like this: no capital returns, means no capital investment – no capital investment means no assets – no assets means no business. Hard to argue with that. OK, OK, I thought the customer was king but now I realise it is the shareholder – sorry. And then we go to the human resources seminars where we are told that the people are the most important asset. It seems the employee is king![6] The argument briefly goes something like this: any organisation is ultimately based on its people – if they are happy and work well, the customers, shareholders and others will be looked after – so no happy people = no sustainable organisation. Hard to argue against that. The functional curse emerges – competing functions, power-hungry hierarchies and conflicting logics. The traditional answer that Type 1 organisations use to overcome these strains is the investment in General Management (a.k.a. referees at a controlled riot) who can divide and rule all these competing factions. The MBA is the sine qua non for those who wish to get on, as the underlying theory is that those who can understand these differing functions can lead better.[7] However, they soon find this does not work because too much time and money is spent sorting out internal problems, and meanwhile more effective competitors steal their customers. As the organisation has worked like this for a long time it finds it hard to react and adapt to a fast changing environment. Type 1 organisations, sooner or later, face death. Those that survive soon enter a transitional stage towards a Type 2 organisation, cross-functional matrices.

Transition from Silo to Matrix

The organisation has found out, mainly due to pain, that functional hierarchies no longer work well. They are too slow and expensive. The first cuts are normally the swathes of management as the hierarchy is flattened.[8] However, cross-functional working is slower to appear and those who remain often end up simply taking on the responsibilities and work of those who left. So more pain occurs. This is much to the frustration of those 'driving' the change, as they thought they were trying to reduce pain. Pretty soon the best managers start leaving, and so more change is introduced as there is a realisation that

---

5   The most famous exponent of the 'shareholder is king' model is Milton Friedman, whose monetarist policies were readily adapted by Thatcher in the 1980s. There have been many critics of the use of the shareholder as king and in the *Financial Times* of 7 June 2003, Friedman himself conceded: *'The use of quantity of money as a target has not been a success ... I'm not sure I would as of today push it as hard as I once did.'*

6   There are many who uphold the 'employee is king' motto – a humorous view can be found at http://blog.cocagne. com/how-to-fire-in-france.htm, accessed: 16 April 2010, with a more serious one, in R. Sachitanand, 'Where Employee is King', *Business Today*.

7   It seems the MBA is under increasing attack – Mintzberg's views are but one example. However, these polemics are just another example of the tension between oligarchical assumption and polyarchic reality. The underlying assumption of the importance of a MBA is that leaders need to *know* the solutions to the problems facing the organisation or at least be able to work them out. Qualifications such as a MBA enable an individual to acquit leadership roles in a better way. However the underlying assumption, as has been seen, is becoming strained.

8   The 'flat' organisation was first explicitly celebrated by J.C. Worthy, in his study of Sears in the 1940s, 'Human Relations Research at Sears, Roebuck in the 1940s: A Memoir'. The term was taken up in the 1980s by M. Hammer and J. Champy in *Re-engineering the Corporation* (see footnote which follows).

a lot of the work being done is a waste of time. So processes go through 're-engineering'[9] to reduce waste, and increase reaction/pro-action times. It is discovered that most of the waste occurs between the functional cracks of the organisation. Typically a 're-engineering' effort would be undertaken with the introduction of new technology, and indeed there was a flurry of such activity towards the end of the twentieth century. So a new kind of organisational structure evolves – functional hierarchies are slimmed down further and cross-functional working evolves. These can be focused on product lines or even market regions. These new areas need 'leading' as well, so new hierarchies emerge. The transitional state continues as the strains between the two hierarchies occur – for example, much time could be spent deciding who reports to whom in a 'solid line' and who reports to whom in a 'dotted line'. Once these tensions ease, other tensions arise – for example the new hierarchies, such as regions or product lines, become unbalanced and cross-product/regional opportunities are missed. So the pendulum swings a bit back to ensuring better balance and the organisation arrives at a Type 2 – with cross-functional working in a more dynamic way.

Type 2 – Cross Functional Matrices

The idea of 'matrix' organisation is not new – but they have becoming increasingly common than when they first began to appear.[10] In these organisations most people are working in a cross-functional way, where a product line or region has its own separate support functions. Reporting and processes are efficient and centralised functions are slimmed down. Focus is on outputs rather than inputs, and many managers have two lines of reporting and are comfortable with that, even though at times tensions occur. Functional specialities are spread through the organisation and reaction times are faster. This type of matrix organisation will work for some time. However as external change continues apace, strains will appear. There will be pressure to reduce costs, so the need to re-centralise some functions will grow. The underlying logic and need of the lines along which the matrix are drawn will change and so strains will appear as new opportunities and needs are 'force fitted' into an old matrix structure. The matrix structure, sooner or later, will become like a straightjacket and the organisation will fall behind again. There will be a need for a more fluid structure and so the next stage of evolution occurs.

---

9   Re-engineering was first proposed by Michael Hammer in his article: 'Re-engineering Work: Don't Automate, Obliterate'. This was followed by a book, M. Hammer and J. Champy, *Re-engineering the Corporation: A Manifesto for Business Revolution*. As the practice spread it was increasingly criticised for being too technocratic, and this was addressed in follow-up books by Hammer such as The *Re-engineering Revolution* and *Beyond Re-engineering*. They argued that far too much time was wasted passing on tasks from one department to another. They claim that it is far more efficient to appoint a team who are responsible for all the tasks in the process. In *The Agenda* they extended the argument to include suppliers, distributors, and other business partners.

10   Business started experimenting with the matrix organisation structure on the 1960s – it first appeared in the US aerospace industry as a response to the need for a more project management-based approach. In the 1970s the structure became more widespread when the West started studying the Japanese kieretsu which has some of the aspects of a matrix organisation. The matrix organisation became more widely adopted following the re-engineering efforts of many companies in the 1990s.

Transition from Matrix to CAS

Whilst issues of power and control are the main themes in the first transition from functional to matrix, the key themes in this transition are communication and understanding. New change management processes are put in such as cross-matrix workshops and mass intervention techniques. The latter would include events exemplified by Harrison Owen's 'Open Space Technology' (OST),[11] 'Future Search'[12] and MITs Real Time Strategic Planning.[13] Whilst content consultants might be used for the first type of transition from function to matrix, in this transition stage it is probably process consultants that would typically be used (although each transition can use a mix). Cross-matrix teams will be put in place to work on needed IT systems, HR support policies and operational processes to speed action and further reduce waste. These teams may themselves serve as the germination of the bubbles which evolve in the Complex Adaptive System (CAS) bubble-type organisation. Key boundaries and a few simple rules are put in place by top management, and the organisation's overarching purpose and vision is clarified, understood and shared by all. The type of work that goes on here in many ways reflects the activities and approaches described in Chapter 7.

Type 3 – The CAS Organisation

The term CAS is meant to reflect a dynamic organisation where teams are formed, perform and then disappear as the need arises. What forms the foundation (or cornerstones) of this dynamic are clear *people* processes and policies, sound and flexible information and communication *technology* systems, and transparent, inclusive and flexible *strategy* development processes. People are very flexible and systems are open so information is shared and total transparency is gained. There are not many organisations like this around yet – early examples which emerged in the 1980s/1990s include Oticon in Denmark, Semco in Brazil, Springfield Remanufacturing Corporation (SRC) and Johnsonville Foods Inc. in the USA, and St Luke's in the UK.[14] They are all very different but they have some common features. Information is shared openly. Hierarchy is informal, and the

---

11   OST came from Owen's increasing frustration that the one item which scored consistently higher in his seminars and facilitative workshops were the coffee breaks. He therefore designed a process which enabled people (in large groups of well over 100) to set the agenda within a defined framework and have a range of rewarding dialogues with specific outcomes – 'one large coffee break' as he calls it. It seems and looks chaotic, but it works very well.

12   'Future Search' is the brainchild of Marvin Weisbord and Sandra Janoff and is a more structured mass intervention technique. It has been used to good effect with complex organisations such as local communities. For more details see M. Weisbord, and S. Janoff, *Future Search: An Action Guide to Finding Common Ground in Organizations*.

13   See C.D. Shelton and J.R. Darling, 'From Theory to Practice: Using New Science Concepts to Create Learning Organizations', *The Learning Organization Journal*.

14   A variety of publications exist for each of these organisations:
- Oticon – Case study of how they changed to such an organisation in N. Obolensky's *Practical Business Re-engineering*.
- Semco – *Maverick* by R. Semler is an enjoyable and instructive read. More recently his article 'How We Went Digital Without a Strategy' is also illuminating.
- Springfield Remanufacturing Corporation (SRC) – Jack Stack as CEO wrote up his approach in his book *The Great Game of Business*.
- Johnsonville Foods Inc. – R. Stayer's article 'How I Learned to Let My Workers Lead' is a good read showing the personal journey a CEO goes through. He went on to co-author 'Flight of the Buffalo' with J.A. Belasco.
- St Luke's case is interesting as it shows how such a company can be formed from inception. The CEO's interview of Andy Law in D. Coutu's 'Creating the Most Frightening Company on Earth' shows how this happened.

formal hierarchy is rather flat, dynamic and more to do with meeting the needs and expectations of external stakeholders than actually 'running' the organisation. There is a great emphasis on personal responsibility and underperformance is not tolerated for long – they are not necessarily 'nice' places to work! There are some clear and strictly followed processes, especially around recruitment, retention, as well as selecting new innovations and getting them to market. Such organisations would certainly understand how to implement the principles described in Chapter 7.

Again it should be stressed that the 'types' above are not fixed but indicative, and they are not 'steps' so much as trends. The evolution and journey will be different for each organisation. For example, the journey above was fairly typical for Semco in Brazil, whilst Oticon in Denmark seemed to jump from functional to CAS. Multi-nationals will also have a mix – even Oticon found it hard to replicate fully its evolution at Head Office in Denmark across national boundaries. Large multi-nationals often have a mix with some countries in a matrix, and some in a transition towards a 'CAS' type of organisation. The stresses and strains which occur in such organisations are entirely natural, and indeed are a sign of a healthy evolution. Much time is often wasted in eliminating the pain of such evolution – such an effort is largely wasted and often runs against what needs to be done.

There are a few other ways of looking at this organisational evolution, beyond the pragmatic experience explored above. What is cause and what is effect can be debated, but the evolution is clear. These ways include using:

- metaphor;
- Taoism;
- management theory;
- feedback;
- strategy development.

Metaphor. One such way is to see that organisations are moving from a machine type organisation which can be 'run' to a more fluid organic type of organisation which runs itself.[15]

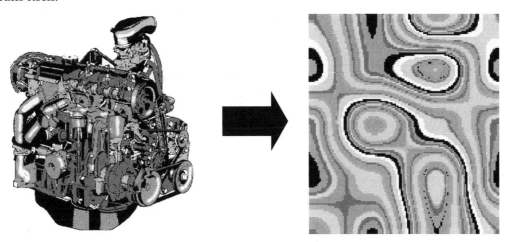

Figure 3.2   Moving from machine to organism

---

15   The concept of 'self-organisation' is key and explored more in Chapters 5 and 6.

Such an organisation will still have oligarchy and hierarchy in place not least to safeguard corporate stewardship and responsibility to the authorities. The internal value of the hierarchy will be more about safeguarding the internal culture to ensure it can be sustained, and ensuring external links are maintained in a world which is becoming increasingly inter-dependant.

Taoism. In terms of Tao, this organisational evolution is a move from Yang to Yin, or better still a re-balancing, so that the benefits of Yang are not lost. This is an important point – the process is evolutionary. At each stage that which is useful is kept and that which is not is discarded. That is different from a revolutionary process where at each stage there is an 'overthrow'. So the *way* these changes and phases are managed is as important as the changes themselves. Organisational change frequently fails due to the perceived need for revolution. Perhaps the maxim 'Revolutionary in thought, but evolutionary in implementation' is a good one.

Management theory. The evolution of organisations in this way, from a deterministic structured machine-type 'organisation' to a fluid, complex/chaotic, organic 'organism' is mirrored by a similar evolution in management science. In 1911, Frederick Taylor published his book *The Principles of Scientific Management*. Taylor saw organisations as machines which leaders could run in a deterministic way. Pulling the right levers would ensure results could flow, and this thinking goes hand in glove with hierarchic functionally based organisations. Although Taylorism is much maligned nowadays, it was farsighted for its day. All Taylor did was to take standard scientific thinking (which was deterministic) and apply it to typical organisations (which were hierarchic).[16] As markets became more complex and dynamic, and as workers became more knowledgeable and effective, strategic planning emerged in the 1960s introduced by, amongst others, Harvard. The MBA then became the ticket for executive success. As the matrix took hold, system thinking emerged as the latest thinking, introduced to organisational management mainly by MIT's Peter Senge in the late 1970s.[17] This evolved into the learning organisation, systemic and more inclusive approaches leading to more 'CAS' type fluid organisational thinking. Whilst these management 'fads' have relatively short life cycles, the concept of polyarchy (based on an old philosophy of Taoism and new complexity sciences) has the potential to act as a foundation on which to re-examine older management models and thus gain better value from them. This is explored with a detailed example in Appendix B.

Feedback. The way personal feedback is done seems to evolve in an organisation from the typical one way process of boss to subordinate towards a more fluid and inclusive 360 degree approach.[18] This evolution often follows organisational change and one way to look at it is shown in Figure 3.3.

---

16   Taylor wrote in his book that a good worker does *'just as he is told to do, and no talk back. When the (foreman) tells you to walk, you walk; when he tells you to sit down, you sit down.'* This would not work so well today. Things have moved on since the early 1900s! But in some ways this book tries to emulate Taylor, as it is simply taking more up to date scientific concepts (which are non-deterministic) and apply them to typical organisations today (which are increasingly less hierarchical).

17   See P. Senge, *The Fifth Discipline: The Art and Practice of The Learning Organization.*

18   The use of 360 degree feedback is relatively new in management, but can be traced back to the use of multi-source feedback in the German military during World War II. The earliest formal process recorded was by Esso in the 1950s. It is now estimated that some 30 per cent of all US companies and 90 per cent of *Fortune 500* companies use such feedback mechanisms.

Type of organisation	Type of feedback	Comment
Functional	90 degree	Boss to subordinate
Transition to matrix/matrix	180 degree	Boss to subordinate, and peer review as well
Matrix/transition to bubble	270 degree	Boss to subordinate, subordinate to boss, and peer feedback as well
Transition to bubble/bubble	360 degree	As above, plus input from other stakeholders such as direct clients/outside suppliers and so on.

Figure 3.3   Possible evolution of personal feedback within an organisation

This evolution reflects a flow towards polyarchy whereby upward and sideways feedback is as important as the more traditional downward feedback. This assumes that individuals will be more 'self-correcting' rather than 'controlled' from above. There is a move towards 360 degree feedback within organisations as the realities of polyarchy and constraints of oligarchy become more apparent. This move again reflects the wider changes explored in Chapter 2. Feedback is absolutely critical for polyarchy to thrive, and this is explored in more detail in Chapters 5, 6 and 7.

Strategy development. Yet another way of looking at organisational evolution is the way that the organisation evolves its strategy. The traditional view is that those at the top formulate strategy and direct those below – the top propose, the bottom dispose. This approach has been the standard view for many thousands of years. Main boards of companies are still expected to be responsible for the strategy of the organisation. However, as Ricardo Semler's article's entitled 'How We Went Digital Without a Strategy' suggests, even the concept of a unified coherent strategy is becoming strained. As the complexities of the world increase, so too do strategy consultants. As the organisation moves from a fixed functional/hierarchic model to a more fluid organic one, so too will strategy evolve in a different way. A possible evolution is shown in Figure 3.4.

There are a variety of ways of looking at strategy. The way it is formulated can be seen as top down, bottom up or a mix of both. The strategy can also be seen in terms of how fixed/fluid it is, how clearly it is understood across the organisation, and how much it is owned through the organisation:

- The extent to which the strategy is clear across the organisation is often a headache for many top executives. Clarity means that everyone in the organisation understands the overall big picture strategy and how they fit within it. This is a perennial problem for top teams. There are, however, stages at which it is natural that the strategy is unclear, normally in a period of transition into matrix or CAS. In many ways the degree of clarity depends not on what the strategy is but how it came about. Similar to the point about ownership below, if there has been no involvement in the

Type of organisation	Type of strategy – possible type of formulation	Comment – possible manifestation	
Functional	Top down	Clear, fixed and not fully owned	Focus on **Content** (what the strategy is)
Transition towards matrix	Top down with input from lower down	Unclear, fixed and owned	
Matrix	Top down and bottom up	Clear, fixed and partly owned	
Transition from matrix towards CAS	Bottom up with top down feedback	Unclear, fluid and owned	
CAS	Bottom up and top down dynamic	Clear, fluid and owned	Focus on **Process** (how the strategy is evolved)

Figure 3.4   Possible evolution of how strategy is set in an organisation

formulation of the strategy, do not expect a high degree of understanding – people need to be engaged rather than preached to. The lack of clarity of strategy is also used as an excuse by followers to do nothing to take the initiative.[19] This is looked at in more detail in Chapter 7.

- Strategies can also been seen in terms of how fixed or fluid they are. In reality this is a continuum, but one can contrast the strategic approach of formulating strategy on, say, a five yearly cycle and having a more fluid approach where strategy is updated on a continual basis. The extent of fluidity and fixed nature will be affected by the market the organisation is in, as well as the organisational evolutionary maturity.
- The level of ownership of the strategy will be dictated by the amount of involvement in formulating and deciding the strategy. The simple rule of 'No involvement = no ownership' often applies. Many senior executives worry about 'buy-in' when in fact they should be concentrating on 'sell-out' – in other words the process used by executives to sell internally is crucial. A key hurdle is the inability to 'let go' which, when you come to think about it, is vital when 'selling' and developing shared ownership. This is explored more in Chapters 9 and 10.

Through this evolution of strategy development there seems to be a move away from *content* (*what* the strategy is) towards *process* (*how* the strategy is evolved). This seems to echo the manifestation of action being as valuable (if not more so) than knowledge discussed in the previous chapter. Another way of looking at strategy development is to

---

19   Here is an interesting exercise which I often use when the issue of an 'unclear strategy' arises within a group of executives in an organisation. Ask them to write out in small groups what they think the key points of the strategy are. You more often than not will find that there is a remarkable consistency between the various groups. It seems that the issue is not so much that the strategy is unclear but the fact that people have a low degree of tolerance towards ambiguity and use a seemingly unclear strategy as an excuse. This point is explored more in Chapter 6.

consider to what extent the strategy is determined (that is, follows the traditional view of strategic thinking) and to what extent it is emergent (that is, follows a more dynamic view of strategy).[20] As the world becomes more complex, the latter is fast replacing the former. There are a variety of strategic tools and techniques which underscore each approach. The traditional view of strategy is the rather linear: 'Know where you are – Decide where you want to go/make the strategic objective – Plan the route – Implement'. Such an approach can also be used to good effect for change management. These linear approaches owe much to the traditional view of strategy. The word 'strategy' first came into regular use in the eighteenth century during the time a certain Corsican-born Frenchman was beating up Europe and winning lots of battles – Napoleon. Around that time two great works on strategy were published. The first, *Traits of Strategy* was by Jomini, a French general who had served on Napoleon's staff.[21] His book laid the foundation of many strategic theories, not least the basic assumption of strategy being a deterministic endeavour where one analyses the situation, sets the objective, makes a plan and then executes. From this flows much of business strategy thinking, where a range of analytical approaches exist. The second book, which came out around the same time, never got the attention as much as Jomini's. Clausewtiz's, *On War*[22] gave a more fluid view of strategy, saying for example that strategy is not so much analysed as being formed in the blink of an eye, and thus analysis is more of a dialect than a process. His work was not as easy to read as Jomini's nor did it get as much attention. However, his approach is gaining more influence, not least through authors such as Willam Duggan and his work *Strategic Intuition*. The two approaches to strategy also reflect both the Yang and Yin approach and can be summarised as:

1. intended, determined strategy using analytics and more traditional approaches – more Yang than Yin;
2. emergent, adaptive strategy using dialectics and more dynamic approaches – more Yin than Yang.

These two approaches, and some examples of the business models that represent them, are shown in Figure 3.5. This is not an 'Either/Or' proposition but a 'Both/And'. Nor should one approach replace another – both are needed, although the teaching and training in the Clausewitz tradition is not yet as common as the approaches in the Jumoni tradition.

It is worthwhile giving a brief description to the more dynamic and dialectic approaches in Figure 3.5:

- Emergent Strategy. Mintzberg first explored strategy as emergent, rather than intended, in his paper 'Patterns in Strategy Formulation'[23] which was expanded

---

20   A brief explanation of 'intended' and 'emergent' strategy is well explained in the Harvard Business School case prepared by Prof. Clayton Christensen and Jeremy B. Dann (1999) 'The Process of Strategy Definition and Implementation'.

21   Jomini, H. (1805). *Traité de grande tactique, ou, Relation de la guerre de sept ans, extraite de Tempelhof, commentée at comparée aux principales opérations de la dernière guerre; avec un recueil des maximes les plus important de l'art militaire, justifiées par ces différents évenéments.* Paris: Giguet et Michaud.

22   Clausewitz, C. von, *Vom Kriege* (3 vols., Berlin: 1832–34).

23   Minztberg, H. (1978) 'Patterns in strategy formulation' *Management Science Journal*, 24(9), May.

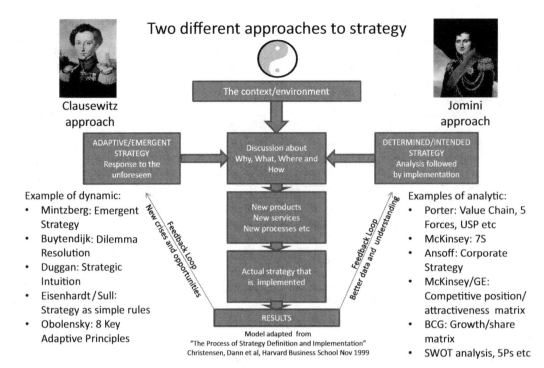

Figure 3.5   Two different approaches to strategy

in his paper 'Of Strategies, Deliberate and Emergent'.[24] Essentially Minzberg sees realized strategies as a mix of deliberate and emergent, where emergent is a stream or pattern of informal decision making in response to changing situations.

- Dilemma resolution. In his article 'Dealing with Dilemmas: Redefining Strategy',[25] Buytendijk proposes that strategy can be defined as a 'Both/And' approach when facing dilemmas rather than the traditional 'Either/Or' approach (for example, making big bets).

- Strategic intuition. In his book of the same title,[26] Duggan explores more fully the Clausewitz concept of strategy being formed as a 'coup d'oeil' (the blink of an eye, or a glance) being a mix of intelligent memory (experience/examples from history), openness of mind (being able to let go of dogma), flashes of insight (being able to make connections) and resolution (determination to see it through).

- Strategy as simple rules: In their first article[27] Eisenhardt and Sull saw emergent strategy working when some simple rules are in place (How to rules, Boundary rules, Priority rules, Timing rules and Exit rules). A decade later in their article 'Simple Rules for a Complex World'[28] they expanded this thinking by saying what needs to

24   Mintzberg, H. and Waters, J. (1985) 'Of Strategies Deliberate and Emergent' *Strategic Management Journal* Vol 6, 257–272.

25   Buytendijk, F. (2010) 'Dealing with Dilemmas: Refining Strategy' *Balanced Scorecard Report*, Sept–Oct 12(5).

26   Duggan, W. (2007) *Strategic Intuition: The Creative Spark in Human Achievement*, Columbia Business School Publishing.

27   Eisenhardt, K.M. and Sull, D.N. (2001) 'Strategy as Simple Rules' *HBR* January 2001.

28   Sull, D.N. and Eisenhardt, K.M. (2012) 'Simple Rules for a Complex World' *HBR* September 2012.

be in place for such an approach to strategy to work. Many of their points reflect the eight principles explored later in this book in Chapter 7.

It should be noted that these dynamic non-linear dialectic approaches to strategy are not meant to replace traditional deterministic approaches – it is 'both/and' not 'either/ or'. A good strategy will have elements of both approaches, paradoxical as it may seem.

Chapter Summary

1. Organisations seem to be evolving from the traditional strict functional and hierarchic type through a more flexible matrix towards a very fluid 'CAS' type. This evolution takes the metaphor of changing from a machine to an organism, and mirrors both Taoism and the development of management theory. It can also be reflected by the evolution of individual feedback mechanisms at the micro level, and the way strategy is formulated at the macro level.
2. This evolution is caused by the rapid pace and extent of change we looked at in Chapter 2.
3. As things become more complex, strategy formulation for organisations needs to evolve and embrace not only the traditional analytical approach but also the more dynamic dialectic approach.
4. Those that get stuck soon face death.
5. Success depends on the ability of the organisation to deal with polyarchy, and to manage the paradox of the existence of polyarchy within oligarchy.

The cracks are beginning to become more apparent, and the trap of a charade is becoming more obvious, as the next chapter will explore.

4 *Finita La Comedia – Stop Playing Charades*

A THOUGHT EXPERIMENT TO OPEN UP YOUR MIND TO WHAT MANY ARE FACING

Research looked at organisations which had achieved 'step-change'.* These changes were sweeping and included strategy, culture and re-organisation, and delivered great results. Such changes do not happen overnight and the typical period of time to achieve such change would be between two to five years. So we are talking about big organisational changes, and a myriad of solutions achieved the changes.

The study looked at organisations that had gone through large changes. The original research was backed up by some action research of some 2,500 executives from over 50 different countries and hundreds of different organisations. They went through the exercise you are about to do. What was studied was where the actual *solutions* came from that made the changes happen. The original research looked at the solutions that made a difference on the ground (the actual action) and then backtracked these solutions over time to who had actually first thought of them – some solutions came from the top of the organisation (the top being the top levels rather than the very top), some came from middle management and some came from the bottom.

Of 100 per cent of the *solutions* that actually make specific changes happen on the ground to get positive results, what percentage of solutions do you think originally come from/are first thought of at the top?

---

*   The original study was done by the Dale Carnegie organisation in the USA with the award-winning Milliken carpet company. This was followed up by action research by the author by taking some 2,500 executives (see footnote 1, Chapter 2) through this exercise. The numbers scored were remarkably consistent throughout the world and thus seem to reflect a global trend.

So Where Are the Solutions…?

The number you choose for the percentage of solutions from the top can also reflect both the background/context within which you operate and also the assumptions you have about leadership. In very general terms:

- The *higher* the number is, the more formal and traditional you may see leadership. In general terms the more junior and inexperienced the person is, the higher the number will be (*except* for the very old/retired who often have a traditional view).

**Of 100 per cent of solutions,
what percentage come from the top?**

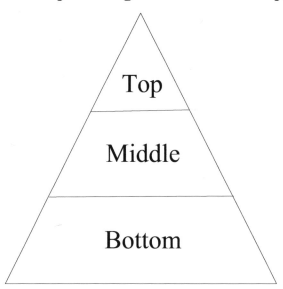

Figure 4.1   Where do the solutions come from? (part 1)

The higher number owes more to the traditions of the past than the realities of the present and trend of the future.

- The *lower* the number is, the more informal and also perhaps more senior the person is. In general terms senior executives will give a low number as they live the bitter reality. They also realise their job is not about knowing and disseminating solutions, but creating the context where solutions can flow naturally.

So the number you give will depend in some ways on the mix of age, culture and experience you have. However, some general trends exist:

- The more formal and structured organisations tended to give a higher number, but the assignation of higher numbers was not so much done by senior management but more often done by middle management. This always engendered a good debate about what roles and responsibilities were.
- There were some cultural trends – more formal European countries (such as Italy and Germany) tended to give a higher number than the more informal countries (such as Denmark and the UK). Asian countries, who tend to be more deferential towards authority and more hierarchical, as well as countries who have a legacy on strong top-down leadership (for example, Soviet military industrial companies), also scored on average slightly higher.
- There were some age differences – in general terms the more junior the level, the higher the number, and the more senior the executives the lower the number. In fact one main board all gave a figure of 0 per cent – the CEO explained, 'We all understand that is not our job any longer.' It is worth noting that the organisation was in a transitional phase from matrix towards CAS (see previous chapter).

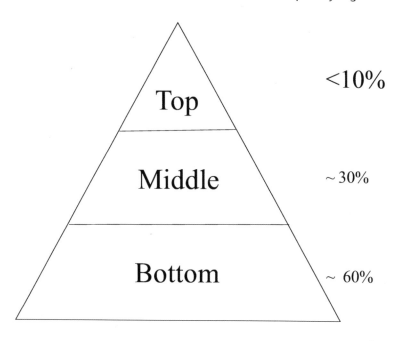

Figure 4.2   Where do the solutions come from? (part 2)

The average figure has *usually* fallen below 15 per cent, and has always been less than 30 per cent. In other words, it is universally agreed that those at the top of the organisations only know a fraction of the solutions needed to overcome the problems faced by the organisations that they lead.

So the fact is those at the top do not know the solutions to the problems faced by the organisations they lead. And generally speaking they *know* that they do not know. However, they cannot *say* that they do not know. When was the last AGM or senior management workshop/meeting you went to where the CEO stood up and said, 'Beats me – any suggestions?' This is because there is an expectation (both by themselves and others) that they *should* know. So they often pretend to know. It is a charade and those at the top get stuck like the Red Queen – running hard to keep informed because they feel they should know when in fact they realise they do not. Leaders are more stressed, challenged and confused today than they have ever been before. Our research showed that the top few layers of a company typically know less than 10 per cent of the solutions to the problems facing the company. In the old days they turned to God – in more modern times they turn to management consultants. And what do the consultants actually do? Amongst other things, they go to the people who know (those closest to the action) and ask them. It seems that the boom of strategy and general management consulting has more to do with top leadership's inability to say to subordinates *'I don't know – what do you think?'* than perhaps anything else...[1]

Meanwhile those at the bottom of the organisation are just as culpable. They know the solutions (or most of them). They also intuitively know that the people at the top do not know. And they often know that the people at the top know that they do not

---

1   Between the mid-1990s and 2000 the size of the global consulting market has more than doubled to more than US $110 billion in total revenues (Kennedy Information 2001: 35).

know! But they still *expect* the top to know – they too seem trapped by the old oligarchic assumption of what leadership is about.[2] In the old days the top *did* know the solutions – but not anymore. And it is far more convenient for those at the bottom to expect people at the top to know as it absolves those at the bottom of any culpability for the unsolved ills of the organisation. After all, they say, it is job of the people at the top to know! So the bottom complain around the water coolers: 'Management should...', 'The company should...'. Having complained they feel absolved of responsibility, and go back to work.

The charade is complete – those at the top pretend to know, those at the bottom pretend not to know, and the organisation waltzes inexorably towards its death. Meanwhile those stuck in the middle have nothing to do except pull their hair out. In reality they do their best to hold the organisation together as they see top managers becoming ever distant and cut out from the reality at the bottom, and the bottom becoming ever distant and uncaring about the strategic issues facing the organisation.[3]

Such a sad state of affairs may explain the typical feeling when top management do a 'road show' to an organisation facing the need for change. Imagine the scene: the top team arrive and show the workers a great 'son et lumiere' PowerPoint slide show – 'Problem this...', 'Strategy that...', 'Solution this...' and so on. And what is the general reaction from the serried ranks of workers, often expressed during the coffee break? 'Bull****!' is a typical comment. The conversations in the coffee breaks are often more realistic than the charade played out in the plenary sessions.

This state of affairs is one that is common and natural as it shows there is a deeper flow towards polyarchy. What we witness are the stresses and strains of the tensions between an organisation clinging onto the certainties and comforts of oligarchy and certainty, whilst the uncomfortable realities of polyarchy and complexity are fast emerging. This may explain why Collins concludes: *'Leading from Good to Great does not mean coming up with the answers and then motivating everyone to follow your messianic vision. It means having the humility to grasp the fact that you do not yet understand enough to have the answers and then to ask the right questions....'*[4] This is remarkably similar to the research done a few years earlier by Hirschorn and Gilmore from Wharton who concluded: *'Subordinates need to challenge in order to follow, and superiors must listen in order to lead.'*[5]

How can one start to get around this? The complexity of the situation should not be underestimated. Behaviour breeds behaviour. Frequently this state of uncertainty drives executives into an ever increasing fixation with details in a vain attempt to stay ahead. This in itself becomes damaging, as employees become more hesitant and wait to see what is expected next. An executive of a large multi-national company was heard to complain:

---

2   The bottom generally expects the top to know the solutions to the organisation's problems. Even further than this, they still in some countries expect leaders to know the details of their own jobs better than they do themselves. Research done by Andre Laurent asked workers in various countries to what extent they agreed with the notion: 'It is important for a manager to have at hand the precise answers to most of the questions that subordinates may raise about their work.' The survey was done in the late 1970s and again in the late 1990s. There was a difference between the surveys (overall a drop of agreement), and also by country with (in Europe) the highest level of agreement being Italy (over 50 per cent) and the lowest being Sweden (under 10 per cent). This also highlights the differences in various countries.

3   See Q.N. Huy, 'In Praise of Middle Managers'.

4   J. Collins, *Good to Great*, p. 75. The study looked at great companies and what common features that they had. These companies had existed for a long time, and were seen by their peers as truly great. It built on the *Built to Last* study by Collins and Porras. And note the word 'yet' – even Collins seems trapped by the notion that the leader should know!

5   L. Hirschhorn and T. Gilmore, 'The New Boundaries of the "Boundaryless" Company'. Such a cultural norm would be typical of a polyarchy.

It's a real pain when the CEO and his staff comes and visits. My whole operation almost grinds to a halt as the managers scurry around to make sure they understand all what is going on because they know that if the CEO asks a question to which they do not know the answer, they are in big trouble. I do not need to know the details – that's what we pay our people at the coal face to do. But when the CEO walks in and points to one of the many trains loading in the siding and asks me 'Where is that shipment going to?' he expects me to know. So I waste a huge amount of time on the details and it causes frustration and demoralisation...

In many respects it is a tragic comedy – and it is best stopped.

How to 'Finita la Comedia'

To change such behaviour takes time and is not done by dictating.[6] In Chapter 10 we look at some strategies and processes which can be put in place to enable polyarchy to flourish and get results. But this also needs a fundamental change of *attitude* to succeed. The charades described above need to be pointed out and stopped at the individual behavioural level. There are a variety of things that one can do to change such behaviours. Here are three effective possibilities which can begin to 'finita la comedia':

1. The 'I do not know' approach.
2. The challenge and support approach.
3. The dynamic approach to Question and Answer (Q&A).

Let's have a look at each in a little detail.

1. Breaking the Charade – The 'I Do Not Know' Approach

If a question is asked to which one does not know the answer, saying 'I don't know' is a good display of honesty.[7] It is also very brave if one operates in a culture of fear and reprisal, and in such a case needs to be done with finesse. There is also a whole cultural element – for example such a bland statement in China by a leader would be taken to mean something else! So such a bland statement should of course be followed up by another statement. For example, agreeing one should know and will find out is one option (for example, 'Does anyone here have the answer?'). Or throwing the question back to explore how a resolution can be found is another (for example, 'What would you or your colleagues suggest?'). Clarifying why the answer is needed and what the interlocutor would actually *do* with the answer is also a good tactic to open debate and dialogue. (for example, 'If you knew the

---

6   A good example of this is R. Stayer's article 'How I Learned to Let My Workers Lead' – he wasted 2 and a half years and half his management team trying to get people to take the lead by telling them to do so before he finally realised the mistake he was making.

7   Collins illustrates this in *Good to Great* by the story of Alan Wurttzel who took over from his father as CEO of a failing family business – his key answer when people asked where he wanted to take the company was, 'I don't know.' Instead of providing answers he led by questions to engender dialogue, and enable a process for the solutions to emerge. This approach seems to echo Richard Leider's 'Land of I don't knows' (R. Leider and D. Schapiro, *Repacking Your Bags*, quoted in R.P. White, P. Hodgson and S. Crainer, *The Future of Leadership*).

answer to that what could you do with it?'). There are some times when one *should* know the answer – again saying 'I do not know but I should' is honest. Saying 'I will find out and get back to you', and actually doing that, gains far more respect than trying to answer the question when one does not actually know the answer! Another powerful strategy can be to say 'I don't know – what do you think?' This often works well when you suspect (as is so often the case) that the person thinks they know the answer and is seeking senior management affirmation. So the strategy employed will differ depending on the context in terms of the task in hand, the cultural situation and the nature of the relationship between the person asking and the person answering. But whatever the context, it is a good strategy to begin to break the oligarchic assumptions which are frequently endemic. In his *Good to Great* study, Collins discovered a 'new' type of leadership which he called 'Level 5 leadership' – a leader having humility and fierce resolve at the same time.[8] To say 'I don't know' does take some humility, but when one understands the nature of the underlying charade and emergence of polyarchy, saying 'I don't know' is perhaps not so much a question of humility as common sense. And it shows a certain comfort with uncertainty. The 'I don't know' approach and follow up question/comment is part of a wider strategy of the challenge/support approach which comes next.

2. Breaking the Charade – The Challenge and Support Approach

Breaking out of the charade of pretending to know, and helping others to break out, takes a brave heart. However, it is not as terrifying or difficult as one thinks, despite the complexities involved. It takes a mix of challenge and support. There are four broad options as shown by the example below in Figure 4.3. This looks at what a leader might be able to do when asked a question to which he does not know the answer. The response will depend on what the needs are. For example if the question could give rise to a good dialogue, but is difficult, high challenge and support would be appropriate. If on the other hand the question is too specific and is of little interest to others then the straight 'I am sorry, I do not know' may be more appropriate. There is no detailed determinism here, it is a matter of fine judgement. Again the task in hand, cultural setting and relationship will need to be taken into account. The key rule is honesty rather than bluff. Embracing and using uncertainty is more positive and useful than trying to discount and avoid it. It does take judgement and can be difficult – in fact seeing the complexity may explain why it is easier to pretend to know! But the ensuing dialogue and honesty gets better results. It is similar to Collins' recommendation for brutal honesty, which he found thriving in great companies.

---

8   Collins' 'Level 5 leadership' is in his book *Good to Great* – Level 5 leadership = 'Executive – Builds enduring greatness through a paradoxical blend of personal humility and professional will'. Collins' research finds that leaders of great companies are not the charismatic types one would expect to find. This paper and the emergence of polyarchy explains why this is so. The other levels of Collins' model are: Level 1 = 'Highly Capable Individual – Makes productive contributions through talent, knowledge, skills and good work habits'; Level 2 = 'Contributing Team Member – Contributes individual capabilities to the achievement of group objectives and works effectively with others in a group setting'; Level 3 = 'Competent Manager – Organises people and resources toward the effective and efficient pursuit of pre-determined objectives'; Level 4 = 'Effective Leader – Catalyses commitment to and vigorous pursuit of a clear and compelling vision, stimulating higher performance standards'.

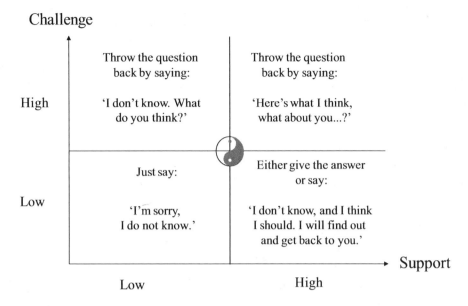

Figure 4.3   Breaking the charade via challenge and support

The two complementary approaches of challenge and support in some way reflect the Yang (Challenge) and the Yin (Support) of Taoism (see Chapter 1, Figure 1.2). Like in all of the approaches in this book, there is a degree of finesse which can be exercised – for example, one might wish to use this approach even if you *do* know the answer if only to gain engagement and (if the answer is obvious) full ownership. Wu wei can be exercised in an effective way.

3. Breaking the Charade – A More Dynamic Question & Answer Session

One immediate change that can begin to help the organisation to evolve is for leaders to look at how they run typical Q&A sessions. In the traditional sense leaders stand and take questions from the followers. The assumption (which was fair enough 100 years ago) was that the leader actually knew the answers! As we have seen this is becoming a strained assumption. So, traditionally, questions would flow *up* and answers would flow *down*. A more dynamic approach would be for questions to flow down and answers flow up *as well* – in other words there could be a two-way intercourse and dialogue rather than just one way.[9] This is *not* proposing that a leader should just stand there and ask questions – that would still be one way, albeit the other way around. And for some it may seem more of an interrogation than a discussion. It is suggesting that the leader should ask questions in a spirit of genuine enquiry and desire for dialogue whilst fielding questions as well. This is a more *dynamic* approach. It is also a lot more honest, an honesty which is invariably appreciated by an audience. And those leaders who ask for questions for such sessions to be submitted in writing in advance should begin to think about retirement (yes, believe it or not, some still do!).

---

9   See D. Bohm, *On Dialogue* for how dialogue can help unlock meaning and potential.

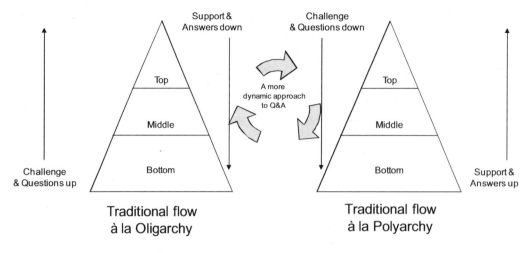

Figure 4.4   A more dynamic Q&A session

The simple suggested approach to changing how a typical Q&A session goes has some deeper consequences, not least when considering the skills that a leader needs. For example, under the traditional oligarchic assumption of leadership the key communication skill was being able to project – public speaking skills were seen as highly desirable. Under polyarchy the key communication skill is to be able to listen. Other examples are shown in Figure 4.5. The implications of such skills needs are considered more in Chapter 10 and Appendix D.

Saying 'I don't know', using challenge and support, and running Q&A sessions more dynamically are just three simple things that can begin to stop the charade. Many other strategies exist. Whatever approach one may try, and one can try a mix of all three, the key thing is to be authentic. This is much easier to say than do, and there will be many slips and bruises on the journey. Such is the way.

Oligarchical assumption		Polyarchical assumption	
Questions and issues coming up	Answers and solutions sent down	Questions and issues flowing down	Answers and solutions coming up
Ability to: • Analyse • Prioritise • Link to strategy	Ability to: • Talk and project • Simplify • Inspire and persuade	Ability to: • Question • Coach • Challenge • Enquire	Ability to: • Listen • Summarise • Support • Understand

Figure 4.5   Skills needed in polyarchy vs. oligarchy – an example

The Challenge of Upward Leadership

As the Complex Adaptive Leadership (CAL) associates have travelled the world in the last two years and taken the CAL approach with us, a common theme we meet is *'This is great – but our bosses do not understand'*. And, perversely enough, when we operate at Executive Board level we often meet, *'This is great – I wish our subordinates would embrace this and challenge us more!'*. When asked, *'How many of you have challenged upwards?'* a typical group of middle to senior managers will have around 90 per cent raise their hands. When asked, *'Of those who raised their hands, how many of you had a better relationship with the boss you challenged?'* most will raise their hands again. Within the charade outlined above is another charade – a fear of challenging due to fear of worsening the relationship, when in fact the opposite is true. So here are a few tips picked up about challenging the boss:

1. Be centered and really know what is important to you, as well as understand the full context and picture. If not, anything thrown your way will leave you hard pressed to say 'No'.
2. Use the Aikido approach. 'Ai' means harmony; 'Ki' means energy; 'Do' means the way = 'The way of harmonious energy'. So, when you have an opposite idea to that proposed by the boss, here are three simple steps:
   a) let go of your idea – this does not mean abandon it, but you need to let it go;
   b) summarise back to your boss his idea, build on it and show you really understand it;
   c) position your idea back and look for common ground and a resolution.
4. Pick your battles – and once committed, do not give up.
5. Diplomacy trumps aggression – never loose your cool!

This subject alone could be a whole book! And indeed a few have been written.[10]

A Nagging Emergent Issue – and Smart Turkeys

When discussing the issues in this chapter with executives a key paradox often emerges – and that is exemplified by one question asked recently in an INSEAD Executive programme: *'This is all very well. But would the turkeys vote for Xmas?'*

Why should managers and leaders move to a situation where they are following as much as managing? Surely they would be out of a job? As will be seen later, that is not the case. *But* the question remains, and for the pedant, here are a few turkey facts:

1. Turkeys originate from North America, and are not very suited to the current natural habitat.
2. There were estimated to be 10 million wild turkeys in North America in 1800 and 3 million domestic turkeys.[11]
3. By the turn of the century the wild species had become all but extinct, due to the destruction of natural habitat by farming and commerce.

---

10   For example, see Useem, M. (2001) *Leading Up – Managing your boss so you both win*, Crown Business.

11   B. Cambell and E. Lack, *A Dictionary of Birds*.

4. The modern US environment is not very conducive to turkeys – for example in the first half of the twentieth century in Maine there were no wild turkeys until the Department of Inland Fisheries and Wild Life released 24 turkeys on Swan Island. They had all died by 1946. Since then a series of releases under careful management has raised the wild turkey population to around 25,000. These are kept and nurtured for hunting.

5. Since the tradition of having turkey at Thanksgiving and Christmas has become established, the turkey population has thrived and exceeded the level of 200 years ago.

So the bottom line reads – if there was no tradition of eating turkeys for Christmas and Thanksgiving, there would be no turkeys. Given a vote for Christmas or extinction, smart turkeys would vote for Christmas! A paradox, but an understandable one.

Chapter Summary

1. Many organisations are stuck in a charade: those at the top know they do not know most of the answers to the problems facing the organisations they lead, but feel they *should* know. So they often pretend to know.

2. Meanwhile those at the bottom know most of the answers, and know the people at the top do not know, yet they *expect* them to know. So they often pretend not to know.

3. This situation is due to the changes discussed in Chapters 2 and 3 and the resultant stress between the oligarchic assumptions which remain endemic, whilst polyarchic realities are fast emerging.

4. There are some simple strategies one can employ to break the charade, and it takes time and patience. Embracing paradox and uncertainty helps. And leadership needs to be exercised upwards and sideways, not just downwards.

5. Smart turkeys vote for Christmas (and Thanksgiving)!

Leadership seems to be more complex than it used to be. We appear to be surrounded by more complexity than we had before. And yet, as we will see in the next chapter, recent advances in science and mathematics can help us see that chaos and complexity, paradoxical as it may sound, are actually quite simple. There is an underlying order and flow that one can tap into...

A Quick Breather between Parts I and II

Part I is over. Let's take a quick breather and recap. In Part I we looked at the *context* of dynamic leadership and polyarchy. Here again are the summary points from each chapter all together:

From Chapter 1

1. The scientific view of complexity and chaos is not the normal view – there are underlying patterns and principles which can be applied. These are paradoxical in nature.
2. Polyarchy is an extension, evolution and synthesis of anarchy (chaos and no leadership) with oligarchy (order and traditional leadership). It sees leadership as a complex dynamic system rather than just an attribute or something only assigned leaders do, and is based on the dynamics and features underscoring complexity science, chaos mathematics and a subset of complexity science – Complex Adaptive Systems Theory – hence the term 'Complex Adaptive Leadership'.
3. A basic understanding of Taoism can help grasp the paradoxes which arise and enable a leader to use polyarchy as well as be more effective within an oligarchic assumption.
4. Complex Adaptive Leadership links modern Western complexity science with ancient Chinese wisdom to offer a new and powerful approach to leadership which can get better results for less effort.

From Chapter 2

1. We have changed the *context* of leadership faster than we have changed our assumptions about *what* leadership actually is.
2. The increase of knowledge in the world is matched by an increase of uncertainty. Knowing more does not necessarily help increase certainty.
3. Oligarchic assumptions are increasingly colliding with fast emerging polyarchic realities.
4. Power has become atomised.
5. The context within which leaders lead is more complex.

From Chapter 3

1. Organisations seem to be evolving from the traditional strict functional and hierarchic type through a more flexible matrix towards a very fluid 'CAS' type. This evolution takes the metaphor of changing from a machine to an organism, and mirrors both Taoism and the development of management theory. It can also be reflected by the evolution of individual feedback mechanisms at the micro level, and the way strategy is formulated at the macro level.
2. This evolution is caused by the rapid pace and extent of change we looked at in Chapter 2.
3. As things become more complex, strategy formulation for organisations needs to evolve and embrace, not only the traditional analytical approach, but also the more dynamic dialectic approach.
4. Those that get stuck soon face death.
5. Success depends on the ability of the organisation to deal with polyarchy, and to manage the paradox of the existence of polyarchy within oligarchy.

From Chapter 4

1. Many organisations are stuck in a charade: those at the top know they do not know most of the answers to the problems facing the organisations they lead, but feel they *should* know. So they often pretend to know.
2. Meanwhile those at the bottom know most of the answers, and know the people at the top do not know, yet they *expect* them to know. So they often pretend not to know.
3. This situation is due to the changes discussed in Chapters 2 and 3 and the resultant stress between the oligarchic assumptions which remain endemic, whilst polyarchic realities are fast emerging.
4. There are some simple strategies one can employ to break the charade, and it takes time and patience. Embracing paradox and uncertainty helps. And leadership needs to be exercised upwards and sideways, not just downwards.
5. Smart turkeys vote for Christmas (and Thanksgiving)!

So what? Well, the worldwide and organisational contexts, and 'resultant' emergence of polyarchy, seem to be more of a dynamic rather than a straightforward cause and effect. The emergence of polyarchy can be seen as a bifurcation.[1] There are many underlying dynamics at play where cause and effect become inevitably entwined and harder to separate. An example is shown in Figure B1.1 below.

We saw in Chapter 2 how better technologies have led to an increase of general human awareness. But increased general human awareness has led to better technologies! The changes leading to the emergence of polyarchy are part of a more complex dynamic than linear cause and effect.

---

1   A bifurcation is a term used in complexity science, originally identified by an Australian mathematical biologist Robert May who studied animal populations and found that biological systems were driven by non-linear mechanisms which can end up in a major change. The concept is studied more in Chapter 6.

So it spells death for leaders to stick rigidly to the old oligarchic assumption that leadership is solely something leaders do within a hierarchy. Leadership is a lot more complex than that nowadays. Leaders need to be more adaptable, and willing to enable others to lead. The paradox of leaders following is not so hard to embrace. Leaders need to be able and relaxed enough to follow and support those they purport to lead, as well as be able to lead them. To do that, leaders need to *let go* by (paradoxical as it sounds) *holding back*. That means holding back on the urge to jump in and lead. Such a state of affairs explains why new leadership models such as Collins' 'Level 5 Leadership' and Badaracco's 'Quiet Leadership' are emerging.[2]

Holding back is hard to do, as chaos can result, and we all hate that. The reason we hate it is mainly due to the fact we do not understand what is happening.

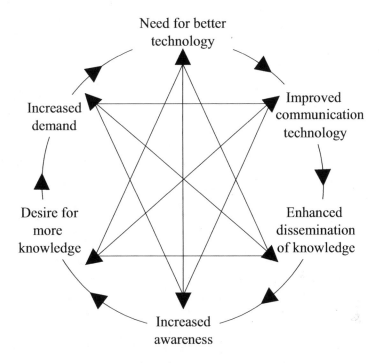

Figure B1.1 Knowledge and technology drive each other

Complexity looks messy, and control seems absent. The typical response to a dynamic and complex situation is for leaders to 'get a grip' and try to exert more control – but that is not what should be done! Such an effort, more often than not, results in waste and the opposite effect to what is desired. An understanding of how chaos and complexity 'works' can help ameliorate such concerns, and it is to this subject that part two is dedicated. First, in Chapter 5 we will look at the emergence of non-deterministic approaches, chaos and complexity sciences in general. This will be followed in Chapter 6 with an amazing exercise which introduces some principles which can be employed – the Four + Four model. These principles are then explored in more detail in Chapter 7 showing exactly how an organisation and their leaders can exploit the dynamics of complexity.

---

2   See J.L. Badaracco, *Leading Quietly*, and J. Collins, *Good to Great*.

Chaos and Complexity

Order in Chaos, Simplicity in Complexity – The Deeper Paradox

A QUICK TEST TO OPEN UP THE MIND

Consider the questions below and score yourself, adding up the scores as you go – select first a category (for example, 'Neutral') and then a numeric score (for example, 5).

1.　　Science is exact and precise.

Strongly Disagree	Disagree	Neutral	Agree	Strongly Agree
1 or 2	3 or 4	5 or 6	7 or 8	9 or 10

2.　　An organisation can mostly be run in a deterministic way (for example, a course of action can be planned to a defined effect).

Strongly Disagree	Disagree	Neutral	Agree	Strongly Agree
1 or 2	3 or 4	5 or 6	7 or 8	9 or 10

3.　　Chaos and ambiguity should be avoided and, if met, resolved and clarified.

Strongly Disagree	Disagree	Neutral	Agree	Strongly Agree
1 or 2	3 or 4	5 or 6	7 or 8	9 or 10

4.　　'KISS' (Keep It Short and Simple) is a key skill for leaders.

Strongly Disagree	Disagree	Neutral	Agree	Strongly Agree
1 or 2	3 or 4	5 or 6	7 or 8	9 or 10

5.　　Complex behaviour has complex causes.

Strongly Disagree	Disagree	Neutral	Agree	Strongly Agree
1 or 2	3 or 4	5 or 6	7 or 8	9 or 10

6.   Different systems always behave differently.

Strongly Disagree	Disagree	Neutral	Agree	Strongly Agree
1 or 2	3 or 4	5 or 6	7 or 8	9 or 10

7.   Simple systems behave in simple ways with underlying simple causes.

Strongly Disagree	Disagree	Neutral	Agree	Strongly Agree
1 or 2	3 or 4	5 or 6	7 or 8	9 or 10

8.   The more you put into something, the more you will get out.

Strongly Disagree	Disagree	Neutral	Agree	Strongly Agree
1 or 2	3 or 4	5 or 6	7 or 8	9 or 10

9.   If you do not control things, sooner or later they will descend into chaos.

Strongly Disagree	Disagree	Neutral	Agree	Strongly Agree
1 or 2	3 or 4	5 or 6	7 or 8	9 or 10

10. Complexity, muddled, complicated – it all the same – difficult!

Strongly Disagree	Disagree	Neutral	Agree	Strongly Agree
1 or 2	3 or 4	5 or 6	7 or 8	9 or 10

Total the scores:

If you score over 75 in the questionnaire at the start of this chapter, you may be surprised and the chapter may open your mind. If you score below 60, this chapter will just reinforce what you already know. And if you score in-between, hopefully you will find this chapter of interest and it sparks off some creative thinking.

In Chapter 1 we saw that polyarchy is an evolution, or synthesis, of the long term trends of leadership. These trends were anarchy followed by oligarchy. Polyarchy is a synthesis of the two. Oligarchy still seems to be the current main assumption of leadership, but there is a discontinuity with the fast changing times as explored in Chapter 2. These fast changes have encouraged the emergence of polyarchy. In Chapter 3 we saw how organisations are evolving from a more fixed hierarchic silo-based type to a more fluid type. This has led to strains as explored in Chapter 4, with leaders more stressed and under the microscope than ever before. The largest barrier to being comfortable with polyarchy is the fact that it has an element of anarchy and chaos. So an understanding of the underlying history and dynamics of chaos and complexity, and the move away from determinism, will help leaders be relaxed in letting go and practising 'wu wei' when such an approach should be taken. The last part is emphasised as this is not to extol 'wu wei' as the only route, or even best route. As will be explored in Part III it is one of a variety of routes, but seems to be the hardest to do well.

Taking a scientific view of chaos and complexity has an advantage. There is a danger (as with many new ideas) that one thinks an almost religious belief and faith needs to be achieved in order to run fully with a new idea, and that old ideas need to be replaced. However, one does not have to become an anarchist in order to embrace the ideas of polyarchy. One does not need to throw away conventional science and mathematics in order to embrace chaos and complexity theories. But one does need to understand the limit to which classical and traditional theory and approaches can go. And by understanding contradictory approaches, the paradoxes can be embraced and used.

So in order to practise Complex Adaptive Leadership and be comfortable with the Tao (flow) of polyarchy, it helps to realise that this is not just a philosophical trend but also a scientific trend as well. So an understanding of the trends in science is useful.[1] Put another way, oligarchy is still important (and very much surrounding us) but, like classical science and mathematics, it does not really help when things are dynamic and complex and so at times can get in the way. What relativity and quantum mechanics is to classical Newtonian physics, polyarchy is to classical leadership thinking.

Before we dive into the science (and for some it may be best avoided if you do not like science!) let's have a quick look at complexity at a more pragmatic level first.

Complexity – Problem or Opportunity?

Complexity as a theme seems to be popping everywhere. For example, some of the boats on the River Thames are sponsored by KPMG with their tagline 'Cutting through complexity'.[2] KPMG sees complexity as something to be cut through, overcome, so clear and practical solutions can be delivered to their clients. At the same time, a plethora of articles and books have emerged recently about complexity. For example in the *McKinsey & Co. Quarterly Review* published in May 2010[3] complexity is positioned as something that creates problems and needs to be managed, put in its place so to speak. Four types of complexity are identified:

- **Imposed complexity** includes laws, industry regulations and forces from outside. It is not typically manageable by companies.
- **Inherent complexity** is intrinsic to the business and can only be jettisoned by exiting a portion of the business.
- **Designed complexity** results from choices about where the business operates, what it sells, to whom and how. Companies can remove it, but this could mean simplifying valuable wrinkles in their business model.
- **Unnecessary complexity** arises from growing misalignment between the needs of the organization and the processes supporting it. It is easily managed once identified.

---

1   It should be stressed that drawing parallels between modern physics/mathematics and the social sciences is fraught with danger. The frequent misuse of such ideas in the social sciences led the physicist Alan Sokal to write a spoof paper entitled 'Transgressing the Boundaries: Towards a Hermeneutics of Quantum Gravity', deliberately full of misunderstandings and illogical arguments. Much to his surprise it was hailed as a seminal contribution until he denounced it as a phoney.

2   'Cutting through complexity' is the tagline to the KPMG new brand and identity, as explained at http://www.kpmg.com/mt/en/issuesandinsights/articlespublications/pages/cuttingthroughcomplexity.aspx, accessed: Feb 2014.

3   Birkinshaw, J. and Heywood, S. (2010) 'Putting complexity in its place' *McKinsey and Company Quarterly Review.*

It is as good an approach as any other that sees complexity as something to be solved and overcome, and assumes a deterministic approach – analyse what type of complexity you are dealing with, and then deal with it – put it in its place. So far, so good. Another view is provided by David Snowden and Mary Boone in their Cynefin Model.[4] This sees complexity compared to other states, and is one step closer to the actual science of it all. Four states exist according to the model, and the basis of definition is the degree to which cause and effect is obvious and to what degree resultant predictability exists:

- **The Simple.** This is where cause and effect are fully linked and known, and so predictability is high. If you do 'This' you get 'That'. It is the area of process and best practice. I would not call an Airbus A380 a simple piece of kit but in this model it is: push the stick forward buildings get bigger, pull the stick back buildings get smaller; keep pulling back and they get bigger again. Cause and Effect. Do 'This' and you get 'That'. It is the area we like things to be and we try to push as much as we can into this box. Something crops up, we categorise it, and then deal with it. In some small respect this is the attempt by the McKinsey article mentioned above – categorise the type of complexity and then deal with it.
- **The Complicated.** This is where cause and effect are there, but the linkages are not so obvious and need analysis to sort it out. Predictability is less than 'The Simple' but with careful analysis and consideration the choices one makes have a fair degree of predictable outcome. It is the area of experts and the traditional 'Jumoni approach' to strategy (see Chapter 3). It is the area of McKinsey and Company's[5] MECE approach (listing parts of a problem that are Mutually Exclusive and Collectively Exhaustive). The analytical tools to deal with 'The Complicated' are those typically taught in an MBA. It is the 'Either/Or' world – either we can do this or we can do that. Analyse the situation using a variety of tools and then make your choices.

And then we have a BIG jump over a boundary. 'The Complex' and 'The Chaotic' are of a very different logic and assumption. They lend themselves to a different scientific tradition. 'The Simple' and 'The Complicated' share the common scientific assumption that lends much to conventional physics and science – that the world is largely deterministic, linear and one can predict once we understand the underlying laws. The boundary into the next two parts of the Cynefin model is into the world of the 'New Science'[6] which are non-linear, non-deterministic and hard if not impossible to predict with a degree of certainty:

- **The Complex.** This is where cause and effect are combined. The multiple 'agents' involved (for example, people, organisations, component parts of the system and

---

4   Snowden, D. and Boone, M. (2007) 'A leaders framework for decision making' *Harvard Business Review*.

5   "The McKinsey Way" is one of a series of three books that talk about MECE: Rasiel, Ethan (February 1, 1999), *The McKinsey Way* (1 ed.). McGraw-Hill. Rasiel, Ethan and Friga, Paul (September 26, 2001), *The McKinsey Mind: Understanding and Implementing the Problem-Solving Tools and Management Techniques of the World's Top Strategic Consulting Firm* (1 ed.). McGraw-Hill. ISBN 978-0-07-137429-3. Friga, Paul (November 24, 2008), *The McKinsey Engagement: A Powerful Toolkit For More Efficient and Effective Team Problem Solving* (1 ed.). McGraw-Hill.

6   The first link of these new sciences to leadership was made by Meg Wheatley in her seminal 1992 book *Leadership and the New Science – Learning About Organization From an Orderly Universe*. Her 1999 Second Edition replaced the tagline with: 'Discovering order in a chaotic world' which more closely resembles the link to the new sciences of, for example, quantum mechanics and chaos mathematics – these are explored later in this chapter.

so on) are interconnected with feedback loops that affect each other in a complex network that is hard to predict. Here one needs to probe and use more modern approaches such as those mentioned with regard to strategy in Chapter 3. One probes, one discovers and one adapts and advances in a dynamic way.

- **The Chaotic.** This is rare and is where there is no discernable cause and effect at all. At one level this is the easiest to deal with as a leader – just act. Just do something and, as there is no discernable cause and effect, do not worry too much about what one should do. Act and then move on towards one of the other three boxes.

So a way to look at the Cynefin Model is to consider each of the four differing states existing on a continuum (Figure 5.1). On the one hand an assumption of determinism is relevant (either, cause and effect is very well known or it can be analysed so the underlying predictability understood). On the other hand, non-determinism is the assumption (cause and effect is interlocked or non-existent and so predictability is low or impossible).

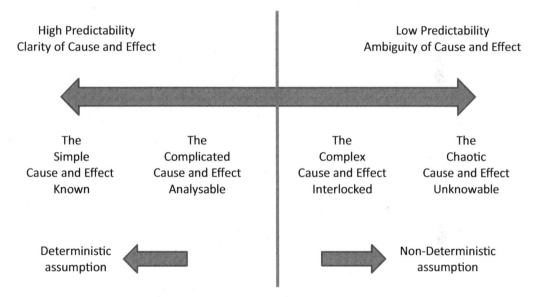

Figure 5.1   The four states on a continuum

Another way of looking at the Cynefin Model is with regard to the Unknown/Known matrix (Figure 5.2).

The reality is that in most organizations the first three co-exist. There will be issues/ situations which are simple, those which are complicated and those which are complex. The trick is to understand the nature of the underlying issue being faced and then deal with it in an appropriate way. Much time is wasted by addressing 'The Simple', for example, by using emergent approach best suited to 'The Complex'.[7] Similarly, much time is wasted trying to solve 'The Complex' by employing things best used for 'The Simple' (such as use of processes).

---

7   Ralph Stacey describes what he calls 'Complex Responsive Processes' (CRP) where human interaction and discussion can interact in a way which is hard to predict. This can happen in meetings which can be great for probing a complex problem but when the problem is simple a more linear disciplined approach to problem solving is better.

Unknown knowns *The Complex* Probe and discover	Known unknowns *The Complicated* Analyse and decide
Unknown unknowns *The Chaotic* Act and move on	Known knowns *The Simple* Categorise and deal

Based on the Cynefin Model

Figure 5.2   The unknown/known matrix

So complexity can be a problem if it is created by applying one approach from one box above, to solve a problem from another box. In this sense complexity can become a value destroying problem. But if complexity is understood, and the underlying science is appreciated, then it can become a value creating opportunity.

This book deals with 'The Complex' and this chapter specifically looks at some of the sciences which have shaped complexity science. Complexity, and the dynamics that drive it, are discoverable. Once discovered, it can help leaders get more result for less effort. What follows is an exploration of some of this science (and for those who do not like science, I would skip straight to the next chapter!). The rest of the book explores how such theory can be applied.

Background to Chaos and Complexity Science

The science of chaos and complexity is relatively new. The glimmers of this new 'science' (or *approach* to science may be a better description) began in earnest just over 100 years ago. However, some argue that the roots of thinking about chaos and complexity can be traced back to the ancient Greeks when Hesiod wrote in *The Theogony* in 8 BC 'First of all chaos came to be and from that emerged order.'[8] Others may argue that the interplay between chaos and order, complexity and simplicity, dated further back to the Taoist *I Ching* which saw the two interlinked as a dynamic.[9]

---

8   *The Theogony* (Genealogy of the Gods) written by Hesiod in the eighth century BC is a poem which recounts the creation of the world out of chaos, the birth of the gods, and descriptions of their numerous adventures.

9   For a good translation of the *I Ching* see R. Wilhelm and C.F. Baynes (trans.), *I Ching or Book of Changes*.

In the Tao Yin/Yang symbol (Figure 5.3), the Yin has within it elements of the Yang (represented by the white dot) and the Yang has within it elements of the Yin (represented by the black dot). The Yin/Yang symbol is called the 'Tai Chi Tu', or 'The power of great polarity'. Chaos comes out of order, and order comes out of chaos. Paradox.

So up until the turn of the twentieth century, the main thinking about the interplay between chaos and order, complexity and simplicity, was largely philosophical. As far as *science* was concerned the universe was ordered. The view of science was that nature was deterministic and based on solid uncontroversial laws. By the late nineteenth century, science had proven rules as described by eminent scientists such as Sir Isaac Newton (proposed 200 years earlier in his *Philosophae Naturalis Principae Mathematica*). Other laws were uncovered by the experiments of scientists such as Faraday and proven formulas of mathematicians such as Maxwell and Laplace (proposed 100 years earlier). Laplace stated the deterministic viewpoint thus:

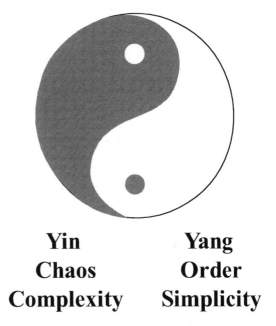

Yin   Yang
Chaos   Order
Complexity   Simplicity

Figure 5.3   Yin/Yang – chaos and order

'If we knew the motion and positions of all the particles in the universe, then we could calculate their behaviour at any other time in the past and the future.'

So by the late nineteenth century it was thought that most of the basic laws that govern our planet had pretty well been discovered and the following uncontroversial assumptions held sway:

1. The universe is like a giant machine following laws in absolute space and time. Newton described it thus 'Absolute, true and mathematical.' He also stated that 'time flows equably without relation to anything external'.
2. All motion has a cause, and every cause has an effect – nature and the universe is deterministic.
3. Light has the properties of a wave, as determined by Huygens, proven by Faraday and Maxwell, and supported by Young's double slit experiment (explained in more detail below).
4. Matter has two models – waves (such as electromagnetic waves, light waves and so on) or particles (such as physical matter), and they are mutually exclusive to each other.
5. Any system can be measured objectively to a degree of accuracy. An observer can be external to the system being observed, in accordance with objective Cartesian scientific investigation.

As an aside here, if one looks at some of the assumptions above, one can see a similar view still apparent in business – for example the assumption that markets respond to the laws of economics and that businesses can be run in a deterministic way. Cause and effect laws are similar to supply and demand. It is assumed that businesses can be measured in an objective way, and run like a machine. In such a world, oligarchic assumptions make sense – but we all intuitively know that it is not the whole story! It appears that business thinking is far behind modern scientific thought and stuck in 'The Simple' and 'The Complicated'.

Let's get back to science. By the late nineteenth century it was felt that there was not very much more that physics and science could contribute. This view was typified by the Nobel laureate Albert Michelson who said in June 1894, *'The more important fundamental laws and facts of physical science have all been discovered, and these are now so firmly established that the possibility of their ever being supplanted in consequence of new discoveries is exceedingly remote. Our future discoveries must be looked for in the sixth place of decimals.'*[10] This was echoed by the head of the US patent office who said around the same time, *'All that is to be invented has pretty much been discovered.'*[11] It had all been 'sorted'. Smugness pretty much reigned, although a very small minority were not so sure …

By the mid- to late twentieth century, all of the above five 'uncontroversial' assumptions had been successfully challenged. What happened? There were four key new theories which undermined the classical approach: relativity theory, quantum mechanics, chaos mathematics and complexity science. A brief understanding of each will help today's busy leader be more relaxed with the many uncertainties of daily life, as well as embrace the paradoxes which ensue. This is because:

- **Relativity Theory** shows how deterministic rules which could be said to contradict each other can co-exist – it is not a case of 'either/or', but 'both/and'.
- **Quantum Mechanics** shows how underlying reality is uncertain and probabilistic rather than strictly deterministic[12] – so reality is a paradoxical and seemingly chaotic dynamic between deterministic and non-deterministic forces and matter is paradoxically both a wave and a particle.
- **Chaos Mathematics** shows how chaos has an underlying order and patterns which can be used to good effect.[13]
- **Complexity Science** shows that complexity has an inherent and underlying simplicity of a self-organising nature.

---

10   Michelson is known for his famous experiment to measure the velocity of the Earth through the ether, a substance that scientists believed filled the universe. This experiment was done with Edward Morley in 1887, and is known as the Michelson–Morley experiment. It ended up showing that the ether did not actually exist. This experiment overturned conventional thinking, created a lot of confusion and helped Einstein's relativity theory evolve. It is clear that Michelson himself did not understand the significance of this accidental discovery when he said eight years later that there was nothing much left to discover in physics.

11   This has been attributed to Charles H. Duel, Commissioner of the US Patent Office in 1899. However there is much legend about such a quotation which is discussed in C. Morgan and D. Langford, *Facts and Fallacies*. There is no evidence that anyone in the patent office really said anything of the sort. However, it was only a few years later that *Scientific American* announced on 2 January 1909 that 'The automobile has reached the limit of its development.'

12   Although some may see quantum mechanics as a 'non-deterministic' science, the way that the underlying probabilities of quantum mechanics unfold is certainly deterministic. It is this strange combination of uncertainty and underlying certainty that helps to give quantum mechanics its reputation of being almost (some would say totally) impossible to understand fully.

13   Chaos mathematics is often a misapplied term, due to the confusion between the everyday and technical uses of the word chaos (that is, complete disorder vs. sensitivity to initial conditions). A more technical term for chaos mathematics is 'chaotic dynamics'; a dynamical system is a mathematical system.

Classical physics
Newtonian and Laplacian universal laws
Maxwell and Faraday's electromagnetic laws
Clausius' laws of thermodynamics

General Relativity
Time is not constant but relative
Mass and energy are linked
Space and time are linked and curved

Quantum mechanics
Non-deterministic nature of matter
Light is both a wave and a particle
Uncertainty principle

Chaos mathematics
Butterfly effect
Phase space attractors
Universality
Bifurcations

Complexity science
Self-organisation
Post-normal science
Complex Adaptive Systems theory

Deterministic certainty

Non-deterministic uncertainty

Figure 5.4   The flow towards chaos and uncertainty

Polyarchy is a paradoxical fusion of anarchy and oligarchy. Whilst we all know and are comfortable (to varying degrees) with oligarchy, we all tend to shy away from anarchy. We dislike chaos – we dislike complexity – 'Keep it simple!' is a frequent cry. If one can gain an idea of how chaos works, and how natural it is from a scientific viewpoint, one can be more comfortable with it. The trend towards polyarchy (a less deterministic approach than oligarchy) is similar to the trend in science towards less deterministic approaches. The underlying trend is natural. And even within the scientific trends there are paradoxes. For example, on one level quantum mechanics seems uncertain and non-deterministic compared to Newtonian mechanics. And yet quantum mechanics has very deterministic mathematics behind it.[14]

Again it is important to stress that non-deterministic approaches do not supersede or replace deterministic ones – they complement them in a powerful way.

An understanding based on science can help to encourage a more dynamic approach to leadership, give insight into chaos/complexity and enable a more effective understanding of how polyarchy can actually work.

---

14   Quantum mechanics has various interpretations. The broad theories usually focus on the paradoxical wave-particle nature of matter. The Copenhagen interpretation states that matter is a wave until the collapse of the wave function occurs and then matter is made up of particles. In the Bohm interpretation, every particle has a definite position and momentum at all times, but we do not usually know what they are, though we do have limited information about them. Some argue that despite the inherent uncertainties within aspects of quantum mechanics, the science is *more* deterministic than classical science. This is because some problems that cannot be solved in classical science (leading to chaos) can be solved exactly by quantum mechanics.

A Very Brief View of Relativity: Innocence Lost

The theory of relativity blew away a few classical foundations. Until relativity came along, there were three solid and uncontroversial foundations for science:

1. time flows independently and constantly;
2. energy and mass are separate; and
3. space is constant and separate.

In 1905 Einstein was working in the Swiss patent office as a clerk third grade (his promotion to second grade had recently been turned down). Physics was his passion, although he had recently failed in his application to teach physics at a local school. Without an affiliation to a university, or access to a laboratory or decent library, he published five papers that year in the *Annalen der Physik*. Three of them were seminal, described by C.P. Snow as '*The greatest in the history of physics.*'[15]

Of the three, one was about the particle nature of light (which contributed to quantum mechanic thinking and for which he later won a Nobel prize). The second was about Brownian motion and how the apparent random motion of particles followed a statistical law. And the third, for which Einstein is more famous, is the theory of relativity. He postulated the special theory in 1905 and ten years later widened it into the general theory (which added gravity).

In the special theory of relativity, Einstein showed that the speed of light was constant and thus time and space are relative. The fact that space is relative is easy to understand, as what is observed in space is dependent on the relative locality of the observer. The fact that time can be relative and thus not constant is harder to imagine, but has been born out by experiments.

In 1959, Harvard University proved Einstein's general theory of relativity, that gravity had an effect on time. This was done by noting the difference of time passing when measured at the bottom of a tower compared to the top. The gravity effect was also noted by Vessot and Levine who fired a rocket containing an accurate hydrogen clock and noted the difference in time when measured against a similar clock on the ground.[16] The closer to a large mass one is, the greater the gravitational force, and so the slower time passes.

Time is also affected by speed, and the special theory of relativity has also been proved. It was confirmed by an experiment by Hafele of Washington University in St Louis and Keating of the US Naval Observatory in 1971. They put two highly accurate atomic clocks on two planes which flew around the world and landed – both clocks showed time flowing differently to the clocks of the US Naval Observatory (against which they had been synchronised).[17] The faster one travelled, the slower time passed. At 99

---

15   See Snow's book *Variety of Men*. He described the papers: '*All of them are written in a style unlike any other theoretical physicist's. They contain very little mathematics. There is a good deal of verbal commentary. The conclusions, the bizarre conclusions, emerge as though with the greatest of ease: the reasoning is unbreakable. It looks as though he had reached the conclusions by pure thought, unaided, without listening to the opinions of others. To a surprisingly large extent, that is precisely what he had done. It is pretty safe to say that, so long as physics lasts, no one will again hack out three major breakthroughs in one year.*'

16   A clock in orbit in space gains a nanosecond (a billionth of a second) per hour. The clock on top of the 25m tower in Harvard University recorded a time warp factor of 0.25–12 per cent.

17   They flew the clocks around the world in a westerly direction as well as an easterly direction. They wanted to see not only if time was affected by speed but also by the spin of the planet, which was suggested by Einstein's Field

per cent the speed of light, time warps by a factor of around seven – in other words one second will pass where a minute would have. The twin's paradox is when a twin goes out to space and back at 99 per cent the speed of light for three years and returns to find the other twin sibling aged by 20 years. In all these experiments (both actual and thought), and many more besides, the time differences which were found responded exactly to the predications made by Einstein's theory and his field equations.[18] Space and time are linked and relative. The only absolute is the speed of light.

The theory of time being inconstant and dependent on who is where and at what speed can give rise to some intriguing conclusions. One is that the reality that one person sees will change due to position and speed. For example, imagine you are on an old fashioned train carriage with doors that open to a small inter-connecting platform at each end. Imagine that you were in the exact middle of the carriage and had a machine which could fire a particle at the speed of light both up and down the carriage and when the particles hit the doors at the end of the carriage, the doors would open. The particles are fired at exactly the same time and go at exactly the same speed. To you (sitting in the carriage) the doors would open at the same time. If there was a clock by each door recording the time that this happened, the clocks would show the same time. But then imagine the carriage is passing an embankment and your friend is sitting there watching the experiment. To him the train is travelling in a direction – thus the particle fired towards the end of the train will arrive at its door (which is travelling in the direction of the spot where the particle was fired) before the particle travelling towards the front of the train. The doors for him will open at different times![19]

So time is not constant. That is hard for the non-scientists amongst us to fathom. It was not just the classical assumption of time that Einstein challenged. His famous equation $E = MC^2$ (energy is equal to mass times the speed of light squared) showed that mass and energy are linked and not, as was generally assumed, separate things. And the speed of light is a big number (675 million mph, or 185,000 miles per second), so that number squared is huge. In other words a gram of matter has within it the energy able to supply the electrical power of a large town for several days. Again this is hard to imagine, but further development by other scientists in the nuclear field showed how true this could be. Nuclear weaponry and energy are still only scratching the surface however – a nuclear weapon only releases around 1 per cent of the total potential energy of its mass.

Finally Einstein showed that space and time are linked into space-time, and it is curved. The basis on which sound mathematical geometry is traditionally founded is shaken under this assumption. The founder of geometry is often held to be Euclid who in ancient Greece

---

Equations. They found that it was, and that the equations were very accurate. The clock on the plane which flew around the world in an easterly direction ran 59 nanoseconds slower. The one that flew westerly ran 273 nanoseconds faster (due to the Earth's spin). See Hafele and Keating, 'Around The World Atomic Clocks: Predicted Relativistic Time Gains'. In 2005, the National Physics Laboratory (NPL) in the UK conducted a similar experiment and got the same result (as reported in *Metromnia*, issue 18, Spring 2005).

18   The availability of computers to make large and complex calculations as well as the atomic clock, has made such experiments possible. The atomic clock is run by a caesium atom which vibrates at 9,192,631,770 per second – if two such clocks ran together they might differ by a second within 500 million years.

19   This thought experiment has been attributed to Eddington (as, apparently, he liked trains while Einstein liked to use trams!). The experiment may seem strange, but not so strange when one considers the doppler effect of sound (a consequence of the Galilean relativity of Galileo and Newton). Hear a siren coming towards you and then going away it will change in sound, and yet to the person in the ambulance it will stay the same – two different realities due to two differing relative positions.

laid out the rules of geometry.[20] We all know that the degrees in a triangle add up to 180. But this does not hold true in curved space. If you draw a large equilateral triangle on an orange, you will find the angles add up to more than 180 degrees. If the apex is on the top of the orange with an angle of 90 degrees and the bottom along the diameter, then they will add up to 270 degrees. The rules of geometry founded by Euclid in ancient Greece, and which are still studied and followed today, are shaken when applied to curved space. This in itself was not new as it was generally known that Euclidean geometry may work for builders but not for ocean navigators. What was new was the theory that the whole of space-time is curved.

Much of the theory of relativity is hard to understand but, rather like the graph of general awareness shown in Chapter 2, many more understand it today than when it was being first aired. Indeed when the theory was being discussed in November 1919, well after publication, an eminent scientist of the day, Sir Arthur Eddington, in reply to Ludwig Silberstein saying he must be only one of three people who understood the theory, said after a long pause: 'I am trying to think who the third person is.' Nowadays any undergraduate of physics will have a good understanding. They will also understand Newton's laws. Both are proven – both can be applied – and both are contradictory of each other. Paradox exists at the most scientific level.

So what? The key point is that the theory of relativity disproved some of the long held firmly rooted and dearly held beliefs and assumptions of classical physics. Yet classical physics still work.[21] In other words, the Newtonian assumptions work for large individual objects moving slowly, but they do not stack up when the speed of light or the whole universe is involved. Put another way, classical theory does not go far enough – they are OK for when things are simple, but not when things are more complex. So in leadership theory terms (and for those tied to oligarchic assumptions), the point shows that a theory such as polyarchy may indicate some of the failings of the assumptions of oligarchy, but both still work, depending on the context.

There is a movement in physics to find a Grand Unifying Theory (GUT) or Theory of Everything (TOE) which squares away all the paradoxes – perhaps the GUT/TOE is that paradox exists and is part of the universe and thus no such GUT/TOE exists. The fact that classical Newtonian physics and the more modern relativity of Einstein are in contradiction and yet both are proved, and work, is also very Taoist – Yin and Yang again.

The ability to hold opposing views and be able to apply each when needed (and sometimes both at the same time) is a *key* attribute that leaders need today. Such an assertion, given the lessons of modern physics, is perhaps not so much a philosophical aspiration as a logical scientific conclusion and common sense. If the very universe in which we exist can allow two contradictory scientific models of Newton and Einstein to be, then it should not be so confusing that oligarchy and anarchy can co-exist in science, within polyarchy. So far, so good, so Taoism – the idea of a paradoxical dynamic. However, the plot thickens.

Both Newton and Einstein were deterministic in their approach and Einstein believed in a rule-driven universe as did Newton (just different rules). His theory was itself challenged by a new science that he himself helped found – quantum mechanics. This

---

20   Euclid lived around 300 BC, and wrote *The Elements*, a 13-volume work on the principles of geometry and properties of numbers. His work was rediscovered in the fifteenth century, when it was translated into Arabic. Until recent years *The Elements* has been the principal source for the study of geometry in schools.

21   The 1969 moon-shot used calculations from Newton's *Principae Mathematica* rather than Einstein's field equations as the latter were seen as too complicated and offered an accuracy not needed.

was not the case of one set of deterministic rules disagreeing with another. This was a far deeper paradox that showed that underlying reality was itself non-deterministic. Einstein spent much time trying to disprove the theory he himself helped found. Indeed he wrote to Max Born, another founder of the theory: *'You believe in a God who plays dice, and I in complete law and order in a world which objectively exists.'*[22]

And yet quantum mechanics still works – without it we would not have the semiconductor, lasers, LEDs, CDs, automatic door opening devices and a whole series of other inventions.

A Quick View of Quantum Mechanics – Underlying Reality is Uncertainty

We operate in a world where we like to think that there is a degree of certainty and that what we see is what exists. In that frame of mind we like to think in classical ways, especially in terms of cause and effect. We like to think that the material things around us are solid. Quantum mechanics challenges this. Having a basic appreciation of quantum mechanics can help us to let go of some of the more deterministic assumptions we may tend to hold onto.

Whilst the theory of relativity looks at the big macro universal picture, quantum mechanics looks at the small micro sub-atomic picture. The theory of relativity answers many questions, whilst quantum mechanics seems to raise more questions than answers. Indeed Richard Feynman, one of the leading scientists in this area stated *'I think I can safely say no-one understands quantum mechanics.'*[23] Neils Bohr, one of the founders of the new science, was reputed to say a person who was not outraged on first hearing the theory about quantum mechanics did not appreciate what was being said. Meanwhile Heisenberg, another founder of the theory, when asked how best to envision an atom, dryly remarked *'Don't try'*. This sounds similar to what the original Taoist thinkers said about Taoism, as mentioned in the Chapter 1. The link between the two is no accident.[24]

Let's take a quick look at the sub-atomic world. Atoms are very small – it was the Italian nineteenth-century scientist Amedeo Avogadro whose work in 1811 led to the calculation that in a litre of gas there are 6.02×10^{23} atoms– that is 6.02 and 23 zeroes, a lot.[25] If an orange was the same size as an atom, the number of oranges to make up the planet Earth would be the same number as the atoms to make up the orange. The fact that atoms exist was identified a long time ago, although subject to much debate. For example, Democritus of Abdera in 370 BC stated *'The only things are atoms and empty*

---

22   This is often quoted and gave inspiration for Ian Stewart's book on chaos mathematics, *Does God Play Dice?*

23   Richard Feynman is rated by some as being as influential to modern physics as Einstein. He invented Quantum Electrodynamic (QED) theory, worked on the Manhattan Project, and was the one who showed that the 'O' rings were responsible for the space shuttle Challenger disaster.

24   F. Capra's seminal and best-selling work *The Tao of Physics* describes the many parallels between Taoism and other Eastern philosophies/religions to modern physics. The linkage of Taoism to modern physics is similar to such a linkage made by Collins and Porras to the lessons from their research on visionary companies in their *Built to Last* study.

25   Avogadro postulated in 1811 that a litre of gas at equal temperature and pressure would contain the same number of atoms. The exact number itself was not calculated until later on that century, when the concept was extended to include not only gases but also all substances.

space.[26] What he did not realise is that atoms are in fact themselves mostly empty space. That was discovered by Rutherford who found atoms consisted of two basic and very small parts – a nucleus (consisting of two types of particles: neutrons and positively charged protons) and negatively charged electrons. The standard view is that electrons 'orbit' the nucleus – in fact it is a bit more complicated than that but such a model helps understand an atom and its particles.[27] If an atom was the size of St Paul's Cathedral, the nucleus would be the size of a pinhead on the floor (accounting for more than 99 per cent of the atom's weight) and the electrons would be the size of a speck of dust whizzing around the nucleus at a distance of the top of the dome – in other words the atom is made up mostly of empty space. The fact that it is solid is due to the movement and energy of the particles within the atom. If that is hard to understand, imagine a propeller – it defines a solid space by its movement. And the particles in an atom whizz around at a very much faster speed than a propeller.[28]

It is the behaviour of such particles that quantum mechanics is concerned. Particles do not seem to follow any of the classical laws. Unlike planetary orbits, the path of the electron follows no predictable pattern – it appears chaotic. Furthermore the particles behave like waves. Classical thinking would have us believe that matter is either a wave or a particle but cannot be both.

To understand this, and to be outraged as Bohr suggests we should be, the double slit experiment sheds some light (no pun intended). This experiment was designed by Thomas Young in 1798, and was first shown in 1801, with the obvious proof and conclusion that light is a wave.[29] He shone a light through a card with two slits onto a dark card behind. When one slit was closed the light on the dark card reflects the slit the light went through. The same occurred when the other slit was closed, as shown in Figure 5.5.

---

26   Democritus developed the atomic theory of the universe that had been originated by his mentor, the philosopher Leucippus. Hardly any of Leucippus' writings remain, but he is generally credited as being the founder of atomic theory.

27   In 1899, Thomson proposed that the atom was a positively charged sphere with negatively charged particles called electrons distributed within the sphere (called the 'Plum Pudding' model). Rutherford discovered in 1911 that the positive charge of an atom was amassed in the atom's centre and the electrons orbited this nucleus like planets. Bohr discovered in 1913 that electrons had certain values of energy which dictated the distance from which they would orbit the nucleus – and that they could change that orbit (the so called 'quantum leap'). Schrödinger in 1925 proposed that electrons do not 'orbit' the nucleus but act like waves around the nucleus travelling at certain distances and energies. This model is generally accepted as the most accurate.

28   The speed of an electron is around 40,000 miles per second, the particles in a nucleus at 80,000 miles per second. Furthermore, solidity is enhanced by what is called resonance. Molecules are made up of atoms – H_2O is water, two atoms of hydrogen and one of oxygen. A single hydrogen atom has a nucleus (itself made up of one proton – positive charged particle – and one neutron – neutral charge particle), and 'orbiting' the nucleus is one electron (negatively charged particle). In a molecule the electrons' 'orbits' of the atoms are shared, which is known as resonance – this also adds to the solidity of the molecule.

29   Young's experiment is better described as a demonstration, as it demonstrated the wave nature of light. It seemed to have settled the great debate at the time as to whether light travelled as particles (as proposed by Sir Isaac Newton) or as a wave (as proposed by Christiaan Huygens). Although not widely appreciated, Young's experiment was actually shining light on a sliver of cardboard, rather than two slits, to show its wave nature. Fresel, along with others such as Babinct, Fraunhofer and Kirchofff, refined the mathematics of interference and diffraction into a predictive mathematical theory which helped Maxwell realise that light is a form of electromagnetic radiation.

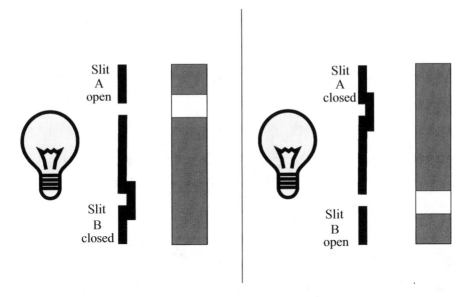

Figure 5.5   Young's amazing double slit experiment – part 1

One would expect when both slits are open, two white areas would occur on the dark card, as shown in Figure 5.6. But this does not happen!

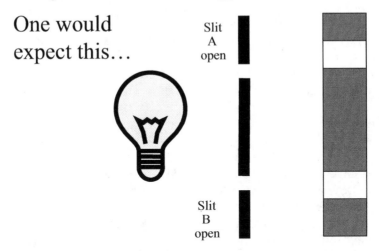

Figure 5.6   Young's amazing double slit experiment – part 2

When both are open, instead of two white areas on the dark card appearing, a *series* of white areas appear, as shown in Figure 5.7.

This is because the light waves interfere with each other. Some waves cancel each other out (hence the dark areas) and some amplify each other (hence the light areas). There was some debate about light being a particle or a wave, but Young's proof seemed to have settled the debate. His proof was reinforced by Fresel in 1815, and also mathematically by Maxwell in the 1860s. However, in 1900 Max Planck showed that heat radiation travelled in packets of particles, which he called 'quanta'. Planck was the one who lent the name 'quantum' to quantum mechanics. Einstein, who showed that all of radiation, including

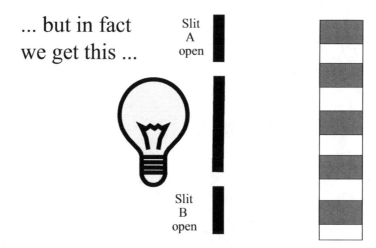

... but in fact
we get this ...

Slit A open

Slit B open

Figure 5.7   Young's amazing double slit experiment – part 3

light, travelled in particles, reinforced this theory. He did this by solving the mystery of the photoelectric effect of light displacing electrons on a metal plate. It was for this work that he received a Nobel Prize.[30] These light particles were later to become called 'photons' by Lewis in 1926 after Bose in India further proved Einstein's theory. So now we have two proofs: one showing light is a wave and another that it is a particle.

If light is a particle (albeit with no mass) then it follows that solid particles might act in the same way. Within the Young double slit experiment, solid particles (such as electrons) might behave like light. Strange as it may sound, they do. And it gets stranger as we go. Firing particles through Young's double slit leads to a similar interference pattern, as was shown when electrons were fired through such a double slit. Stranger still, when *individual* electrons are fired *one at a time* the *same* interference pattern in Figure 5.7 above occurs over time. In other words it seems that a single solid particle can travel through both slits at the same time, interfere with itself and produce the pattern – this defies common sense. Even stranger, when one tries to see which slit the particle goes through, the interference pattern ceases and the pattern shown in Figure 5.6 emerges. The particle behaves like a solid particle. *The very act of observation changes the outcome.* So much for the Cartesian concept of independent and objective observation. And stranger even still, as shown by Wheeler and Aller,[31] when one *retrospectively* measures (that is, *after* the particle has gone through the slit, but before it hits the screen) the same thing happens. If one does not retrospectively measure, we get the pattern in Figure 5.7 (that is, the electron passes through both slits as a wave) and if one does retrospectively measure we get the pattern shown in Figure 5.6 (that is, the electron passes only through one of the slits). This seems to defy the arrow of time, as an action in the future seems to affect something in the past.

---

30   Although Einstein is more famous for his theories of relativity (Special theory in 1905, and General theory which added gravity effects in 1915), it was for his work on light particles that he won his Nobel prize. The effect that he explained was why light, when shone onto a metal plate which had an electrical charge passed through it, would dislodge electrons from the surface of the plate.

31   See K. Minas and R. Nadeau, *The Conscious Universe: Parts and Wholes in Physical Reality*, p. 42 – Minas describes how the University of Maryland and the University of Munich both independently confirmed Wheeler's experiment. Paul Davies also described this as 'Teleology without teleology' in his *Goldilocks Enigma* (yet another paradox).

The strange wave-particle duality led to Heisenberg's 'Uncertainty Principle'. This states that one could not measure the precise location and motion of a particle at the same time: one could either measure its location but not its motion, or one could measure its motion but not its location. Heisenberg used the German word 'Unbestimmheit' which can also be translated to mean 'non-deterministic'. The uncertainty also reflects the atom itself: one can state that the electron particle will be within the 'orbit' of a nucleus, but one cannot state its exact orbit or path. So quantum mechanics replaced certainty with probability.

Quantum mechanics theory also breaks with Einstein's law that nothing can travel faster than the speed of light. It was Wolfgang Pauli's 'Exclusion Principle' which suggested in 1925 that twinned pairs of particles can affect each other instantaneously no matter what the distance between them is. This instant link (or 'non locality') was further developed and proven by Bell in the UK, Bose in India and Aspect in the USA. Einstein called it 'spooky action at a distance'. Experiments conducted in the particle accelerator in CERN outside Geneva in Switzerland in the late 1990s has shown that paired particles, whose spin is affected when one of the pair is changed, effect such a change at the *same time* even when several miles apart (that is, the 'message' that one particle spin is changed is received instantaneously by the other particle). To date no one has managed to explain why this is so and how the law regarding the speed of light can be broken. So quantum mechanics raises doubts about the theory of relativity – Stephen Hawking said *'The two theories are known to be inconsistent with each other. They cannot both be correct.'*[32] But they both seem to be.

What quantum mechanics shows us is that the underlying nature of things is chaotic, uncertain and hard to understand fully as it breaks classical thinking (which after all is proved as well). It shows that seemingly absolute truths, laws and logic that work within one context do not necessarily work within another. The theory also shows that the underlying nature of things is very dynamic. Atoms are a collection of very small particles moving at incredible speeds creating the solidity we gain by knocking on wood.

What has quantum mechanics got to do with leadership? Well, if the underlying nature of reality is indeed chaotic and uncertain, but within this chaos and uncertainty there is some order, then chaos is not necessarily something to be abhorred as much as understood. This is not to say one should induce chaos and then just stand by and watch gleefully as everything falls apart. Nor is it to say that one should replace oligarchy with anarchy and forget trying to create some order. If one is to use polyarchy, and the types of polyarchic systems that are explored later on, one needs to remember that polyarchy is a fusion of *both* anarchy and oligarchy. The two are opposite and contradict each other, yet can work together in a powerful way. Such a state of affairs flows naturally. The greatest barrier to letting go and using 'wu wei' leadership is the fear that loss of control results in chaos – to some extent this is true but chaos itself has a useful dynamic. So quantum mechanics shows us that:

1. There is more than one logic, and 'reality' is not what it seems to be. One needs to be flexible in thinking and not tied to one approach. Taking a more dynamic approach is more natural and enables a better chance of success.
2. Underlying nature seems contradictory and somewhat chaotic. But within contradiction and the chaos there is some order. This is a paradox. An understanding of that order can help one appreciate chaos, and so gain better results, and so embrace paradox more easily.

---

32   See Stephen Hawking's *A Brief History of Time*.

3. Probability is more attuned to reality than certainty – understanding probability is better than trying to ensure a certain determined outcome.

So far the exploration of chaos and uncertainty has been fairly theoretical with only some attitudinal application. How can one actually apply such theories into organisations? It is the third area of chaos mathematics that lends the best examples, and it is to this we will now turn.

Chaos Theory – Underlying Order

Chaos mathematics (more commonly called chaos theory) is relatively new.[33] The mathematician Ian Stewart wrote in his book *Nature's Numbers*, '*Chaos behaviour obeys deterministic laws, but it is so irregular that to an untrained eye it looks pretty much random. Chaos is not just complicated, patternless behaviour; it is far more subtle. Chaos is apparently complicated, apparently patternless behaviour that actually has a simple deterministic explanation.*'

Tien-Yien Li and James Yorke of the University of Maryland were the first two mathematicians credited with the using term 'chaos' in their 1975 paper 'Period Three Implies Chaos'. At the same time Mitchell Feigenbaum was working on chaos in the Theoretical Division of Los Alamos (founded three decades earlier by Robert Oppenheim). They were unaware of each other's existence. Feigenbaum, Yien and Yorke were fairly representative of a group of disparate mathematicians, physicists, biologists and chemists all working in the mid-1970s on chaos in splendid isolation to each other. In the true spirit of the subject, the theme of chaos and complexity emerged from a variety of different places, in a chaotic way.

What is it all about? One simple way of understanding what chaos theory is about is to look at how smoke comes out of a cigarette – you will see that it goes straight up and then, for no apparent reason, begins to swirl in a seemingly chaotic way. Understanding exactly why it begins to swirl is a typical area of chaos science. The study of chaotic instances uncovered some surprising findings – chaos was not so chaotic after all ...

There are many concepts within chaos theory. This section will consider ones that are applicable to Complex Adaptive Leadership, with some examples of how they can be applied:

- attractors
- universality
- fractals
- bifurcations.[34]

---

33   Simple deterministic mathematics (for example, $1 + 1 = 2$) is fine as far as it goes, but it cannot deal with complex dynamics. So it was in 1657 that Girolamo Cardano published *The Book of Games of Chance*. The theme of such non-linear thinking in maths was also explored by Laplace who published in 1812 his *Théorie Analytique des Probabilités*. This was built on by Quetelet in 1846 with his error law and normal distribution. The work done in mathematics in the nineteenth century was also mirrored in science where Galton (anthropology), Edgeworth (economics) and Pearson (philosophy) turned statistics into more or less and exact science. Maxwell built on this in 1873 by proposing statistical methods for molecular motion. So by the end of the nineteenth century, science had two paradigms for mathematical modelling – the deterministic approach of differential equations, and statistical analysis for probabilities. There was no common ground between the two. It was Henri Poncaré who united the two in his topological phased space theory. See D. Gillies, *Philosophical Theories of Probability*.

34   It is sometimes hard to delineate where chaos theory ends and complexity theory begins – bifurcation is often aligned to complexity theory. I include bifurcation in chaos theory as it has some very mathematical aspects. It is sometimes called phase transition theory by complexity scientists.

ATTRACTORS

An attractor is the plot of movement of an object in 'phase space'.[35] Phase space is an illustration such as an x/y axis graph (Figure 5.8). So, for example, if we plot a pendulum swinging, the phase space we could plot its movements against could be its velocity at any one moment on an x axis and the angle it is at any one moment on the y axis.

If we were to plot a pendulum swinging non-stop against velocity and angle, we would see a circle, as seen in Figure 5.9. This assumes the pendulum has no friction to slow it down, or has a mechanism to drive it against friction. The resultant plot is called a periodic attractor. In reality the pendulum would have friction and so would slow down to a stop. In this case it would be plotted as a spiral (see Figure 5.9). The resultant plot is called a point attractor. The pendulum is 'attracted' to a steady state, a particular point – hence the term 'attractor'. The same plot would result from a ball swung around the rim of a round basin and then let go – the ball would travel around and around until finally settling in (attracted to) the bottom of the basin.

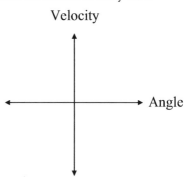

Figure 5.8   Example of phase space

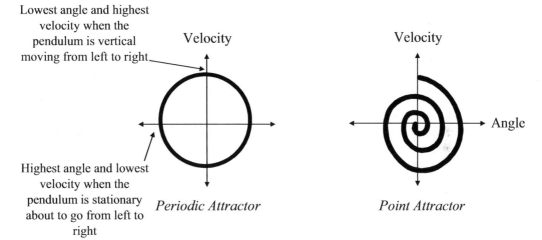

Lowest angle and highest velocity when the pendulum is vertical moving from left to right

Highest angle and lowest velocity when the pendulum is stationary about to go from left to right

Periodic Attractor

Point Attractor

Figure 5.9   Examples of attractors

These plots have a specific and easily understandable pattern. However, some attractors do not and they are called 'strange' attractors. Perhaps the most famous and useful strange attractor is known as the butterfly effect, or Lorenz's Strange Attractor. Of all the chaos theories this one has special importance for Complex Adaptive Leadership.

Much work was done in the 1970s when the new theories of chaos were really beginning to emerge. Strangely enough, most papers in various different fields began

---

35   Phase space was first proposed by the Irish mathematician William Hamilton. It was later used by the French mathematician Henri Poncaré as a way to plot a chaotic or non-linear system, and he was one of the first late nineteenth-century mathematicians who anticipated chaos theory.

to appear independently of each other in 1970. Sadly very few were aware that a lot of work had already been done ten years earlier. It seemed no one thought of looking in the *Journal of Atmospheric Sciences*, volume 20, pp. 130–41, published in 1963. Over a decade before the term 'chaos mathematics' was first coined an article entitled 'Deterministic Non-Periodic Flow' by Edward Lorenz described one of the most famous manifestations of chaos mathematics – the butterfly effect. Its more technical term is 'Lorenz's Strange Attractor'.[36]

Edward Lorenz was a keen mathematician but actually worked as a research meteorologist. He built a mini-weather system simulator on a Royal McBee computer in 1960. In the winter of 1961 he wanted to study again a weather simulation he had just spent several days running, and so typed in the starting parameters once more. These consisted of a very lengthy list of numbers each with a long decimal point such as 0.501675. The numbers represented changes in three variables of temperature, pressure and wind speed. To save time, he left the final few numbers off as this in meteorological terms was insignificant – 'Like a seagull fart in a hurricane' was the apparent significance he was reported to comment to a colleague. The simulation ran at first exactly as before, but after a couple of days some very small differences occurred to the first run. After a while these differences grew to an outcome that was vastly different – the simulation ended in a weather state poles apart from the first run, despite such a very small change at the start. Lorenz made an accidental but very significant discovery – that a very small change within a complex system (such as weather) can produce a very large difference to what would have otherwise happened. In other words, when a situation has a great sensitivity to initial conditions a small change can have a disproportionate effect. When he worked out why this was, he found that even complex and chaotic systems, which are unpredictable in the long run, have an underlying pattern. This accidental discovery was given the technical name 'Sensitive Dependence on Initial Conditions'. When Lorenz presented his paper several years later to the 139th meeting of the American Association for the Advancement of Science in Washington in 1972, he titled his paper 'Predictability – Does the Flap of a Butterfly's Wings in Brazil Set Off a Tornado in Texas?' His answer was, predictably, ambiguous whilst focusing on the instability of the atmosphere. Lorenz's butterfly effect can be explained by three (temperature, pressure and wind speed) simultaneous non-linear differential equations which have an infinite number of possible solutions. When graphed, these equations give a picture as shown in Figure 5.10, which shows why the term 'butterfly' is used.

Since that time the butterfly effect is one of the most well-known phenomena of chaos mathematics. It has given rise to many manifestations in films, literature and TV.[37] It also has historic manifestations, a recent one being Mohamed Bouazizi, the Tunisian fruit seller in the rural town of Sidi Bouzid, who upon having his wares confiscated and being unable to gain an audience with the mayor, immolated himself in front of town hall on 17 December 2010. His desperate action set off a series of events which became known as the Arab Spring. An unforeseen, unprecedented and dramatic political, social, cultural and economical realignment across the Middle-East, has gone on to dramatically

---

36   Attractor theory was developed in the 1970s by David Reulle. He was a mathematical physicist who discovered how to explain turbulence using strange attractor theory. Naturally he was thrilled when he discovered Lorenz's work that had been done a decade earlier. He even went to see Lorenz but was reportedly disappointed that they never really had the discussion about the ins and outs of attractor theory that Reulle was hoping for. Apparently they spent most of the time taking their wives to an art gallery.

37   For example see http://en.wikipedia.org/wiki/Butterfly_effect_in_popular_culture, accessed: February 2014.

change the daily lives of over 200 million people. Although the story of Mohamed Bouazizi is tragic in the extreme, his actions were, in fact, the wing flap of Lorenz's butterfly.[38]

The butterfly effect is very significant as, on the face of it, it seems to break the first law of thermodynamics, sometimes known as the Law of the Conservation of Energy, which can be summarised as: the effort you put in will dictate the result you get out. Yet within complex organisations, *small* changes can yield *large* results. A practical example of this is the concept of 'catalytic mechanisms' that Collins reports in his research. These are small changes to company policy which yielded large results.[39] Examples of this include:

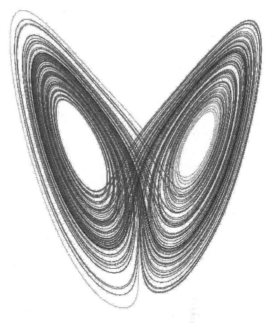

Figure 5.10 The butterfly effect

- Granite Rock[40] wanted to be the market leader in customer service. They decided to allow customers to 'short pay'. At the bottom of each invoice one can find the following: *'If you are not satisfied for any reason, don't pay us for it. Simply scratch out the line item, write a brief note about the problem, and return a copy of this invoice along with your check for the balance.'* Collins reports that over the years this small addition to the invoice has had a profoundly positive impact.

- Mike Jackson, then CEO of financial services company Birmingham Midshires in the UK, included his personal phone number on complaint forms. These forms stated if the complaints were not dealt with in a quick and polite way, the customer could phone him personally. The company was struggling to survive, and it identified customer service as a critical opportunity. The number of calls the CEO actually received was negligible but such a small change had a large and beneficial effect on staff handling complaints, as well as on customer perceptions. The company's poor situation was turned around and it became an award winner for customer service.

---

38   This example was written up by Douglas Dean, a CAL Associate.

39   J. Collins, 'Turning Goals into Results: The Power of Catalytic Mechanisms'. Strangely enough the concept of 'catalytic mechanisms' did not make it into the final outcome of the research which uncovered it. In his book *Good to Great* 'catalytic mechanisms' are not mentioned at all, although the stories of Gore and Granite Rock are. Perhaps this was due to the fact that 'catalytic mechanisms' are more of a polyarchic feature, and the book seems to have an oligarchical assumption. For example Collins and his team are very surprised by the level of 'humility' they see in leaders of great companies. Perhaps the application of Complex Adaptive Leadership would be seen as 'humility' within an oligarchic assumption, albeit common sense in a polyarchic one.

40   Granite Rock is a company over 100 years old in Watsonville, California and is one of the 'Great' companies in Collins' book *Good to Great*. They sell crushed gravel, concrete, sand and asphalt, and are the best performing company in the industry. It charges a 6 per cent price premium to its competitors, has consistently gained market share and won the Baldridge quality award in 1992.

Again this initiative was but one of a variety of efforts taken, and shows how a relatively simple thing can help achieve a larger effect.[41]

- Bill Gore, founder of W.L. Gore & Associates,[42] wanted the company to have a 'natural leadership' style (similar to polyarchy). So they have a policy which allows staff to 'sack' their bosses. They cannot sack them from the company, but if they feel their boss is not providing the right support, they can simply bypass them and choose to another person to report to.

- National Vulcan, in order to enable a more team-based self-organising culture, removed without warning the time punch machines used by staff to clock in. This small move had a huge effect on changing the culture in the desired direction.[43]

- 3M[44] has a strong commitment to innovation, aiming to have 25 per cent of revenue from products less than five years old. To support this, they have the policy of 'bootleg time' which allows each employee 15 per cent of his time and available resources to be devoted to pet projects. Staff are encouraged to take the lead and define new products – the most well-known which resulted from this was the Post-it™ note.

These are relatively small policies but they have a big effect on the organisation. According to Collins, such catalytic mechanisms have five characteristics:

1. They produce results in unpredictable ways. In some ways this links to the principle of needing to have a degree of tolerance to chaos and ambiguity. No one could have

---

41   For the full case see N. Obolensky, *Practical Business Re-engineering*.

42   W.L. Gore & Associates is a fabric company worth over $2Bn and founded by Bill Gore in 1958. His view of 'natural leadership' is that leadership could not be bestowed by hierarchical position. He felt that the best came from people who could make commitments freely and not when told to do so. This is what is posted on their web site <http://www.gore.com/en_xx/aboutus/culture/index.html>, accessed 18 April 2010:

How we work at Gore sets us apart. Since Bill Gore founded the company in 1958, Gore has been a team-based, flat lattice organization that fosters personal initiative. There are no traditional organizational charts, no chains of command, nor predetermined channels of communication.

Instead, we communicate directly with each other and are accountable to fellow members of our multi-disciplined teams. We encourage hands-on innovation, involving those closest to a project in decision making. Teams organize around opportunities and leaders emerge. This unique kind of corporate structure has proven to be a significant contributor to associate satisfaction and retention.

We work hard at maximizing individual potential, maintaining an emphasis on product integrity, and cultivating an environment where creativity can flourish. A fundamental belief in our people and their abilities continues to be the key to our success.

How does all this happen? Associates (not employees) are hired for general work areas. With the guidance of their sponsors (not bosses) and a growing understanding of opportunities and team objectives, associates commit to projects that match their skills. All of this takes place in an environment that combines freedom with cooperation and autonomy with synergy.

Everyone can quickly earn the credibility to define and drive projects. Sponsors help associates chart a course in the organization that will offer personal fulfilment while maximizing their contribution to the enterprise. Leaders may be appointed, but are defined by 'followership.' More often, leaders emerge naturally by demonstrating special knowledge, skill, or experience that advances a business objective.

Associates adhere to four basic guiding principles articulated by Bill Gore:

1. Fairness to each other and everyone with whom we come in contact.
2. Freedom to encourage, help, and allow other associates to grow in knowledge, skill, and scope of responsibility.
3. The ability to make one's own commitments and keep them.
4. Consultation with other associates before undertaking actions that could impact the reputation of the company.

43   N. Obolensky, *Practical Business Re-engineering*.

44   3M (Minnesota Mining and Minerals) is one of the 'visionary' companies in Collins and Porras, *Built to Last*. It was founded in 1902 to supply abrasive minerals. It never succeeded as a mining company and had to be bailed out several times by investors. In 1905 it moved out of mining into manufacturing sandpaper.

foreseen the emergence of Post-it™ notes. Other innovations which have come out of their process include reflective licence plates, and a machine which replaces the heart during operations. Since its introduction, 3M has seen its revenues and profits increase 40 times.

2. They distribute power, often to the discomfort of those who traditionally hold power. For example Granite Rock's short pay gives power to the customers. Gore's gives power to the employees. In many ways the mechanisms support the atomisation of power looked at in Chapter 2. And this point helps explain why a devolved style of leadership is needed, as explored in Chapter 10.

3. They have teeth. Catalytic mechanisms need to be specific and cannot be half measures! For example the steel manufacturer Nucor pays its staff a base pay which is 25–33 per cent below the national average, but has a bonus of 80–200 per cent of base pay based on team productivity. This simple mechanism has teeth and encourages the teams to be self-policing.

4. They help 'eject viruses'. A lot of controls are geared at getting people to act in a certain way, the 'right way'. Catalytic mechanisms help organisations get the right people in the first place. Gore's mechanism soon gets rid of managers who are unable to lead in a certain way.

5. They produce on-going effects. They are not like the one-off rousing speech or motivating event. Catalytic mechanisms run themselves and produce on-going effects as 3M's shows.

Catalytic mechanisms are not new, even if the term is. Such approaches have existed in the field of change management for a long time. They can be seen in the context of change strategies, as shown in Figure 5.11 below. Catalytic mechanisms in some sense are the more scientific name of 'low hanging fruit' – small effort, big effect.

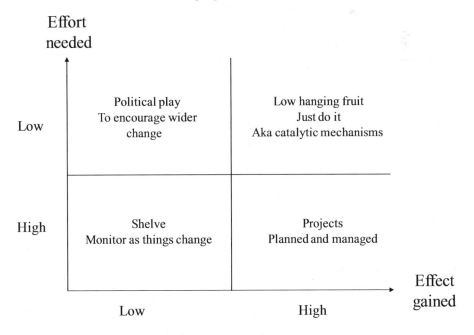

Figure 5.11 Where do catalytic mechanisms fit?

Collins suggests some guidelines for introducing such catalytic mechanisms:[45]

1. Don't just add, remove. Many catalytic mechanisms are geared to removing previous policies. For example, when HP removed the restriction whereby components had to be bought from internal divisions, those divisions were catalysed into improving efficiency and quality. Many policies are legacies from more hierarchic times.

2. Create, don't copy. The best way is to involve people in their creation, rather than copying them from outside the organisation and enforcing them. Some of the best ideas for catalytic mechanisms come from lower levels, as the research in Chapter 4 would suggest (most solutions are known at the bottom).

3. Use money, but not only money. They need not cost money. Fifty per cent of the catalytic mechanisms identified by Collins' team did not involve spending money.

4. Allow them to evolve. They need to evolve with the time. For example, 3M started in 1956 when scientists were urged to work in their labs on lunch breaks on whatever they wanted. This was formalised in the 1960s as the '15 per cent rule', whereby scientists could use any 15 per cent of their time. In the 1980s it was extended to all staff. In the 1990s, worried that not enough people were using the rule, a task force 're-invented' it with more bonus schemes and recognition rewards for those who used it.

5. Build an integrated set. A single catalytic mechanism is not going to work in isolation. They need to be coherent with overall goals and direction (for example, the 3M example supports their innovation policy). There also needs to be more than one catalytic mechanism to gain overall effect.

So Lorenz's Strange Attractor, the butterfly effect, is exemplified by catalytic mechanisms – small changes which over time gain a big effect. There are other examples of using the butterfly effect including NASA's use of hydrazine fuel to manage satellites, 'intelligent' pacemakers, Japanese dishwashers and a UK spring manufacturer.[46] These examples are scientific application of chaos theory. 'Catalytic mechanisms' are a good example of chaos theory being applied in leadership. The idea is not new, as the famous poem *'For want of a nail the shoe was lost, For want of a shoe the horse was lost, For want of a horse the message was lost, etc. etc.'*[47]

Another way to look at attractors is to see them as a 'flow'. In Taoism a critical skill is to go with and add to the flow of what is happening. If there is an underlying flow, then a small change can be a big encouragement. Catalytic mechanisms therefore need a flow

---

45   The *Good to Great* study identified hundreds of different catalytic mechanisms, catalogued by Collins' research colleague Lane Hornung.

46   NASA directs trajectories of spacecraft using the butterfly effect – one example was the International Cometary Explorer. They used the fact that the butterfly effect applies to trajectories in the solar system. With tiny amounts of hydrazine fuel, they created little puffs that steered the spacecraft halfway across the solar system to meet up with comet Giacobini-Zinner. That's how they achieved the first ever scientific cometary encounter. For how the Japanese are using chaos engineering in the design of dishwashers, see K. Aihara, 'Chaos Engineering and its Application to Parallel Distributed Processing with Chaotic Neural Networks'.

47   The concept of a nail leading to the loss of a horse and wider implications first appeared in John Gower's *Confessio Amantis* in 1390 ('For sparinge of a litel cost, Fulofte time a man hath lost) and was also written up by T. Adams in his *Works* in 1629. Starting at the nail and then escalating to the shoe, horse, rider, messenger, battle, and kingdom is a popular rhyme. It was partially used by Benjamin Franklin in the preface to *Poor Richard's Almanac* of 1753 where he started by stating 'A little neglect may breed mischief'.

within which to operate. And attractors, when plotted in phase space, show a physical flow. The application of this to leadership is considered in detail in Chapter 10.

UNIVERSALITY

Universality is the next concept of chaos theory that has a practical application to Complex Adaptive Leadership, although the research for such applicability is much thinner. The concept was discovered by Mitchell Feigenbaum[48] – had he seen Lorenz's work he would have perhaps been able to advance his thinking a lot faster. As it was, he made some significant advances without Lorenz's thinking. The key concept he introduced was that different chaotic systems have similar universal laws.

An example of 'universality' is what is called 'Feigenbaum's Delta'. An example is how the dripping of a tap changes when the tap is slowly opened (towards a chaotic flow). You can try this at home! At first the tap drips in a pattern drip, drip, drip and so on. A gradual turn moves the pattern to drip-drip, drip-drip, drip-drip and so on. Another gradual turn moves it to drip-drip-drip-drip, drip-drip-drip-drip and so on. Sooner or later the drips give way to a chaotic flow. You can discover that the turn of the tap by a factor of 4.669201 to each previous turn changes the dripping by these stages towards the chaotic flow. What is more surprising is that this numeric factor ('Feigenbaum's Delta') shows up in a whole load of other chaotic dynamics – the formation of helium, the initial swing of pendulums, the behaviour of random moving magnets, and the vibration of train wheels to name a few. In other words, there is universality within the dynamics of chaos in different systems.

The application of Feigenbaum's Delta has hitherto been confined to science and engineering. However, the significance of universality has a wider application – chaotic systems, which were hitherto thought of as unique, do in fact have underlying patterns and shared laws.

You may notice in the exercise explained at the beginning of the next chapter that the flow seems to come together, then fall apart a couple of times before finally coming to the resolution. The time factor of this happening decreases by a factor of 4.669. So it seems that Feigenbaum's Delta can be applied not only to a steady state becoming chaotic, but *also* to a chaotic state becoming steady.

FRACTALS

Fractals are simple shapes or patterns that are repeated many times and gain increasing complexity along the way. They were 'discovered' by a Polish-born French mathematician called Benoît Mandelbrot.[49] He studied chaotic systems in the 1960s and discovered that

---

48   Dr Mitchell Feigenbaum received his PhD in theoretical high energy physics from the Massachusetts Institute of Technology in 1970. He was a research associate at Cornell University from 1970 to 1972, and at Virginia Polytechnic Institute from 1972 to 1974. He then moved to Los Alamos National Laboratory, where he was a staff member from 1974 to 1981 and a fellow from 1981 to 1982. While creating his work on chaos, he shared his office with Murray Gell-Mann who went on to found the Santa Fe Institute. From 1982 to 1986 he was a Professor of Physics at Cornell University. Dr Feigenbaum was a visiting member at the Institute for Advanced Studies at Princeton in 1978 and 1984. He joined Rockefeller University in 1986. In addition to being the university's Toyota Professor, he is also director of the Center for Studies in Physics and Biology.

49   Benoît Mandelbrot was born in Poland in 1924 and is a French mathematician who specialised in chaotic systems (for example, movement of prices over many years; telephone line errors) and found patterns – he called them fractals, which show underlying patterns of chaos.

there were underlying patterns. He called them fractals, after seeing the word in his son's Latin homework. The famous fractal shape from chaos theory is called the 'Mandelbrot Set'. This is generated by a simple mathematical formula repeated again and again. The variety and complexity which arises is unbelievable, with repetitions of the overall picture as part of the pattern (Figure 5.12). It resembles the psychedelic effects that LSD is said to produce. Strangely enough, fractal geometry, the Mandelbrot Set and LSD appeared on the scene roughly at the same time....

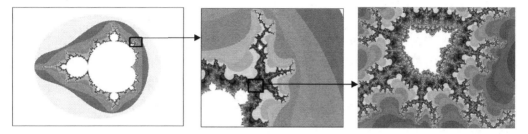

Figure 5.12 Fractal geometry and Mandelbrot set

A simpler example of a fractal is the Koch snowflake[50] (or its similar Koch curve) shown below (Figure 5.13). A triangle is replicated to a third of its size, and placed halfway along its sides. This is repeated many times and an image like a snowflake emerges as shown in Figure 5.11 below. As the 'coastline' of the snowflake becomes more and more complex, it is possible for an infinite coast to be included in a finite space, another seeming paradox. Indeed such a possibility was discussed in Mandelbrot's paper 'How Long Is the Coast of Britain?' in which he stated: *'The concept of "dimension" is elusive and very complex, and ... the field abounds in paradoxes.'*[51]

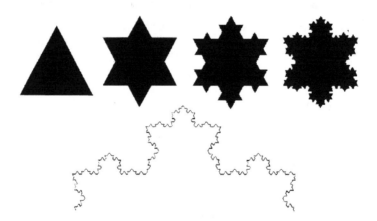

Figure 5.13 Koch snowflake – example of a fractal

---

50   The Koch snowflake (or Koch star) is a mathematical curve and one of the earliest fractal curves to have been described. It appeared in a 1904 paper entitled 'On a continuous curve without tangents, constructible from elementary geometry' (original French title: *'Sur une courbe continue sans tangente, obtenue par une construction géométrique élémentaire'*) by the Swedish mathematician Helge von Koch. The lesser known Koch curve is the same as the snowflake, except it starts with a line segment instead of an equilateral triangle.

51   B. Mandelbrot, 'How Long Is the Coast of Britain? Statistical Self-Similarity and Fractional Dimension'.

The 'Sierpinski gasket'[52] is similar to the Koch snowflake. This is formed by adding a triangle inside the triangle (instead outside as in the Koch snowflake) and then repeating the exercise for each triangle remaining. This is a deterministic pattern and process – the build-up of which is shown in Figure 5.14. A simple deterministic process can build up a complex pattern.

Figure 5.14 Sierpinski gasket – 1

The Sierpinski gasket above uses an equilateral triangle – the same effect can be seen in a right angled triangle.

As can be seen the gasket is created by the repetition of a simple rule – each side of the triangle is halved, and the resultant triangle removed – this is repeated for the triangles that remain, and over time a complex fractal emerges.

Figure 5.15 Sierpinski gasket – 2

What is surprising is the application of a similar rule to a completely different shape (a square) results in the same complex pattern emerging as can be seen in Figure 5.16.

---

52   The Sierpinski triangle is a fractal described by Sierpinski in 1915 and appeared in Italian art from the thirteenth century. It is also called the Sierpinski gasket or Sierpinski sieve. Waclaw Siepinski was born 1882 and died in 1969 in Warsaw. He was known for outstanding contributions to set theory (research on the axiom of choice and the continuum hypothesis), number theory, theory of functions and topology. He published over 700 papers and 50 books. Three well-known fractals are named after him (the Sierpinski triangle, the Sierpinski carpet and the Sierpinski curve), as are Sierpinski numbers and the associated Sierpinski problem. In some ways his work pre-dated Benoit Mandelbrot, who is known as the founder of fractal pattern theory.

Figure 5.16   Sierpinski gasket – 3

So the application of a simple and deterministic rule can create a complex pattern. In other words within complexity there lies simplicity and complexity will have simple underlying rules. However, the gasket yet has another surprise. What is remarkable is that exactly the same pattern is produce by a random process. Called 'The Chaos Game',[53] it shows how random (presumably chaotic) chance produces great order. First, draw three points (the vertices of a triangle, which don't have to be equilateral or isosceles), and label the points 1, 2 and 3. Then choose a starting point S, at random (the chosen point below is not within the triangle, but it can be – it matters not). Then begin the game. Choose random numbers, 1, 2 or 3 (with a dice – 1 spot and 4 spots can equal point 1, 2 and 5 = point 2, 3 and 6 = point 3). Each random number defines where a new point halfway between the latest point and the point towards which the random number directs you. For example, the first random number below was a 1; so a point halfway between S (the random starting point) and 1 is plotted. Then the dice is thrown to get another random 1, then 3, 2, 1 and 3. After drawing 6 points, I perceive no obvious pattern. With a computer, it is easier to continue to choose many more points.

Below, we have three pictures of the chaos game. The first has 60 dots. The second has 600 dots, and starts to show a pattern. And the third has 6,000 dots, and the pattern is clear – the Sierpinski gasket. Surprised? You should be, as this shows that a deterministic approach (as described above Figure 5.14) and a random approach can have exactly the same result.

Perhaps the best real-life example of how a simple pattern repeated time and again can lead to great complexity and diversity is DNA – there are only four base parts of DNA. These bases are repeated millions of time to give the unique diversity we have.[54]

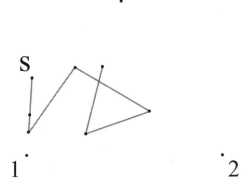

Figure 5.17   The beginnings of 'The Chaos Game'[55]

53   The 'Chaos Game' is described by the mathematician M. Barnsley in his book *Fractals Everywhere* See <http://www3.sympatico.ca/waynerp/IFSA1.htm>, accessed 17 April 2010. You can have a go at playing the game at <http://www.jgiesen.de/ChaosSpiel/ChaosEnglish.html>, accessed 17 April 2010.

54   The importance of DNA (Deoxyribonucleic acid) was discovered in 1944 by a group of US scientists who showed it was responsible for transformation in bacterial cells. In 1953 the UK biophysicist Francis Crick and US biochemist James Watson discovered that DNA was made up of three kinds of sub-molecule: phosphate, deoxyribose (a sugar), and various bases. DNA contains four kinds of base: adenine (A), cytosine (C), guanine (G), and thymine (T). The base A, C, G and T are repeated millions of times in differing sequences to give each organism its own unique DNA. 99.5 per cent of our DNA is similar to monkeys, and 99.9 per cent of human DNA is the same – the small 1 per cent, incredible as it may sound, explains much of the rich diversity we have in our species.

55   <http://www.jimloy.com/fractals/sierpins.htm>, design by Jim Loy, accessed 17 April 2010.

After 60 rolls of the dice...   After 600 rolls of the dice...   After 6,000 rolls of the dice...

Figure 5.18   Order out of chaos ...

The Sierpinski gasket has a few more surprises. Perhaps the most surprising was the analysis done by four academics in Brazil of the Yuan/US Dollar exchange rate.[56] They looked at the Yuan/US Dollar exchange rate over a period of some 20 years. With a few odd exceptions, the yuan seemed to track the dollar according to market dynamics. However, by applying sophisticated analytical techniques instead of a graph showing a typical rate movement, the Sierpinski gasket emerged leaving the researchers to conclude that there was some global determinism in the data and that perhaps the rate was in fact being managed in a subtle way by the Chinese. Perhaps no surprise then after all!

Fractal thinking is a new and powerful way of looking at things within the context of business. I say new, but in fact it has been around for a while. For example, Hans-Jurgen Wanrnecke talked about Fractal Companies in the early 1990s.[57] This concept was further researched by Straus and Hemel who described the turnaround of a manufacturing company in Germany, Mettler-Toledo Albstadt GmbH, which was losing millions in the 1980s before it was turned into a 'fractal' company. This saw its workforce reduced by 65 per cent, suppliers reduced from over 80 to 10, finished goods stocks reduced by 95 per cent, and delivery times greatly increased. Order volumes can fluctuate between 50–200 per cent but the fractal self-organisation of the workforce and processes ensure a highly adaptive and flexible approach.[58] The company is now a leading global player. Fractal thinking is a 'Both/And' approach to thinking rather than an 'Either/Or' and is more suited to 'The Complex' as exemplified in Figure 5.19.

Fractal theory underpins much of the recent theories of 'Big Data', and is generating much investment. For example, the firm 'Fractal Analytics' in 2013 received a US$25 million to help fund its rapid growth.[59] How does fractal thinking work in 'Big Data'? Mandelbrot's investigation into fractals started with the concept of measurement and borders – with his famous, initial paper entitled 'How Long is the Coast of Britain –

56   Matsushita, Raul, Iram Gleria, Annibal Figueiredo, and Sergio Da Silva, (2003) 'Fractal structure in the Chinese yuan/US dollar rate.' *Economics Bulletin*, Vol. 7, No. 2, pp. 1–13.

57   Warnecke, H.J. (1993) *The Fractal Company – A revolution in corporate culture.*

58   Strauss, R.E. and Hummel, T. 'The new industrial engineering revisited: Information technology, business process re-engineering and lean management in the self-organising Fractal Company'. Paper published for Engineering Management Conference, 1995. Global Engineering Management: Emerging Trends in the Asia Pacific, Proceedings of 1995 IEEE Annual International.

59   http://www.datacenterknowledge.com/archives/2013/06/24/ta-associates-invests-25m-in-big-data-analytics company-fractal analytics/, accessed: February 2014.

Modern Fractal Thinking for 'The Complex'	Traditional Analytical Thinking for 'The Complicated'
CAL's 'MICI': Mutually Inclusive Collectively Inter-dependent	McKinsey's 'MECE': Mutually Exclusive Collectively Exhaustive
Items within a system have holographic repetitions of each-other and are inter-linked	Items within a system are distinct and unique, and no repetitions exists

Figure 5.19 Fractal thinking

Statistical Self-Similarity and Fractional Dimension.'[60] He ended the paper by saying: '*I cannot avoid quoting here these lines by Alfred North Whitehead (the co-author with Bertrand Russell of Principia Mathematicae), "To come very near true theory and to grasp its precise application are two very different things as the history of science teaches us. Everything of importance has been said before by somebody who did not discover it." There is a French saying, that what is true on one side of the Pyrenées is false on the other.*' The key to the Mandelbrot Set is that the equation's solution will either go to zero or infinity depending on the variables. The graph of the solution has vast areas that are uniform and boring: in these areas, the solution goes unfailingly to either infinity or to zero regardless of the equation's parameters. However, there are a few areas where the solution will swing between zero and infinity. Graphing these areas produces the famous patterns. So, for the Mandelbrot Set in the border condition, the solution becomes highly interesting. The trick is to look for interesting self-similar patterns in the noise. The US retailer Target is a good case in point. The retailer's 'Big Data' analysis of its premium card holders shows similar patterns to Mandelbrot's Set: there are vast periods of time when the shoppers buy the same things, at more or less the same rate and at the same time. There are few to no changes and it is very difficult to motivate the shopper to change. However, Target's analysis also showed that there are periods in their premium card holders' life when they change buying patterns and the most marked period occurs before and after having a baby. Therefore, the transition period between no child and child (that is, pregnancy) becomes an incredibly important and interesting boundary condition – because during this time, you can influence the shopper to change his/her shopping patterns and this new pattern will last a very long time. This insight led Target to dive deep into their shoppers' buying patterns during pregnancy and to

---

60   Mandelbrot, B.B. (1967) 'How Long is the Coast of Britain? Statistical Self-Similarity and Fractional Dimension', *Science* 156, pp. 636–638.

analyse in-depth what they bought and when. They became so good at understanding the buying patterns of 'pregnant households' that they can define the baby's due date to within three weeks. Target's analysis is similar to deep diving the Mandelbrot Set; the deeper you go, the more interesting it becomes. I guess the major difference is that Mandelbrot dives result in pleasing aesthetics while the Target dives generate pleasing bottom lines. However, 'Big Data' can have a double edge – Target suffered due to the recent hack of their consumer database that harvested about 40 million debit and credit card numbers as well as personal information for another 70 million people. The hack occurred due to a single email sent to a small air-conditioning repair and maintenance shop in Sharpsburg, Pennsylvania. Fazio Mechanical Services had a supplier contract with the local Target store and was therefore linked into their system. This is a good example of the butterfly effect, a tiny, incremental event causing a huge effect. It was through this minuscule hole, in a corner of the system, that the hackers gained access to the complete database. This hack has had a huge, negative impact on Target's brand image and bottom line.[61] 'Big Data' may be fractal and an opportunity, but it can have big risks too!

The application of fractal theory is also present in the design and engineering fields. Zakka Hadid used fractal geometry to design the award winning Cardiff Bay Opera House, and Michael Batty used fractal geometry and strange attractor theory for spatial analysis and city planning. The relevance to Complex Adaptive Leadership is more philosophical than scientific but has some practical applications to leadership. Leadership behaviour breeds behaviour – the way leaders behave will soon be repeated. There are many patterns that are repeated that can be applied – catalytic mechanisms are like a fractal of the butterfly effect. So a small change in leadership behaviour, especially from the top of a hierarchical organization, can have a disproportionate effect. We will see in Chapter 10 how the patterns of attractor theory can be repeated in the application of the Complex Adaptive Leadership model. There are many such similar patterns and repetitions when exploring how chaos theory can be applied in leadership terms. Some would call such similarities 'remarkable coincidences', but in fact they are entirely natural when one considers the existence of fractals. The similarity between the evolution of science and leadership theory referred to earlier in this chapter is perhaps a fractal of a deeper emergence, explained by Fritjof Capra as a rebalancing of a very Yang type world to a more Yin one.[62]

Let's summarise the story so far: a small change can get a big result (butterfly effect), chaotic systems seem to share some universal laws (Fiegenbaum's Delta), and the underlying patterns of scientific development and leadership theory evolution seem to share the same patterns (fractals). These are not isolated aspects of chaos theory but interrelated. For example, within the butterfly effect there are fractal patterns which show how universality can work (as you may see when you do the exercise at the start of the next chapter). There does not seem to be a rational or indeed even mathematical formula which ties these aspects together, and they seem to co-exist in an intuitive way, which is both compelling and intriguing.

---

61   Again I am grateful to one of our CAL Associates, Douglas Dean for this piece of research.

62   F. Capra in his book *The Tao of Physics* identifies this deeper trend, which empirical evidence supports. The world has been traditionally Yang dominated – for example, more male, assertion, consumption, competitive orientated. But in recent times issues such as women's equality, integration, conservation and collaboration are gaining significance.

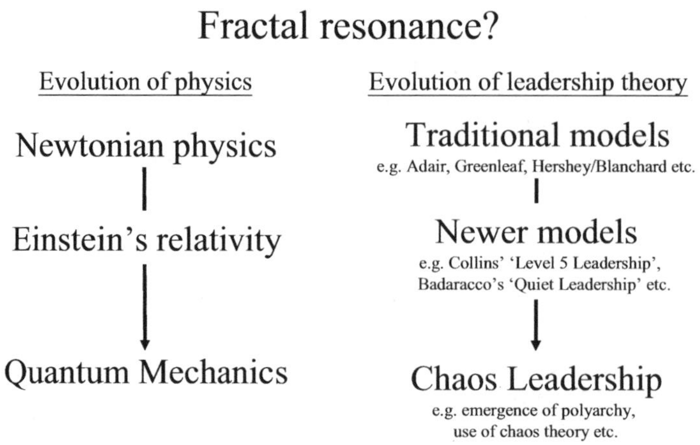

Fractal resonance?

Evolution of physics	Evolution of leadership theory
Newtonian physics	**Traditional models** e.g. Adair, Greenleaf, Hershey/Blanchard etc.
↓	↓
Einstein's relativity	**Newer models** e.g. Collins' 'Level 5 Leadership', Badaracco's 'Quiet Leadership' etc.
↓	↓
Quantum Mechanics	**Chaos Leadership** e.g. emergence of polyarchy, use of chaos theory etc.

Figure 5.20 Fractal resonance of Science and Leadership Theory

BIFURCATIONS

Another mathematical pattern is what complexity scientists have called bifurcations.[63] Bifurcations are sometimes called by complexity scientists 'phase transitions' – traditionally they were used to describe the transition of, for example, steam into water and water into ice. It is also a big jump or a change. We saw examples of these in Chapter 2, although they were not then identified as such. A visible trend will suddenly change direction in a radical and visible way. In Chapter 2 we saw how the context within which leadership is practised has bifurcated away from the trend it has followed for thousands of years. Another bifurcation is the recent explosion in knowledge, the trend line of which also seems to follow that of volatility.

Bifurcations are similar to what has become known as 'tipping points', many examples of which are given in the book of the same title by Malcolm Gladwell.[64] A tipping point is a point in time when an underlying pattern that has been going on for some time suddenly produces a large change. If the butterfly effect describes the input of the process (that is, a small change to a situation sensitive to initial conditions), a bifurcation is often (but not always) what happens downstream.

A good example of this is what complexity scientists refer to as the 'Buttons and thread' simulation. 'Buttons and thread' is a computer simulation and Figure 5.22 shows the end result. In the bottom half of the figure one can see a number of 'buttons' randomly spread across a table which have been joined at random by cotton 'thread'. The top left part of the window shows the number of buttons in the largest cluster – this obviously starts with two and then builds up as pairs of buttons are connected into larger clusters. The top right window shows the number of buttons connected on the x axis, with the number of buttons in the largest cluster on the y axis. You will note that the graph jumps twice – each being a bifurcation/phase transition.

---

63   A bifurcation is a term used in complexity science, originally identified by an Australian mathematical biologist Robert May who studied animal populations and found that biological systems were driven by non-linear mechanisms which can end up in a major change.

64   See M. Gladwell, *The Tipping Point*, for examples.

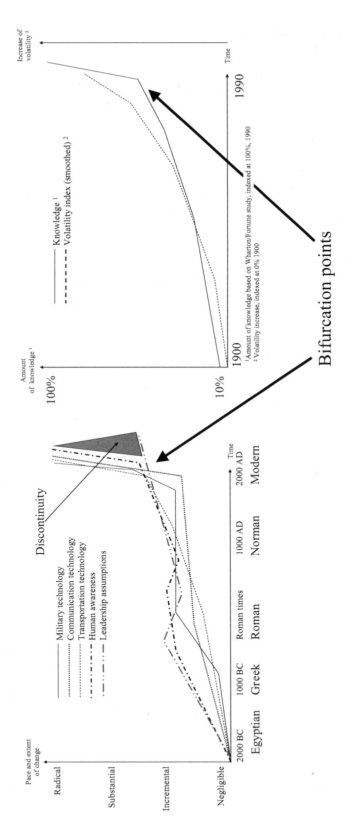

Figure 5.21 Examples of bifurcation points

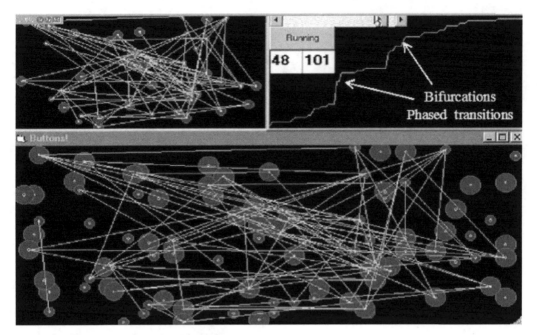

Figure 5.22 Buttons experiment[65]

Another way of looking at this is shown in Figure 5.23. The number of buttons in this simulation is 400. There is a huge jump in the number of buttons in a cluster when the 0.5 ratio of threads to buttons is reached. The larger the number of buttons, the steeper the curve.

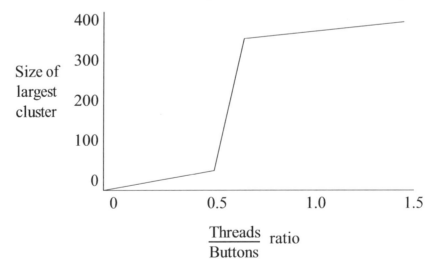

Figure 5.23 Buttons and threads experiment

Source: S. Kauffman, *At Home in the Universe.*

---

65   Illustration from DVD Embracing Complexity by Ernst & Young's Centre for Innovation distributed at the Ernst & Young conference in Paris 2000 'Embracing Complexity: Exploring the application of complex adaptive systems to business.'

If one can imagine that the buttons are not buttons, but people within an organisation, and that the thread is not thread but random conversations, then the number of buttons in a cluster can become connected insight, and the phased transition/bifurcation graph can illustrate the 'Ah-ha!' phenomenon. You have seen this yourself. You have a random conversation at the coffee machine, and then later on you have a conversation on the train home with a stranger, and then you have a conversation at home and suddenly – *wham!* – you make a connection and get an insight. An *'Ah-Ha'* moment. This equates to a bifurcation of meaning, a phase transition from random conversations into deeper meaning.

Bifurcation theory as exemplified by the buttons simulation has some important lessons:

- The process is random and messy – but is recognisable and often called 'coincidence' or 'synchronicity'. Synchronicity has been applied to leadership before, perhaps the best example being the seminal book by Jo Jaworski, *Synchronicity – The Inner Path of Leadership.*[66]
- A 'critical mass' of randomness is needed to get meaning. This is randomness that cannot be controlled but is vital for obtaining a controlled result, paradoxical as that may sound.
- Things progress in messy steps and not in a smooth line. So one needs to be comfortable with a messy process – this seems antithetical to most management theory.

Can this be applied? Can the bifurcation in meaning be applied to business? An example of Xerox may give an answer.[67] There was a period of time when their photocopiers would break down, but by the time a Xerox engineer turned up to repair it the fault had vanished. These 'ghost' faults were a large drain on the Xerox engineers, who operated in vans and were tasked on one-way radios centrally by a controller who took the calls. They called in a range of experts, including a team from the Santa Fe Institute[68] (set up for complexity science research). It was suggested that the van drivers be given two-way radios. Soon the drivers were using the radios for random conversation – and the effectiveness of repairing ghost faults rose by 80 per cent in all areas except one. The exception to the improvement was the area where the manager of the team heard

---

66   Jo Jaworski was heavily influenced by the writings of Robert Greenleaf who wrote in his *Servant Leadership* that the essence of leadership is the desire to serve one another and to serve something beyond ourselves, a higher purpose; Greenleaf described this as 'servant leadership', the leader as the servant of the people he or she leads. Jaworski describes how a meeting in 1980 with David Bohm, the physicist, had a profound effect. Bohm had just published *Wholeness and the Implicate Order*, and told Jaworski that the concepts of time, space and matter no longer applied. They discussed Bell's theorem, which proves that the world is fundamentally inseparable. Bohm said that everything is connected to everything else, and told Jaworski that, *'The oneness implicit in Bell's theorem envelops human beings and atoms alike.'* For Jaworski, with his growing sense of the interrelatedness of everything, these ideas made perfect sense. He saw relatedness as the organising principle of the universe.

67   This story is a good example of Received Based Communication, or RBC. This is what birds use to flock. RBC allows frequent open two-way communication between individuals allowing a greater level of self-organisation. This is described by E. McMillan in her book *Complexity, Organisations and Change*. See also A. Battram, *Navigating Complexity: The Essential Guide to Complexity Theory in Business and Management*.

68   The Santa Fe Institute for complexity science was set up in 1984 by the quantum mechanic scientist Murray Gell-Mann, the particle physicist who discovered quarks (sub-particle matter).

them having random conversations and told them to stop. In that case it was clear that the critical mass 'tipping point' was never achieved.

Another example of seeing bifurcation theory in action is the physical design of offices. The days of closed doors and people working in relative isolation are fast being consigned to the past. Open plan, communal eating areas, coffee areas and so on all allow a large degree of socialisation and random conversations. The head office of Microsoft in the UK, for example, resembles more a shopping mall than a head office with café and sitting out areas under a large atrium. Wireless networks allow people to move their working area and socialise more. A similar example can be found in the car parts manufacturer Unipart in the UK. The head office is actually called 'The U', short for 'University', and the whole atmosphere owes more to one of a campus than a corporate headquarters. The move towards informality and socialisation is not a 'nice to do' – it can yield significant results. A study in the productivity of open plan vs. closed office revealed an increase in productivity.[69] Bifurcation theory when applied to random conversations perhaps indicates why this is so.

So let's review briefly where we are: a small change can get a big result (butterfly effect), chaotic systems seem to share some universal laws (Feigenbaum's Delta), the underlying patterns of scientific development and leadership theory evolution seem to share the same pattern (fractals), and significant changes can occur in steps (bifurcations). Can all these factors actually be used to get results? The story of a call centre below may give an answer.

APPLICATION

The application of chaos theory in fields outside of mathematics is not new. For example William Shaffer in the US used data from chicken pox and measles using strange attractors and phase space reconstruction to see when mass inoculation should occur, a result which he could not get using more traditional linear methods done by standard epidemiology. We have mentioned that fractal theory has been used in design work from city planning to architecture. And we have seen examples of chaos and complexity theory existing in business such as catalytic mechanisms and the butterfly effect, bifurcations and Xerox engineers and so on. However, the *deliberate* application of chaos and complexity theory in business and the management of organisations is still in its infancy. Some examples do exist. These include:

- Revco Drugstores achieved a 34 per cent increase in productivity by moving its warehouse picking from a centrally controlled to a self-organising system. It can be proven mathematically that workers spontaneously gravitate towards the most optimum way of working.[70]
- General Motors saved $1.5m a year by scrapping the centrally controlled paint spraying approach of trucks that came off the line at its operation at Fort Wayne. This system, which was normally controlled centrally, was replaced by a bidding

---

69   See A. Brennan, J. Chugh and T. Kline, 'Traditional Versus Open Office Design: A Longitudinal Field Study', *Environment & Behaviour*.

70   C. Anderson and J.J. Bartholdi III, 'Centralized Versus Decentralized Control in Manufacturing: Lessons from Social Insects'.

system for the ten painting booths which was far more efficient. The bidding system is based on a single simple objective (paint as many trucks as possible) and a few simple rules (for example, use as little paint as possible, if there is a long queue in front of the booth – bid zero and so on).[71]

- In 'John Deere Runs on Chaos', Paul Roberts describes how the world's largest machinery maunfacturer put compelxity and chaos theory into use through a project called Vision XXI. This involved enabling a wider viewpoint for all employees (so each understood the whole rather than just their part), ensuring information flows at all levels, and freedom of action for employees to get things done, and solve problems.[72] In many ways the John Deere story also resembles some of the principles of a fractal self-organising approach.

Below is another example of how, in a management rather than technical sense, the application of complexity science can make a difference.

Hal was studying for his part-time MBA and ran a technical call centre of 300 technicians covering the market in Europe, Middle East and Africa. The call centre provided technical support for users of software sold by the company. It was during his MBA that he first saw the buttons simulation and was exposed to chaos theory. And it was then that he finally, in a great *'Ah-Ha'* moment, realised why smokers in his call centre were more productive. He found out that his smokers were more productive in the first place due to a detailed productivity improvement study recently completed. The call centre was facing closure with operations moved to India, unless productivity could be improved. Hal had done a very deterministic re-engineering programme, helped by experienced productivity consultants who had done things like reposition the coffee machines around the call centre to cut down on the walking-to-and-from time and so on. This and other measures had seen productivity increase around 5 per cent but that was not enough. One of the facts that came out of the research done in the productivity improvement study was that smokers in his call centre were more productive. He could not work out why this was – until he saw the buttons simulation. Then he realised that smokers would, at random, get up and go outside to smoke and whilst they did they had random conversations. Whilst doing this they gained knowledge from each other to solve issues in new ways, which enabled them to handle more calls faster. This is similar to the Xerox experience. Hal realised then that he needed a place where people could, at random, gather to have 'smoke' breaks. So he introduced one small change and waited to see what would happen. He created a space where people could have a break and moved all the coffee machines into it. He put bean bags in the space as well. The results, which are astonishing, are shown below in Figure 5.24 with productivity measure shown by the time spent by callers waiting to get through (the lower the number, the lower the wait time and thus the higher the productivity). Numbers have been withheld due to commercial sensitivity.

This study was part of Hal's MBA and, as such, these figures and the causes for them were subject to academic scrutiny. As can be seen there are two phased transitions/bifurcations – first, things get better, then worse, then better, then worse, then the long

71   David Berreby, 'Between Chaos and Order: What Complexity Theory Can Teach Business', *Strategy + Business*, second quarter edition, issue 3.

72   P. Roberts, 'John Deere Runs on Chaos', *Fast Company Magazine*, issue 19.

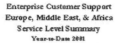

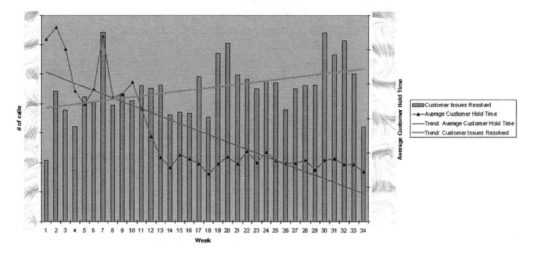

Figure 5.24 Call centre result

term result was suddenly gained. It was tempting for Hal to step in and interfere when the results started to get worse during these phased transitions/bifurcations, but his basic understanding of complexity and chaos helped him to hold back and not interfere (wu wei). His operation achieved well over 40 per cent increase in productivity.

So from chaos mathematics we can see how there can be an underlying order to a seemingly chaotic state of affairs. And the mini-case studies of Xerox engineers, the call centre and others show that the use of non-deterministic approaches can yield good results with two examples of an increase of 30 to 40 per cent in productivity.[73]

Complexity Science – The Dawn of a New Era

So far we have used the term chaos and complexity fairly inter-changeably. But they are really two different things. Chaos theory shows that simple systems can exhibit complex behaviour. Complexity theory shows us that complex systems can exhibit simple 'emergent' behaviour.[74] As shown back in Figure 5.4, complexity science came along after

---

73   For more examples see James Yorke and Ceslo Grebogi, *The Impact of Chaos on Science and Society*.

74   This distinction is not so simple, and within the field there lie contradiction and paradox, somehow reflecting, like a fractal, the subject matter itself. For example in their book *The Collapse of Chaos*, Cohen and Stewart propose the distinction on page 2: '*Chaos theory tells us that simple laws can have very complicated – indeed unpredictable – consequences. Simple causes can produce complex effects. Complexity theory tells us the opposite: complex causes can produce simple effects*'. On page 22 the distinction seems to reverse: '*On pragmatic grounds, the most useful way forward seems to be to stick to the naïve definition of complexity, to accept simple rules may not produce simple results....*' On page 29, they seem to suggest complexity is a mix of order and chaos: '*We've explained how simple laws can give rise to complexity. But at the bottom of the funnels that lead downward from the complexity of our daily lives, we find two apparently contradictory things: order and chaos.*' In many ways the differing definitions are complementary in a Taoist way, and reflect the paradox and uncertainty that the theories seek to grapple with. Be that as it may, it is best to see chaos and complexity as two sides of the same coin.

the emergence of chaos mathematics. If any place or date can mark the full emergence of complexity science, it is 1984 and the establishment of the Santa Fe Institute by the quantum mechanic particle physicist and Nobel Prize winner Murray Gell-Mann.[75] He defines complex systems as thus: *'Complex systems are neither ordered or random, but combine both kinds of behaviour in a very elusive but striking manner.'*

The Santa Fe Institute was the first to attempt to bring together people from differing disciplines who seemed to be working on a similar phenomenon – the emergence of complexity and non-determinism. This included mathematicians, scientists from disciplines such as chemistry, physics and biology, economists, anthropologists and others. Traditionally people worked in these areas in complete isolation from each other. They were looking at complex systems as diverse as how birds flock, to how capital markets operate, from how atoms in lasers behaved, to how train wheels resonated. It very quickly became apparent that such diverse areas of complexity had some common features.

Complex systems seem to be on the 'edge of chaos' – that means that they are able to balance order and chaos. What does that mean? The (perhaps apocryphal) story of the Hofplein Roundabout in Rotterdam, Netherlands provides a good example. The Hofplein intersection has several roads. When the large roundabout was first introduced to try to ease traffic flows it did not work – the ensuing chaos of giving drivers choice seemed too much. It was then decided to put traffic lights on each entrance to the roundabout – again this did not work very well and the traffic flowed as badly as ever. Then one day, the traffic flowed smoothly – this was when the lights developed a fault and all stuck on amber. When the roundabout had no lights, it was too chaotic. When it had lights, it was too ordered. When the lights stuck on amber it was on the edge of chaos, and the traffic flowed.[76]

Complex systems have four common features:

- self-organisation
- inter-relatedness
- adaptive nature
- emergence.

Let's look at each of these in a little more detail.

1. **Self-organisation.** Complex systems have a high degree of self-organisation. Self-organisation emerged as an area of study through various scientific disciplines in the

---

75   M. Gell-Mann, *The Quark and the Jaguar*.

76   This story perhaps inspired the approach which was implemented in the Netherlands, where transport planner Hans Monderman pioneered a new method which involves removing traffic signs, lights and in some cases, road markings. This allows a bit more randomness towards chaos. This concept has been successfully tested in the small Dutch town of Drachten, which has had traffic lights removed. Other changes included the installation of a children's playground in the middle of one of the roads to force drivers to slow down. *'When you don't exactly know who has right of way, you tend to seek eye contact with other road users'*, he said. *'You automatically reduce your speed, you have contact with other people and you take greater care.'* The 'Shared Space' is being tried in seven pilot projects across the Netherlands, Denmark, Germany, the UK, and Belgium. In the US, officials in West Palm Beach, Florida, have been successful in slowing down traffic and reducing accidents by also following the concept.

mid-twentieth century.[77] A good example is the work done by Ilya Prigogine,[78] the Belgian chemist, who identified three features of self-organisation:

a) Open feedback loops, with internal structures which can be organised independently of external cause but are linked firmly to the environment within which the system exists. Feedback loops create the complexity where cause and effect are blurred and become one, a catalytic dynamic. The feedback loops thus make cause and effect hard to identify.

b) The flow of energy allows for a 'far-from-equilibrium' condition. In other words there is a degree of ambiguity and uncertainty, and the system is not in a steady state (steady being inactive).

c) A high number of causal inter-related and inter-connected relationships exist, too complex to map or calculate.

Although Prigogine was working on chemical substances, his findings about self-organisation could be found (like a fractal) in many other areas of science – Hermann Haken and lasers,[79] Manfred Eigen and enzymes,[80] Humberto Maturana and Francisco Varela in neurology,[81] James Lovelock in atmospheric sciences and ecology,[82] and so on. What is remarkable is that the individuals mentioned were working in very different areas, were unaware of each other's research, but came

---

77   The concept of 'self-organisation' is central to polyarchy, as it is to complexity science. Self-organisation emerged in many areas of research. Its earliest signs can be traced back to the world of cybernetics in 1943 when the neuroscientist McCulloch and mathematician Pitts published their seminal paper 'A Logical Calculus of Ideas Immanent in Nervous Activity'. It was in the 1970s that self-organisation began to emerge fully in a variety of scientific fields.

78   Ilya Prigogine solved the mystery in the late 1960s of 'Bernard's Instability'. This was discovered by Henri Bernard at the turn of the century when he found that heating a liquid in a non-linear way led the liquid to form an ordered honeycomb cell-like pattern. Prigogine's work showed that when the liquid moves away from equilibrium, self-organisation occurs. He also used this theory to explain the Belousov–Zhabotinski reaction where two chemicals mixed with a catalyst and moving away from equilibrium can produce patterns in an autocatalytic way. The significance of Prigogine's work is often underestimated – it was the first solid proof that went against the hitherto sacrosanct second law of thermodynamics, that the dissipation of energy was always association with the growth of entropy (disorder). He presented his findings at the Nobel symposium in 1967 and published his theory of dissipative structures with Glansdorf in 1971.

79   Hermann Haken studied Light Amplification through Stimulated Emission of Radiation (LASER). It was well known that atoms emit radiation (heat and/or light) when their electrons are 'excited' (moved to a higher 'orbit' of the neutron). However, Haken realised that for this to happen the atoms need to be in a state far from equilibrium and that the atoms self-organise to achieve the light radiated. He published his findings in 1970. Haken subsequently founded a new area of scientific research called 'synergetics' which is the study of the formation and self-organisation of patterns and structures in open systems far from thermodynamic equilibrium.

80   Manfred Eigen proposed that life emerged from a progression of chemicals which self-organised in a far from equilibrium way. This was the pre-biological origins of life. He called this 'molecular self-organisation' and studied catalytic cycles in enzymes in the 1960s. Eigen showed that self-replication may have occurred before the emergence of life.

81   Humberto Maturana studied and researched at MIT, and was influenced by cybernetics before returning to his native Chile where he specialised in neuroscience at the University of Santiago. He worked on cognition and published his findings in 1970. He began a long collaboration with one of his former students, Fransisco Varella, and coined the term 'autopoiesis' from the Greek 'auto' = self and 'poiesis' = making. Their Santiago Theory of Cognition stated that neural networks were self-organising, and that cognition can exist without a brain or nervous system (for example, plants can tell the difference between light and darkness).

82   James Lovelock proposed that Earth was a self-organising living system. This theory is often known as the Gaia theory. He proposed that for a planet to be alive it needed an atmosphere that was far from equilibrium. Earth's atmosphere has a lot of methane and oxygen which reacts with each other, and a little CO_2. This is opposite to Mars whose atmosphere is in chemical equilibrium and thus no life exists. Earth's atmosphere is far from equilibrium and therefore life exists. He published his ideas in 1972.

to similar conclusions and published their findings all within a few years of each other, many in the same year – 1970. In all these areas, the three principles above were applicable. The principles also seem resonate in many organisations today. Self-organisation has been the subject to a lot of study and there has been a growing interest in so called 'self-managed' teams.[83] These are explored more in Chapter 7.

2. **Inter-relatedness** is linked to point 1c above. Complex systems have a high degree of inter-relatedness between their constituent parts. Some view this as the defining aspect of complexity – the more connection points there are, the higher the complexity as Figures 5.22 and 5.23 show.

Complex systems are often seen as networks rather than hierarchies – and as the number of 'nodes' or connection points grows, complexity grows even greater. This is similar to network theory,[84] and another factor which seems to support the notion that a strict oligarchic and hierarchic approach is becoming less and less effective for leading an organisation. A leader needs to be *part* of the network, rather than an entity somehow above it and trying to manage it (which would be impossible due to its complexity).

If we cycle the example in Figure 5.25 a few times, we see that complexity (defined by the number of relationships within a network) increases in an exponential way as shown in Figure 5.26. If we take this definition of complexity, and count people as nodes, then the increase in communication technology has greatly increased the complexity of the world in recent times (as discussed in Chapter 2).

Complexity

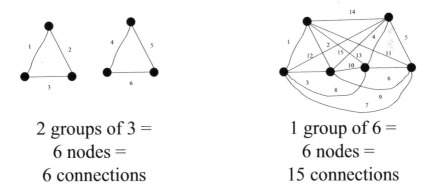

2 groups of 3 =
6 nodes =
6 connections

1 group of 6 =
6 nodes =
15 connections

Figure 5.25 The more connection points, the more the complexity

---

83   The concept of self-managed work teams is not new and is a direct result of socio-technical systems theory and design developed by Eric Trist and his colleagues at the Tavistock Institute. The theory contends that organisations intimately combine people and technology in complex forms to produce outputs. This process is supported through sub-systems. The social sub-system includes the work structure that causes people to interact with both technologies and each other.

84   Network theory is part of graph theory and applied mathematics, and within social science is perhaps the only theory which is not reductionist. A network is a set of relationships and connections. Network theory looks at the nature and dynamic of such connections, and the symmetrical and asymmetrical relations within.

Relationship growth in a network

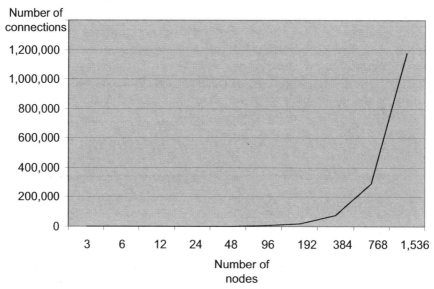

Figure 5.26 Exponential complexity

This increasing complexity is reflected in the thought experiment of Ludwig Boltzmann, a physicist and founder of statistical mechanics, as shown below.[85] This demonstrates how the addition of objects to be sorted adds to the complexity in terms of the number of possible ways of doing the sorting. Although intuitively this makes sense, what the experiment shows is that rising complexity in this case also has a similar exponential curve to the one shown above.

1. **Adaptive nature.** Complex systems are highly adaptive to the environment within which they exist. As we saw in Chapter 3, organisations can be seen as evolving towards Complex Adaptive Systems. CAS emerged from the Santa Fe Institute.[86] Their adaptability depends very much on the open systems and feedback loops described under the self-organisation feature above. An adaptive system will have a 'sense and respond' approach – a good, adaptive system will have a high degree of awareness to its local context as well as a high capability to change internally. In some ways this is similar to Stephen Haeckel's *Adaptive Enterprise*.[87] This is an organisation which 'senses' (by picking up external messages/trends and

---

85　In the original experiment he proposed colour balls – letters are easier to print! Ludwig Boltzmann is in some ways a tragic figure. He worked on theories such as black body radiation, energy and movement of particles within atoms. His views seem to be only expressed by him and his work was strongly criticised by scientists of the day, most of whom are now long forgotten. He committed suicide in 1906. He did not know that Einstein had proved some of his theories just before he killed himself, or that Planck had also done the same, and that the subsequent science of quantum mechanics would fully validate the views for which he had been so strongly criticised.

86　See for example Morowitz and Singer (eds), *The Mind, The Brain And Complex Adaptive Systems – Santa Fe Institute Studies in the Sciences of Complexity Proceedings*, and (for a more up to date and wider view) Shan and Yang, *Applications of Complex Adaptive Systems*.

87　See S. Haeckel, *Adaptive Enterprise – Creating and Leading Sense-and-Respond Organizations*.

How many ways of distributing the scrabble tiles in the partitioned box?

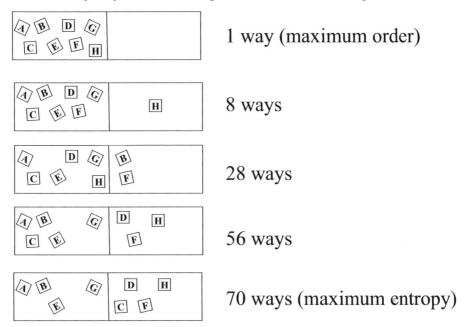

1 way (maximum order)

8 ways

28 ways

56 ways

70 ways (maximum entropy)

Figure 5.27 Boltzmann thought experiment on complexity

correctly identifying them for what they are) and responds (by deciding what to do, planning if needed, and then acting with the right response which enables it to influence the outside environment, ready to sense again). Haeckel reckons the only kind of strategy that makes sense in the face of uncertainty is a strategy which is adaptive – this resonates strongly with the observations in Chapter 3. His book is full of examples of companies which have followed such a route. Complexity scientist Seth Lloyd sees successful adaptive organisations as being able to translate apparent 'noise' at a faster rate as it arrives. Thus the 'sense' requires intuition and fast learning. 'Respond' needs the principles described later in Chapter 7. Seth Lloyd takes this one step further and proposes the entire universe is like one big interconnected computer.

2. **Emergence.** Complex systems have a process of emergence. For example in a system as complex as a species, evolutionary changes emerge. Emergence is the way complex systems and patterns arise out of a multiplicity of relatively simple interactions.[88] Fractals described above are good examples. Within this is the theme of 'morphic resonance' – that is when a species discovers something of importance, it is 'discovered' independently but at the same time by more than one part of the species.[89] The emergence of self-organisation as a theme in so many different

---

88   For a good overview of the concept of emergence see P.A. Corning, 'The Re-emergence of emergence – A Venerable Concept in Search of a Theory'.

89   Morphic resonance is a term coined by Rupert Sheldrake in his 1981 book *A New Science of Life*, (which was described by *Nature* as a book for burning!). Morphic resonance is apparent when two seemingly unconnected parts of a species comes up with the same idea or invention. He uses the expression to refer to what he thinks is 'the basis of memory in nature ... the idea of mysterious telepathy-type interconnections between organisms and of collective memories within

scientific fields at the same time has an element of morphic resonance about it. And within complexity as a science itself there was morphic resonance as the science emerged from many differing disciplines at roughly the same time. Emergence as a theme in business is best encapsulated by Henry Minztberg's 'emergent strategy' where he proposes that most successful strategies are those which are allowed to emerge naturally rather than those which are forced down into the organisation.[90]

Although the four features above are described separately they are very much inter-linked. For example the *adaptability* of an organisation is greatly enhanced by its ability to be *self-organising*, which itself depends on how well connected (or *inter-related*) the various component parts are. This adaptability will enable the organisation to have *emergent* structures and strategies to cope with changing circumstance around it.

Sometimes the different elements can combine to get astonishing results. For example the Boolean network research by Kauffman has shown that although one could have a huge amount of connections, with theoretically millions of possible states, in fact the mathematics show that only a few ordered states would emerge. A network of 100,000 interconnected nodes, each with two possible states (on and off) would in theory have $2^{100,000}$ possible states, or 10^{60}. This is a very large number, bearing in mind the number of hydrogen atoms in the universe has been calculated to be 3×10^{79}. In fact the possible states in such a network settle to just 317. This is an *astonishingly* low number. Kauffman asserts that such emergent self-organisation within a highly connected network may have made life inevitable on this planet.[91]

Complexity science seems to go against the second law of thermodynamics which suggests that disorder can only increase. If chaos theory observes unstable aperiodic behaviour and underlying patterns, complexity science looks at how things happen and why.

Complexity studies gave rise to 'Post-Normal Science', the brainchild of two philosophers of science, Sylvio Funtowicz and Jerry Ravetz. Ravetz wrote: *'The task is no longer one of accredited experts discovering the "true facts" for the determination of "good policies". Post-normal science accepts the legitimacy of different perspectives from all those stakeholders around the table.'*[92]

Post-normal science does not seek to overthrow the fundamentals of the traditional sciences which came before it; rather it seeks to have its roots in the experience of uncertainty, impermanence, ambiguity and non-determinism. Ravetz's use of the term

---

species.' An example of this is when Karl Schwarzschild in Germany wrote his famous solutions to Einstein's gravitational-field equation. The very same month in 1915, Walter Adams in the USA independently solved the reason why Sirrius B was so dim: using the same new approach as Schwarzschild. A few months later Schwarzschild's solution was discovered independently in 1916 by Dutch physicist Johannes Droste. Another example is how the year 1970 has already been shown to have morphic resonance regarding the science of complexity and the year in which so many papers were published in independent fields reflecting the same findings – this would otherwise be called coincidence. There is a clear link between synchronicity (which is a more philosophical theory) and morphic resonance (which is a more scientific one).

90   See H. Mintzberg, *The Rise and Fall of Strategic Planning*. *'Deliberate strategies provide the organization with a sense of purposeful direction.'* Emergent strategy implies that an organisation is learning what works in practice. Mixing the deliberate and the emergent strategies in some way will help the organisation to control its course while encouraging the learning process. *'Organizations ... [may] pursue ... umbrella strategies: the broad outlines are deliberate while the details are allowed to emerge within them.'*

91   See Kauffman's *At Home in the Universe*.

92   S. Fontowicz and J. Ravetz quoted in Z. Sardar and I. Abrams, *Introducing Chaos*.

'stakeholders' seems to have a resonance with many other studies. There is a degree of morphic resonance with what Ravetz writes, and studies such as those by the Caux Round Table in France, the *Built to Last* study by Collins and Porras in the USA and the UK's RSA *Tomorrow's Company Inquiry* – all proposed a more inclusive approach to leading organisations.[93] Sylvio Funtowitz wrote: *'We confront issues where facts are uncertain, values in dispute, stakes high and decisions urgent … The style of discourse can no longer be demonstration as from empirical data to true conclusion. Rather it must be dialogue, recognising uncertainty, value-commitments and a plurality of legitimate perspectives.'*[94]

The approach of Ravetz's and Fonowitz's post-normal science is shown in Figure 5.28. When decision stakes and system uncertainties are low, applied science/knowledge can work well. Day-to-day management practice works well in such a situation. However, as the stakes and complexity rise, so too does the need for experts. So for example an organisation will frequently turn to consultants with 'expert knowledge' to help resolve certain issues, or depend on 'talented' and 'knowledgeable leaders'. However, when the decision stakes and complexities are very high, then there will be the need for a wider dialogue involving key stakeholders, and a more dynamic approach including a Complex Adaptive Leadership approach.

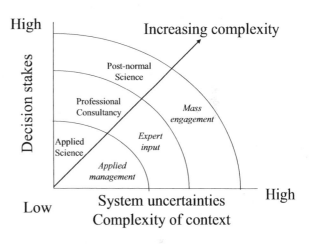

Figure 5.28 Post-normal science when stakes and complexity are high

In reality, an organisation or situation will not fall neatly into one of the three categories where the various approaches are needed in isolation. An organisation will typically need all three, albeit at certain times but sometimes combined.

Perhaps another indication that the world is becoming more complex is the rise of mass engagement techniques to engage the whole organisation and enable the wider dialogue with key stakeholders that Fontowicz and Ravetz propose. Such techniques are becoming more common and include large scale joint management and employee workshops, as well as more specialised approaches such as 'open space technology', 'future search' and 'real time strategic planning' which we considered briefly in Chapter 3.[95] We

---

93   The *Built to Last* study was undertaken in the USA by two Wharton professors, Jim Collins and Jerry Porras. At the same time the Royal Society for the encouragement of Arts, Manufactures and Commerce (RSA) in the UK were doing a three-year inquiry entitled 'Tomorrow's Company'. During this time the Caux Round Table in France (which consisted of a group of senior executives from Japan, Germany and France) were doing a study on corporate success. All were concerned with what sustainable success looked like, and all came to similar conclusions – that a more 'inclusive approach' needed to be taken, which involved stakeholders more. They were unaware of each other whilst they were doing their research. This has a resonance with the discovery of self-organisation, in terms of both the conclusions as well as the emergence of such conclusions in such a fractal way.

94   S. Funtowicz and J. Ravetz, *Uncertainty and Quality in Science for Policy*.

95   See footnotes 10, 11 and 12 of Chapter 3.

visit the use of mass engagement again in Chapter 10 when we look at involvement as a leadership strategy.

The conclusions of post-normal science seem to be echoed by the findings of James Surowiecki in his work *The Wisdom of Crowds*.[96] He concludes that allowing a talented leader to make decisions often is not as good as tapping into the wider wisdom: *'The more power you give a single individual in the face of complexity and uncertainty, the more likely it is that bad decisions will be made. As a result there are good reasons for companies to try to think past hierarchy...'*[97]

In his book he quotes many stories where the collective knowledge of a group of people was superior to a group of experts or leaders. Surowiecki studies many examples, including the Spanish fashion company Zara who seem to have put in place many of the Complex Adaptive Leadership principles explored in more detail later in this book.[98]

Another recent piece of research by Goldstein et al.[99] takes this one step further and shows how traditional visionary leadership can in fact kill innovation. *'Complexity science shows how the typical focus on "heroic" and charismatic leaders can result in a lack of innovation in modern organisations'.* This seems to echo Collin's *'A charismatic visionary leader is absolutely not required for a visionary company, and in fact can be detrimental...'*[100] So what sort of leadership *is* needed? The rest of the book explores this question.

Chapter Summary

1. The trend in leadership practice from the traditional deterministic approach (for example, oligarchic) to a more non-deterministic approach (for example, polyarchic) is matched in the trend in science.
2. An understanding of this scientific evolution, as well as how chaos theory and complexity science can work, lays a good foundation for Complex Adaptive Leadership to be practised skilfully.
3. Relativity theory shows how deterministic rules which contradict each other can co-exist – it is not a case of 'Either/Or', but 'Both/And'.

---

96   J. Surowiecki, *The Wisdom of Crowds*.

97   In *The Wisdom of Crowds*, Surowiecki shows many examples of how the collective knowledge of a group exceeds the knowledge of experts and/or leaders. He states that the best way to tap into such knowledge is to ensure three things: (1) Diversity: that the group has a wide diversity (for example, differing backgrounds, skills, knowledge and so on); (2) Independence: that individuals can express their opinion independently (for example, are not in any way influenced by others' opinion); and (3) Aggregation: that the opinions can be aggregated in an objective way. He states in his study that not many companies seem to put in processes which tap into this kind of wisdom.

98   The retailer Zara has expanded rapidly by mobilising the collective wisdom of its employees. The latest designs are the result of feedback from staff, comments from customers and actual sales recorded in the network of 300 stores. The team of designers interprets this information and relays updated creations to Zara's highly automated factories. New fashions are in stores faster than the competition can manage, and they are also guaranteed to reflect anticipated customer demand. Decisions in Zara are, to a great extent, coordinated by the employees and not directed by senior management. The Zara case study serves as an excellent example of how decentralisation can have an impact on the retail industry. Martin Christopher offers industry insights in *Logistics & Supply Chain Management* with reference to Zara's business model. Other useful information about Zara's management success can be found in P. Ghemawat's and J.L. Nueno's case analysis 'ZARA: Fast Fashion' and D. Bovet and J. Martha, *Value Nets: Breaking the Supply Chain To Unlock Hidden Profits*.

99   Goldstein, J., Hazy, J. K. and Lichtenstein, B.B. (2010) *Complexity and the Nexus of Leadership: Leveraging Nonlinear Science to Create Ecologies of Innovation* Palgrave Macmillan.

100   Collins, J. and Porras, J. I. (1997) *Built to Last – Successful Habits of Visionary Companies* Harper Collins.

4. Quantum mechanics shows how underlying reality is uncertain and non-deterministic – so reality is a paradoxical and seemingly chaotic dynamic between deterministic and non-deterministic forces.
5. Chaos mathematics shows how chaos has an underlying order and patterns which can be used to good effect. The key concepts include strange attractor (for example, butterfly effect), universality, fractals and bifurcations.
6. Complexity science shows that complexity has an inherent and underlying simplicity. The key concepts include: self-organisation (made up of far from equilibrium state, open feedback and complex connections), inter-relatedness, adaptiveness and emergence.
7. Post-normal science proposes that, when times are complex and decision stakes are high, a wider dialogue with key stakeholders is critical. Leaving decisions to a talented few is dangerous. And traditional, charismatic leadership can kill innovation and is not required for a company to be visionary.

A scientific background can thus make it easier to appreciate, and perhaps to embrace, chaos and complexity. There are some underlying principles to complexity that can be put to good effect. Perhaps the best way to appreciate them is on an experiential and emotional level, rather than a purely intellectual one, and so it is to the most surprising, and fun exercise that we now turn.

6 *Getting to Grips with Chaos and Complexity*

AN EXERCISE TO OPEN UP YOUR MIND AND GET A VIEW OF HOW COMPLEXITY CAN WORK

This exercise/game has been around for some time. I wish I knew who invented it so I could give credit. It has changed many people's attitudes. It is used by a variety of places to help develop leadership – for example, it has been used in the past on the first day of officer training for the Royal Marine Commandos to show there is more to leadership than meets the eye. The exercise is also a great way to show how chaos and complexity has an underlying order and simplicity which is a rather counter-intuitive notion. The first time one organises this exercise is terrifying because it seems impossible. But one soon realises that the impossible is very possible. You will need at least eight people and it can be played by over 80. The ideal number is around 25. I am not sure if you have access to 25 people willing to undertake what will seem an impossible task – but this is well worth the experience! It is a working experiment that shows how simple complexity can be, and it leads to a very counter-intuitive and intriguing conclusion about leadership within complex tasks.

Here is a description of how to run the exercise.

The first thing is to find an empty space – 50 people would need the area of a tennis court – 25 people would need at least half that. The space needs to be clearly delineated (using white tape can help here if needed, given the absence of clear boundaries like a fence/wall/verge and so on). This is what to tell the people, after a scene setter appropriate to your context (all verbal instructions to be given are shown in italics – if you follow them verbatim you should not go too far wrong).

> *'Please note the boundaries of the exercise area.'* – Point out and describe the boundary.
> *'I would like you to position yourselves at complete random within the area and be at least a good arms length from anyone.'*

After they are in their starting position:

> *'Now that you are positioned in the area, please pick at complete random two other people participating within the exercise area BUT you are not allowed to indicate who you have picked in ANY WAY. Do not pick me – I am not participating.'*

> *'These two people are now your reference point – you cannot change your reference points, nor can you indicate to them that they are such (even though, as the exercise goes on, you will have a strong desire to!).'*

> *'Let me explain a few more important and simple rules to help you before I give a specific objective:*

Stay within the boundaries.

Use the space when you start and continue – you will want to gravitate towards each other but this will make things harder – so keep your distance from others and use the space.

Move slowly and make the minimum needed minor adjustments to your position. Cover the least possible ground – if you make big and/or fast movements across the area you will be unpopular and also be breaking the rules.

You can only stand still when your objective is achieved.'

'Now let me explain your objective – it is very simple – what you need to do is to adjust your position slowly and gradually so that you are at an equal distance from each person you have chosen as your reference points – equal distance does NOT necessarily mean in-between.'

Here you can slowly move to show yourself at the top point of an isosceles triangle with two others as an example:

'For example if this person here and that person there were my two reference points, by moving slowly and gradually and covering the least possible ground to here I would be at equal distance. Remember that equal distance does NOT necessarily mean in-between.'

Having shown what an example of equal distance looks like you can continue:

'So you will need to adjust your position gradually staying within boundaries, using the space, keeping distance from others, moving slowly, making minimum needed adjustments, and only being still when you are at equal distance (in other words do not wait for others to stop before you re-adjust!!). And just to remind you, you are not allowed to change or indicate who your reference points are even though at some stage you will have a very strong desire to tell them what to do!'

'Remember too that you can only stand still when you are at equal distance from your reference points –so if they move, you will need to move and adjust as well. Once all have achieved their objective the exercise will be over. How long do you think this will take?'

At this stage some people may well laugh and some may say it is impossible – after all if everyone is trying to adjust at the same time it will seem like they have been set an impossible and never ending on-going loop. It will seem like a recipe for chaos (and in fact it is!). But if the rules are followed they will achieve steady state in the very rough proportion of time of one to one and a half minutes per ten people (so 25 people should take around two and a half to four minutes). Do *not* tell them this! But you can say

'Don't worry, it will go faster and easier than you think – you may be surprised!'

Then say:

'OK? Ready, steady, go!'

There will be a big urge on your part to step in and help/give directions when it seems to fall apart – do not do so! You will see that it will oscillate between coming together and seemingly falling apart – but let it flow. You will need to practise 'wu wei'[1] – holding back and allowing the natural flow.

Once all are still, just check by asking:

'Are you all now at equal distance from your reference points?'

Assuming they all say yes, tell them how long it took and congratulate them! After all as a group they self-organised and self-managed a highly complex task. Ask them:

'Given the number of possible solutions, how complex was this task?'

Many will say it was highly complex, which indeed from a mathematical perspective it is. And then ask (which often gets a laugh):

'What would have happened if … we had put one of you in charge?'

Why do many people laugh at this question? Because it is apparent that if someone had been 'put in charge' the exercise would probably go on for a very long time indeed.

The counter-intuitive and intriguing conclusion is that the *more* complex the situation and task, the *less* directive traditional leadership is needed.

To enable a good debrief (or as a reflection for you if you cannot actually do the exercise) say (ask yourself):

'You have achieved in a very short period of time a task that some of you thought impossible, and most of you thought would take a long time to do. What enabled you to do such a thing? What was in place that enabled you to achieve this?'

Make a list – you will find that it will be quite similar to the list which appears in this chapter. The aim here is to get some underlying principles of how to get complexity to work for you (rather than against you) – you will find it is, in fact, quite simple!

---

1   'Wu wei' was briefly mentioned in the Preface. It is a fundamental Taoist concept which is key to Complex Adaptive Leadership. It is explored more in Appendix A.

The outcome of the exercise at the beginning of this chapter often surprises people. It seems impossible, yet it works out very quickly. The counter-intuitive (and for some disturbing) conclusion is: the *more* complex things are, the *less* traditional leadership one needs. Instead a leader needs to put in place certain key principles so that the organisation being led can become self-leading, and the leader can then practice what is recognised in Chinese philosophy as the highest form of leadership – wu wei.

The implications of this simple axiom are immense, and form the basis of Complex Adaptive Leadership. The exercise is complex in that the number of possible solutions, and the way to get those solutions, is huge. As an example, it would take over 100 years just to count the number of possible solutions with 25 people in the exercise. Most agree that if someone was put in charge, then the exercise would take a very long time if the leader practised a typical oligarchic approach (that is, took charge and took responsibility for coming up with the solution).

But what is needed in place of traditional leadership? The debrief question *'What enabled you to complete a highly complex task?'* typically results in a list.[1] The list below is rank ordered by frequency:

- clear individual objective;
- a few simple rules;
- continuous feedback;
- discretion and freedom of action;
- skill/will of participants.

In addition to the five principles above, the following three often came out in subsequent group discussion. They are not perhaps as obvious as the first five:

- underlying purpose;
- clear boundary;
- a tolerance of the players for uncertainty and ambiguity.

Other principles sometimes emerge during the debrief of the exercise but the eight above are the most important ones. One which is not mentioned above, and is often discussed, is the issue of trust. However, if the principles above are applied with integrity then individuals can proceed independently of trust.[2]

Let's look at each in a little detail. We explore how they can be applied and what they look like organisationally in more detail in Chapter 7. At this stage it is just intended to see how they can fit generally:

- **Clear individual objective.** Each person has a very clear idea of what they are trying to achieve. Although they cannot say exactly where they will be, how far from their reference point they will end up or even how (that is, the route) they will get there, the objective they have is clear enough to get them moving. Note the objective is specific enough to give a clear indication if it is achieved or not, but not so specific as to tie the individual down (for example the angle and distance, as well as the route, is flexible). In other words, the individual sets the specific objective (by choosing the two specific people) within a broad objective. It would be very counter-productive to even try to specify the detail of the objective! How many times do we fall into the trap of trying to fathom out the objective to the 'Nth degree'? Although this can work well for relatively simple tasks and projects, when things are complex and dynamic such detailed working out of the objective does not help at all. In fact it gets in the way, taking up time, and demotivating those involved. What is sufficient is that each individual knows what needs to be achieved and, as important, will know immediately when it has been achieved. As the situation changes, and if that achievement then is lost, the individual has enough clarity to adjust and adapt.

---

1   I have run this simulation with over 50 groups taken from the main research group outlined in footnote 1 to Chapter 2. You can see a video of it at: http://www.complexadaptiveleadership.com/organisationalleadership.html, accessed: 18 April 2010.

2   Proceeding independently of trust is one of the approaches which supports the principle of 'separating the people from the problem', part of principled negotiation as described by Fisher, Ury and Patton in their book *Getting to Yes – Negotiating Agreement Without Giving In.*

Another important aspect is that each individual has a sense of ownership of their own objectives, as they could choose which two people were their reference points.

- **A few simple rules.**[3] The rules are sufficient to enable effective action, and enough to keep the system from descending into too much chaos. However, they are not so many as to cause the system to slow down and become cumbersome. The balance between having enough rules to fulfil obligations, and allowing enough freedom to act, is a fine one. The Disney Corporation found that it had gone too far down the route of having rules and procedures for everything. When they tried to move that concept to Europe and a new Disney-world in France they found that it did not work. This experience then forced a look at how they used rules and procedures in general. This saw a major simplification and the results which flowed enabled the new resort to stay afloat, and the current resorts to improve their operations.[4] The move from a heavily measured organisation to a more complex adaptive one is mirrored in the evolution of Semco in Brazil. This is described in the book by their CEO Ricardo Semler called *Maverick*, mentioned in Chapter 3.[5]

- **Clear boundary.** The boundary gives a definition where the action is. For the exercise, the boundary is both the area within which it takes place, as well as the boundary of how the game is to be played (that is, by looking at the two reference points and then moving following the rules to adjust one's position). We typically define boundaries as 'who-is-in-charge-of-who', with the 'organogram' being an all-too-typical way of showing how the organisation is structured. Rather than focusing on the boundary of the organisation per se, Complex Adaptive Leadership looks at the nature of the relationships *across* the boundaries outside of the organisation as well as the internal networks. This is a different way of looking at things – typically we look at the objects within a network (the departments, units, individuals and so on). The other way of looking at it is by seeing the relationships as the main thing, with the objects as the background, as illustrated by Figure 6.1.

At a more macro level, the boundary conditions of an organisation also includes its strategy – what does it deliver, to who and how. Under the oligarchic assumption, strategy is something defined by the leaders and executed by the followers. Under a polyarchic assumption, strategy is defined by the dynamic of the relationships within which the organisation exists. At the end of the day, that dynamic needs to be clarified, so the techniques used in clarification may be the same as within an oligarchic assumption, although the process may differ (for example, the use of mass intervention techniques

---

3   The concept of 'a few simple rules' is the same as 'simple guiding principles' that are often quoted as a necessary function of a Complex Adaptive System. The term is often attributed to Craig Reynolds, who built a computer simulation in 1986 that showed how birds flocked. His theory shows how birds travel in large groups, perform complicated routes, do not collide, and seem to act as a unit on the basis of a few simple rules. Reynolds' three fundamental 'laws' of flocking are: (1) separation – steer to avoid crowding local flockmates; (2) alignment – steer towards the average heading of local flockmates; and (3) cohesion – steer to move toward the average position of local flockmates. See <http://www.red3d.com/cwr/boids/>, accessed 18 April 2010, and also Potts' 'The Chorus-line Hypothesis of Coordination in Avian Flocks'.

4   There were other elements at play which meant that EuroDisney did not work well to begin with. The training was very directive and one employee complained it was like being brain-washed. The style of management was centralised which meant managers, remote from the operation in the US, took decisions which were less than optimum. For more details see H.M. Packman and F.L. Casmir, 'Learning from the Euro Disney Experience – A Case Study in International/ Intercultural Communication'.

5   See footnote 13 to Chapter 3.

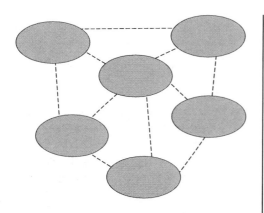
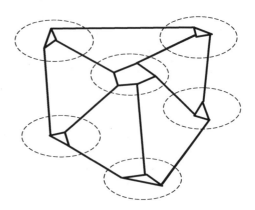

Objects as key part of a network | Relationships as key part of a network

Figure 6.1 Network of relationships is key

as described in Chapter 3). The establishment and maintenance of boundary conditions takes time. So whilst in the more traditional days of oligarchy a leader is looking down into the organisation and defining the strategy and resultant organisation, the polyarchic leader will be looking across and outside the organisation, realising that his organisation is itself a node in a complex network.

- **Continuous feedback.** Every individual knows at any time where they are in relationship to achieving their objective. And they are able to interpret the data they see – in other words they can judge distance. They 'sense' what the reference points are doing and 'respond' – a very real experience of being adaptive. This relates to Key Performance Indicators (KPIs). There are huge debates over the use of measurement, both what should be measured, how it should be done and how reported. Suffice it here to say that an organisation needs a range of measures, and individuals need both to understand them and to understand how they influence them. These should not only include 'hard' measures such as financial and operational metrics, but also 'soft' measures ranging from staff attitude (at an organisational level) to personal behavioural 360 degrees feedback (at an individual level).
- **Skill/will of participants.** Each person has the ability to judge distance and move accordingly (skill) and also wants to do the exercise (will). Translated into organisational terms, this would mean each person has the skills needed to do their job as well as the motivation to do it well. Again the field of skills development and motivation theory is a huge area. People are generally more skilled and motivated than their leaders would often suppose (if their actions are anything to go by, as explored in Chapter 8). The best way a polyarchic leader can develop skills is to ensure a process of knowledge transfer is available, as well as necessary development courses. And the best way a polyarchic leader can develop motivation is to understand how leadership behaviour can demotivate – and then eradicate such behaviour! This issue is explored further in the application of the skill/will model in Chapter 9 and the Complex Adaptive Leadership model described in Chapter 10.

- **Discretion and freedom of action.** Each person is free to act without having to wait for 'permission', or needing guidance on which way to go. This takes both an organisational culture and a personal attitude which encompasses Stuart's Law of Retroaction (it is easier to seek forgiveness than obtain permission). Having discretion and freedom of action within well-defined boundaries is critical for complexity to work. And people need to feel confident in taking risks and using initiative.
- **Underlying purpose.** There is an implicit and unifying underlying purpose to the exercise. When I run this exercise it is normally as part of a course in a business school. I do not need to remind people they are in a business school wanting to learn new things – it is the underlying purpose that unites people and thus it is easy for me, the professor, to ask people to do a strange exercise. If we had all been strangers on a bus, then the underlying purpose would not support the exercise (that is, wanting to go somewhere, and not get off the bus to do a crazy exercise, no matter how compelling the learning).
- **Ambiguity and uncertainty.** Within the exercise there is a degree of chaos, and the situation is far from equilibrium. Whilst for some, if not all, there may be an uncomfortable feeling that things are looking chaotic, and that the exercise may be impossible, people still enter into the flow. This 'far from equilibrium' and uncertainty is the very essence of life itself, is therefore natural and something to be embraced rather than avoided, even if we prefer order and control. And the paradox is that we should not abandon order and control either!

There is also a Yin/Yang element to the eight aspects above. The eight principles can be paired, with each pair having two principles which are complementary and in some way paradoxical to each other.

Complexity works well when you have:

• Underlying, implicit and unifying common purpose	⟷	• Clear, explicit and individual objectives
• Discretion and freedom to act	⟷	• Boundaries enclosing the action
• Skill/will of the individual people	⟷	• A few simple rules of the organisation
• Ambiguity, randomness far from equilibrium	⟷	• Continuous and unambiguous feedback

The 4-plus-4 model for leading complexity

Figure 6.2   Yin/Yang and the Four + Four model for leading complexity

These four pairs are in some way paradoxes as they seem to contradict (that is, implicit–explicit, freedom–enclosure, people power–rules power, ambiguity uncertainty–unambiguous measurement). And surrounding the pairs is the uncertainty of deeper reality, as well as the fact that it is uncertain that these rules work all the time! It is not for nothing that the sub-title of this book is 'Embracing paradox and uncertainty'.

Chapter Summary

1. The more complex things are, the less traditional directional leadership one needs if certain principles are in place.
2. These principles form four pairs of paradoxical principles which together allow complexity to work within an organisation.

7 Getting Chaos and Complexity to Work

A QUICK TEST TO SEE HOW READY YOUR ORGANISATION IS TO EXERCISE POLYARCHY

Consider each question below with respect of your own organisation. Each question has one of five possible answers (from Strongly Disagree to Strongly Agree) and each answer has one of two possible scores. So, for example, if in question 1 you are Neutral, select either a 5 (if your neutrality has a slight tendency towards disagreement) or a 6 (if your neutrality has a slight tendency towards agreement).

1. People in the organisation have a strong shared sense of common purpose.

Strongly Disagree	Disagree	Neutral	Agree	Strongly Agree
1 or 2	3 or 4	5 or 6	7 or 8	9 or 10

2. Each individual has clear, measurable individual objectives.

Strongly Disagree	Disagree	Neutral	Agree	Strongly Agree
1 or 2	3 or 4	5 or 6	7 or 8	9 or 10

3. People are encouraged to take the initiative and act on opportunities when they arise.

Strongly Disagree	Disagree	Neutral	Agree	Strongly Agree
1 or 2	3 or 4	5 or 6	7 or 8	9 or 10

4. The boundaries of responsibilities between people and teams/departments are clear.

Strongly Disagree	Disagree	Neutral	Agree	Strongly Agree
1 or 2	3 or 4	5 or 6	7 or 8	9 or 10

5. People are well qualified and skilled to do their work.

Strongly Disagree	Disagree	Neutral	Agree	Strongly Agree
1 or 2	3 or 4	5 or 6	7 or 8	9 or 10

6. The rules of the organisation are clear and understood by all.

Strongly Disagree	Disagree	Neutral	Agree	Strongly Agree
1 or 2	3 or 4	5 or 6	7 or 8	9 or 10

7.   There is an effective, well defined process for continuous feedback.

Strongly Disagree	Disagree	Neutral	Agree	Strongly Agree
1 or 2	3 or 4	5 or 6	7 or 8	9 or 10

8.   Although there is an element of chaos in this organisation things still seem to work well.

Strongly Disagree	Disagree	Neutral	Agree	Strongly Agree
1 or 2	3 or 4	5 or 6	7 or 8	9 or 10

9.   The organisation has a shared idea of how it contributes to society/the wider world.

Strongly Disagree	Disagree	Neutral	Agree	Strongly Agree
1 or 2	3 or 4	5 or 6	7 or 8	9 or 10

10.   Everybody knows what is expected of them and what they have to achieve.

Strongly Disagree	Disagree	Neutral	Agree	Strongly Agree
1 or 2	3 or 4	5 or 6	7 or 8	9 or 10

11.   People are free to decide how to do their work and do not feel controlled.

Strongly Disagree	Disagree	Neutral	Agree	Strongly Agree
1 or 2	3 or 4	5 or 6	7 or 8	9 or 10

12.   It is clear what each team/department/unit is responsible for.

Strongly Disagree	Disagree	Neutral	Agree	Strongly Agree
1 or 2	3 or 4	5 or 6	7 or 8	9 or 10

13.   People have a high degree of motivation in this organisation.

Strongly Disagree	Disagree	Neutral	Agree	Strongly Agree
1 or 2	3 or 4	5 or 6	7 or 8	9 or 10

14.   The rules of the organisation are few but effective.

Strongly Disagree	Disagree	Neutral	Agree	Strongly Agree
1 or 2	3 or 4	5 or 6	7 or 8	9 or 10

15.   There is a degree of ambiguity about how things are achieved, but objectives are met.

Strongly Disagree	Disagree	Neutral	Agree	Strongly Agree
1 or 2	3 or 4	5 or 6	7 or 8	9 or 10

16. Individuals know how well they are doing towards achieving their objectives at any given time.

Strongly Disagree	Disagree	Neutral	Agree	Strongly agree
1 or 2	3 or 4	5 or 6	7 or 8	9 or 10

Add up the scores. The following should be a guide:

More than 120 = Excellent score – if polyarchy is not apparent then individual leaders may need some development work – Chapter 7 should help, whilst this chapter should reinforce what is already there.

100–120 = Good – some individual areas may need attention and this chapter may give some ideas.

60–100 = Danger zone – the organisational effectiveness is sub-optimal, attention across the board is needed, and this chapter will lay a good foundation for the type of work to be done.

30–60 = Severe danger – action needs to be taken if individual and organisational effectiveness are to be safeguarded, and this chapter as well as the references used will need careful study.

Less than 30 = still existing?

Figure 7.1 gives a template for more detailed analysis:

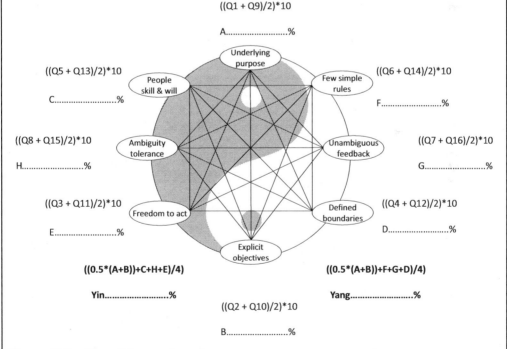

Figure 7.1   Exercising polyarchy

It should be noted that this tool is not about gaining an absolute picture – its real value is by being shared with others who subsequently come together for a powerful dialogue. The key is to first get balance (between Yin and Yang – more than 2 per cent difference is out of balance) and then go for strength (that is, target lowest scores). Balance first – then strength.

The exercise at the beginning of Chapter 6 showed how a group of people can achieve a complex task with little leadership. The counter-intuitive conclusion is that the more complex things are, the less directive leadership should be used. Eight principles were identified which enables a seemingly impossible exercise to be done. Seen as a fractal, these principles can be applied at an organisational level to help them work more effectively.

The exercise at the beginning of this chapter shows to what extent your organisation has these principles embedded. This chapter looks at examples of how these principles can work in practice. As will be seen the mix and method differs and is unique to each organisation. The journey of embedding these principles is probably more important than the principles themselves.

These principles, and the Four + Four model, form the basis of the organisational level of Complex Adaptive Leadership, and this chapter looks at how these principles can be applied.

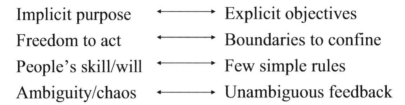

Implicit purpose	←→	Explicit objectives
Freedom to act	←→	Boundaries to confine
People's skill/will	←→	Few simple rules
Ambiguity/chaos	←→	Unambiguous feedback

Figure 7.2   Four + Four principles

Underlying Meaningful Purpose

Purpose is what lends an underlying meaning to day-to-day activities. It's what unites people. It's the fundamental reason for being, and taps into people's motivation. In the paperback version of *Built to Last*, which was a study in the 1990s of visionary companies who had consistently outperformed, Collins and Porras added a chapter where they said: *'Pushed to choose between core purpose and core values, we would likely choose core purpose as the more important of the two for guiding and inspiring an organisation.'*[1]

Purpose needs to be as meaningful to the organisation as possible. It is what sets the organisation apart and gives it a sense of identity, pride and 'raison d'être'. It does not need to be directly linked to the output of the organisation. For example, the CEO of an elevator company once said he considered the purpose of his company was to enable green spaces in cities – without the elevator, many would never be able to work or live in high rise buildings, so more space for cities would be needed with less space available for parks.[2]

Many businesses see their purpose as creating shareholder value. Shareholder value is critical and businesses that do not create a return for their shareholders do not last long. Even public sector organisations have a responsibility to deliver value for tax payer investment. However, an organisation which sees its unique *purpose* as creating shareholder value is making a big mistake for the following reasons:

---

1   J.C. Collins and J.I. Porras, *Built to Last – Successful Habits of Visionary Companies*, p. 224.

2   Presentation by KONE CEO to Leadership Development course at London Business School 2003.

- Such a purpose is not unique – *all* businesses should create shareholder value, and wealth for the wider society. If a business cannot create a financial return for those who invest (and not just the shareholders, but also wider stakeholders) then it will soon be out of business. So shareholder value is a *result* and not a unique purpose.
- It is not inspiring – how many workers do you know leap out of bed with a surge in their heart to create shareholder value? And whilst those at the top may wax lyrical about shareholder value it is slightly hypocritical as a firmly held belief. Most leaders of businesses do not even know who their *real* shareholders are. If you ask the main board of a publicly quoted company who the main shareholders are, they will probably know who the shareholder representatives/middlemen are (such as financial institutions) but they will not know who the real shareholders are (and it is likely they will not care).
- It can lead to the opposite effect. Research by the RSA in the UK in the 1990s showed how companies who focused on shareholder value, and whose annual reports stated shareholder value being its primary purpose, ended up destroying value in the long run.[3]

According to the *Built to Last* study, those organisations who state shareholder value as their purpose have not yet identified what their true purpose is.[4] One could go further and say those organisations who do, are giving a good reason to sell their shares! When Marks & Spencer began to decline, a new CEO was brought in and he stated that the purpose of Marks & Spencer was to ensure shareholder value. Needless to say their results got worse. Marks & Spencer results began to decline in the first place when they lost their sense of purpose and strayed from their values. This began to become apparent in the 1980s in their supply chain and how they treated suppliers. The rot spread like a cancer to their other relationships, including their customers who began to leave them in droves.[5]

So purpose is something deeper and meaningful. Some companies state their purpose clearly. Examples are shown in Figure 7.3 below:

Company	Stated Purpose
3M	To solve unsolved problems innovatively
Hewlett-Packard	To make technical contributions for the advancement and welfare of humanity
McKinsey	To help leading corporations and governments be more successful
Sony	To experience the joy of advancing and applying technology for the benefit of mankind
Walt Disney	To make people happy

Figure 7.3   Examples of purpose

---

3   'Tomorrow's Company Inquiry' by the Royal Society for the Encouragement of the Arts, Manufactures and Commerce (RSA) London, UK.

4   Collins and Porras, *Built to Last*, p. 227.

5   Marks & Spencer results began their decline in the late 1990s when profits went down from £815m in 1998 to £372m in 1999. They then slumped to £2.8m.

The purpose can be used to underlie many things, even language. For example in Disney the concept 'To make people happy' is aligned to entertainment. They have a different language in their theme parks: employees are called 'cast', a work shift is a 'performance', off duty areas (such as canteen and so on) are called 'backstage' and so on. At the end of the day a clear purpose provides a simple question everyone can ask themselves if in doubt about what they are doing: 'Is what I am doing helping us live up to our core purpose?' If the answer is 'No', then it is a simple decision to stop it. Unique and meaningful purpose allows key decisions to be made quickly, especially in a crisis. A company without a deeper and meaningful unique purpose can struggle in a crisis. A good example of this is how two different companies reacted when faced with the similar problem of contaminated products – Johnson & Johnson in the USA with Tylenol in the 1980s and Coca Cola in Europe in the 1990s. Johnson & Johnson was founded by Robert W. Johnson in 1886 'to alleviate pain and disease'.[6] In 1935 his son laid the foundation of the Johnson & Johnson 'credo' which put customers first, employees and managers second, and stockholders (mainly his family) last. He added the community ahead of stockholders in 1943.[7] So when it was discovered in 1982 that one of their leading products, Tylenol, had been tampered with and seven people in Chicago died, the product was withdrawn from every shelf. The decision was made very quickly and at a low level as it was so obvious that the situation went against the core purpose of the company. The company lost wealth in the short term (it suffered a $1.24 billion wealth decline due to the depreciation of the company and Tylenol brand names) but its reputation remained intact.[8] Coca Cola faced a similar situation in France when it became apparent that their product had been contaminated in France and Belgium in the 1990s. However, their purpose was to maximise shareholder value – so the cost of withdrawing the product mitigated against a wide withdrawal. They could not bring themselves to withdraw Coca Cola until the French Government took the decision for the company, by banning Coca Cola across the whole country. It was only then that the company began to withdraw product. Coca Cola's reputation was dented for some time, and its position was badly damaged in France. The bad luck for Coca Cola is that detailed subsequent reports found that there was no contamination and that the sickness was mass hysteria. However the delay in acting was acknowledged as a PR disaster.

So a strong sense of purpose is like a foundation of rock, a constant compass to help point the way. It defines what is at the heart of the organisation.[9] And the heart is central for an organization's health. Taking this one step further, an organisation's health will, to a large extent, dictate its ability to perform[10]. Purpose is often implicit and stays constant in a sea of change. Organisations that last have purpose. The question is to what extent is it understood? The questionnaire at the start of this chapter should give some insight to what extent purpose exists and is shared. If it is not, then a variety of options exist,

---

6   L.G. Foster, *A Company That Cares*.

7   Collins and Porras, *Built to Last*, p. 58.

8   M. Mitchell, 'The Impact of External Parties on Brand Name Capital: The 1982 Tylenol Poisonings and Subsequent Cases'.

9   The issue of 'Heart' is gaining more attention. See for example Beddington-Behrens, S. (2013) 'Awakening the universal heart – a guide for spiritual activist', Umbria Press; and also McGovern, G. (2014) 'Lead from the Heart' *Harvard Business Review*, March 2014.

10   See for example S. Keller and C. Price (2011) *Beyond Performance: How great organisations build ultimate competitive advantage*. John Wiley & Sons.

depending on the context. Chapter 10 will give some possible strategies to be employed (for example, push it or pull it). The following questions may help meanwhile if a sense of purpose is lacking:

Did a sense of purpose ever exist? If it did, what led it to be lost?

To what extent is there agreement that a sense of purpose is important in the first place?

Has the top team agreed what the purpose of the organisation they lead is?

If the top team agrees what it is and why it is needed, to what extent is this shared by subordinates?

They say a fish rots from the head. If a sense of purpose is lacking in the organisation then a discussion needs to start with the top team. Once it is agreed amongst them, then beware – the work has just begun. Cascades rarely work and a sense of constant purpose needs to be *owned* across the organisation. The heart of an organisation cannot be imposed – it needs to be uncovered as it is usually already there. The question is, is it a healthy heart generating health? An involvement strategy is best to uncover the true heart of an organisation. Paradoxical as it may sound, once a sense of purpose is clarified by a top team, they need to be ready to give it up, as it is further explored by the organisation. Chapter 10 gives some further insights on this paradox.

Clear, Explicit and Individual Objectives

Management By Objectives (MBO) was a trend which emerged in the 1970s.[11] When combined with the other Four + Four principles it is a vital component. It seems axiomatic that people who do not have clear objectives do not work well, but clear measurable objectives are often lacking in people's day to day work. The reasons for why this happens include:

Clear explicit and measurable objectives put pressure for performance, and make things more transparent; people naturally avoid such pressure and are often more comfortable when their performance criteria are vague.

Transparency makes it harder for people to hide poor performance, and adds additional stress.

It is hard to keep objectives up to date in a fast moving environment – it is easier to have objectives vague.

Having clear objectives for each individual is not just about having a clear target. It also means that the objectives have to *make sense*, and allow the individual to see how his targets fit into the greater whole. This is easier said than done – there needs to be a clear link to boundary conditions (for example, the strategy of the organisation) as well as the feedback processes).

---

11   Management By Objectives is not a new concept, but was first popularised by Peter Drucker in the 1950s – see *The Practice of Management*.

Objectives need to be:

- Set mutually and involve the individuals concerned so that the individuals can fully own the objectives rather than have them imposed. The process of setting objectives can be as important as the objectives themselves.
- There needs to be enough flexibility – if the objectives are set too tight they constrain, if they are too loose they can miss the target. Sadly there is no clear cut formula here, except for common sense and a good understanding of the context and individual involved. As a general rule the more complex and dynamic the context, the more flexibility is needed in the objectives (the game of choosing two people is a good example – people choose their own reference points, and equal distance can be a myriad of possible solutions).
- They need to be simple – a long list of objectives can confuse and sometimes contradict. The best is to have one simple objective, under which action follows.
- They need to reflect *action* – that is, what you *do*, rather than what you get. The common mistake is to confuse measures of success (financial targets and so on) with objectives. A measure of success could be an increased level of sales – an objective could be to recruit 20 more salesmen in the first half of the year. The achievement of the objective is what gets the result.
- They need to be SMART:
  - Specific (but not constraining);
  - Measurable (for individual to judge progress);
  - Action-orientated (to enable focus on delivery);
  - Realistic (mindful of the context); and
  - Time-orientated (so progress can be measured over time).

So far we have looked at individual objectives. The organisational ones can be more complex. However, they can be simplified by linking them to the key stakeholders. An example of this is the 'Framework for success'[12] below. This can be particularly helpful in a change management situation where the context is complex and fast moving, as it sets out what is trying to be achieved. The first thing to do is to step back and take a broad view of what it is the organisation is trying to achieve. This needs to be summarised into a clear succinct statement such as a Vision or Mission statement. Most organisations stop there, but more detail is often needed. The Framework for success is an organisational version of a project Work Breakdown Structure (WBS) and can be used to bridge the gap between lofty vision and specific earthly action. It is from the Mission and Values statement that goals and initiatives can flow. These initiatives can then be broken down into specific objectives which form the basis of the change/operations. The goals which flow from the Mission Statement can reflect the five key stakeholder groups of the organisation: the Customers, the Suppliers, the Employees, the Shareholders and the Community. However they can reflect other broad themes.

Organisational missions and goals can also have meaning, and be inspiring/motivational in their own right. An example of this is what Collins and Porras called

---

12   N. Obolensky, *Practical Business Re-engineering – Tools and Techniques for Achieving Effective Change.*

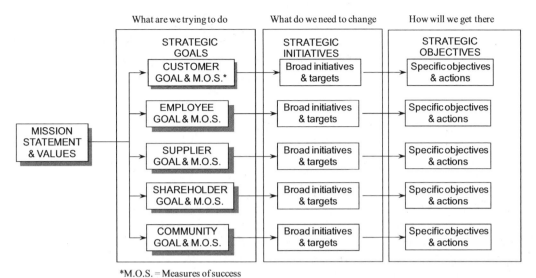

Figure 7.4   **Framework for success**

'BHAGs'[13] (Big Hairy Audacious Goals). Their study showed how BHAGs can replace the need for traditional charismatic leadership. Examples of this include:

- The original moon mission – although the goal of a man in the moon was set by John F. Kennedy, his leadership style alone did not drive the achievement. After all he was killed in 1963, a few years before the goal was achieved in 1969.
- Wal Mart's goal of becoming a major retailer and reaching $125 billion in revenue was set by Sam Walton, who died before the achievement of the goal.
- Boeing's pursuit of the 747 was first set by the CEO William Allen but he had long left when the 747 came to fruition. In fact when he left, the 747 was still only at the design stage – the hard part was yet to come.

So when clear objectives are coupled with an enduring purpose, then the need for traditional leadership dissipates. The question is: can such objectives be set by those who would normally be directed by a leader? (that is, 'followers'). Ricardo Semler from Semco describes in his article 'How We Went Digital Without a Strategy' how this can happen. In one example the team working on a contract servicing offices came up with a whole new business which they subsequently ran.[14] Semler called this approach 'Management Without Control' – another good example of a paradox.

Discretion and Freedom to Act

Once a purpose exists and the objectives are clear (and assuming the other principles are also in place) then people should be left to get on with it. The issue of trust is often quoted

---

13   Collins and Porras, *Built to Last*. The whole of Chapter 5 explores BHAGs in detail.

14   R. Semler, 'How We Went Digital Without a Strategy', *Harvard Business Review*.

by many as being key. But within an effective polyarchy, individuals should be able to *proceed independently of trust* as the system works like an organism – does the brain 'trust' the heart to beat? Trust only becomes an issue if the Four + Four principles are lacking.

Discretion and freedom to act covers three key areas:

- empowerment;
- willingness of leaders to 'let go' and followers to take initiative;
- self-organisation.

EMPOWERMENT

The theme of 'empowerment' became a buzzword in the late 1980s.[15] The reason for this seems to be that as hierarchies were flattened and management layers taken out, there was a need for people to take the initiative. However, such a move came after decades of command and control management, and it seemed most people had become programmed to be unempowered (for example, wait to be told what to do). One of the key reasons why the re-engineering efforts failed in the 1980s was the cultural shock that inevitably accompanied such efforts.[16] The problem with empowerment, however, is that it is fundamentally an oligarchic concept. In other words the leaders 'empower' the followers – they have the power to do so, and they 'give' the power to their subordinates. By definition then they can take the power away. Indeed many leaders' actions are more unempowering (and even overpowering) than empowering. So self-empowerment, and the context for that to emerge and thrive, is more important than 'giving' empowerment.

WILLINGNESS FOR LEADERS TO LET GO AND FOLLOWERS TO TAKE INITIATIVE

Why do leaders find it hard to let go? There are a variety of reasons, and they overlap and are repeated in follower behaviour as well:

- A positive intention for wanting a good result, taken to excess. Everyone generally wants to see a job done to the best possible effect. A leader usually has more experience and often sees the overall context better, so will have a wider view of how the job should be done. If a leader sees a subordinate do something which appears sub-optimal, or might lead to a sub-optimal result, then more often than not, the leader will step in. Indeed, many are taught that is the role of leadership![17] This then leads the follower to be more hesitant and seek approval more often – this

---

15   Empowerment is not a new concept, and its first debated use in organisations was in the late nineteenth century in the USA, where the Chinese approach which favoured efficiency collided with the American approach which favoured control. On his site at http://www.motivation-tools.com/workplace/history.htm, accessed: 18 April 2010, Robert Webb outlines how in the mid-nineteenth century, empowerment approaches helped lay track and dig for gold better. He comments: *'If responsibility leadership is so efficient, why are not more companies using it? Answer: Most leaders do not want to give up control. Control is job security and/or a feeling of importance. The typical CEO will let a company go bankrupt before trusting others with responsibility he thinks should be his.'*

16   See M. Hammer, *Beyond Re-engineering*.

17   If you get bored of reading this book and need a break, Google 'the role of leadership is to' and you will get a good overview of what many see leadership as. They mostly boil down into the three E's – Envision, Enable, and Energise (the 'Triple E' model proposed by Stephenson and Cowan). The assumption of most is mainly based on an oligarchical view, which is what this book is trying to complement through proposing a more polyarchic view.

in turn leads the leader to have less faith in the employee who seems hesitant, and thus a vicious cycle is entered. The way a leader behaves will often drive follower behaviour.

- Fear of poor performance leading to lack of trust. If things go wrong, there is an inevitable 'blame storm'. And leaders are often the first to be blamed if an organisation fails. This means that the fear is real and it is a brave leader indeed who can let go fully and 'trust' the followers. The underlying intention is sound: the desire for a good outcome. However, the consequence of failure also plays a part. How an organisation deals with failure will influence how much leaders are prepared to let go. This can also affect the decision-making process. If decisions are based always on their outcomes, rather than the process employed for the decision to be made, then fear of failure will be increased.[18]

'Letting go' is hard to do ...

... as is 'taking the lead'

Figure 7. 5 Barriers for leaders and followers

- Lack of awareness and understanding. Many leaders do not fully understand the concept of allowing others to take the lead. Many traditional leadership models have leaders 'leading' – that is what they do. Letting go and allowing others to take the lead is seen as weak or, worse, a cop out. For some it is a question of ignorance and poor leadership development. For others it is a question of culture. What is surprising is that no matter the level of leadership knowledge or culture, all recognise the issues presented in this book when faced by them. Coupled with this there also seems to be a lack of understanding of what is really happening on the ground and what the issues are. This gives rise to two issues. The first issue is that leaders are becoming increasingly distanced from reality, and the problems they concern themselves with are often far from those faced on the ground. The second is what I call the 'Coffee Machine Syndrome', which is a little trite, but illustrates the point. This came from consulting work done with a financial services company facing the need for major change in the market. During a culture change programme in the early 1990s, the management tried to get the employees involved in defining the strategy, but initial efforts did not work well. The problem the employees saw as the biggest was the coffee machines which did not work. This exasperated some of the senior managers who could not understand why the employees could not get engaged with the more serious problems of having to redefine the market strategy. The coffee machines were fixed, as were other niggling issues raised, and needless to say at the next workshop the employees began to get more engaged with the strategic issues. Leaders often do not understand why those on the ground do not seem concerned by the strategic issues facing the organisation. But if the problems of the employees on the ground are not sorted out, then they are unlikely to. If the coffee machines are not working, that will be the major issue for the employees! Fix the machines and they will lift their sights up. Another area of 'unawareness' is the

---

18   See Z. Degraefe and N. Nicholson, *Risk: How to Make Decisions in an Uncertain World*.

ignorance regarding chaos theory and complexity science – this is not to propose that leaders should become mathematicians and scientists, but they should have at least a basic understanding (which is provided in the previous chapter). The lack of such understanding adds to the fear of letting go, as well as causing the 'red queen' effect of working harder and harder but achieving little.

Letting go is hard to do, and yet it is central to the idea of wu wei, which according to ancient Chinese wisdom, is the highest form of leadership. One often finds that when one lets go, things tend to sort themselves out often faster and better than if one tried to control it – it is clear that leaders spend far too much and unnecessary time 'leading', as our research shows in the next chapter when we look at individual behaviours.

If there are issues on the leadership side of the equation, so too are there issues on the follower side. Why do followers hesitate to take the initiative or act with discretion? This is explored more in Chapter 9 but suffice to say here that the reasons can be seen as the flip side to the reasons why leaders find it hard to let go:

- A good intention of not wanting to cause upset can be taken to excess. Followers are often hesitant to take the lead as they are unsure of how the leader will see it. How many meetings have you been to where people dance around an issue in a non-committed way until it becomes clear where the leader's thinking is. And for some strange reason, the thinking then expressed by the followers seems to reflect the way the leader sees things. It is almost as if people lose the power of independent thought.
- Fear of failure and negative consequences is also a strong influence. Doing nothing and not sticking one's neck out is a very typical feature of hierarchic organisations. Many cultures share similar metaphors from 'tall poppies' and 'sticking your head above the parapet' in English to 'tall hay' in Holland. In fact the stronger the hierarchy and leadership the less followers are willing to take the lead. There is a pressing need for leaders to see how they exercise their role in a different way – the *Built to Last* study concluded that '*A charismatic visionary leader is absolutely not required for a visionary company and, in fact, can be detrimental....*'[19] Collins later reinforced this finding in his *Good to Great* study. A hierarchy of talented leaders is becoming less of a factor for success. He concluded: '*When you have disciplined people you don't need hierarchy; when you have disciplined thought you don't need bureaucracy; when you have disciplined action you don't need excessive controls.*'[20]
- Lack of awareness and understanding of followers is similar to that of the leaders. Many followers do not behave as though the days of leaders knowing everything are fast disappearing. Note that behaving is not the same as knowing – when pushed, most will admit to knowing intuitively that leaders no longer know the solutions and followers need to take the lead more. But if asked why this is so, most will not be able to demonstrate an understanding. So whilst most have an emotional intuition,

---

19   J. Collins and J. Porras, *Built to Last*, paperback version, p. 7. Porras and Collins conclude that the organisation's core ideology (which consists of its core purpose and core values) serve as the leadership of an organisation.

20   J. Collins, *From Good to Great*, p. 12.

they lack the intellectual understanding – a real heart vs. head conundrum. Faced by such a conundrum, most will prefer to keep their heads down and not take a lead.

SELF-ORGANISATION

Self-organisation is the third part of this principle of discretion and freedom to act. This is linked to the themes of empowerment and willingness of leaders to 'let go'/ followers 'take initiative'. We already saw in the previous chapter how self-organisation emerged as a key theme in the late 1960s and early 1970s in different areas of science as diverse as chemistry, ecology, enzymes, lasers and neuroscience. At the same time self-managed teams were beginning to emerge in business.[21] Like the findings in science, self-organisation needs some underlying principles to work. There is a fractal symmetry here as some of these principles are the same as some of the Four + Four principles which this forms a part of.

So the principle of freedom to act can be seen in terms of empowerment, willingness of leaders to let go/followers to take initiative, and self-organisation. An important balance to this is the need for clear boundaries within which such freedom to act can gain best effect, and it is to this principle that we can now turn.

Boundaries Enclosing the Action

Boundaries exist in every organisation. The issue is how boundaries can be managed in a way which enables freedom to act without complete chaos on the one hand, and not stifle initiative and flexibility on the other. The boundary dictates the 'edge of chaos' or the point that is 'far from equilibrium', so is not a simple point to define. It seems to be more of an art than a precise science. Boundary theory is not a well-developed science.[22] For the purpose of this study, boundaries can be considered in four ways:

- traditional organisational reporting (organograms);
- supply/value chain considerations;
- the defined *who*, *what* and *how* of strategy;
- invisible boundaries.

ORGANOGRAMS

The assumption of an organogram is that the organisation is shown by who reports to whom. It is very oligarchic as the higher you go the fewer people there are. And yet outdated as it is, it is used by just about every organisation of size. This is because it does have value. There are some however who have a different approach to the organogram. A

---

21   See footnote 13 in this chapter re. empowerment. Self-managed teams by definition are empowered. They differ from self-directed teams as their goal/direction (that is, what they do) is normally set for them and then they get on with it (that is, decide and implement how they do it). Self-managed teams began to emerge in business in the late 1970s and early 1980s. Volvo's CEO Gyllenhammar devised self-managed teams of from 15 to 20 workers, who put together a car at their own pace. These teams proved to be 10 per cent to 15 per cent more productive than the normal Volvo's assembly lines.

22   Boundary theory exists in social sciences as a cognitive theory of social classification that focuses on outcomes such as the meanings people assign to home and work and the ease and frequency of transitioning between roles. See E. Zerubavel, *The Fine Line*, and C. Nippert-Eng, *Home and Work*.

sign perhaps of an attempt to move on from the traditional top-down pyramid shape of the organogram is turning the pyramid upside down and showing the people at the 'bottom' of an organisation as being at the 'top'. This is a symptomatic, though not necessarily typical, sign of an organisation which is grappling with the polyarchic realities it faces whilst being gripped by its traditional oligarchic assumptions. The problem with the organogram is that it is often out of date the day it is published. This is not only due to the turnover of people within the various jobs in the organisation, but also the changing role of people's jobs to meet fast moving changing environment. Many pull their hair out to keep it 'up-to-date' – they should learn to relax as it never can be, and should only be used to help people understand only one, albeit important, aspect of the network of relationships that exist. It also serves to show the various boundaries of authorities in an organisation and who is responsible for what. As such it is a valuable boundary defining tool, even if the oligarchic assumption upon which it is mainly based is becoming rather strained. Perhaps a better way of looking at an organisation is using network theory and seeing who is connected to whom, and who is dependent upon whom. This type of analyses invariably shows that cross boundary actions, crossing functional and departmental boundaries, happens frequently. This is critical for helping an organisation navigate complexity. A leader's time spent looking across and outside traditional boundaries is time well spent.

SUPPLY/VALUE CHAIN CONSIDERATIONS[23]

Traditionally the company has been seen as a distinct organisation. But the boundaries within the supply/value chain are becoming blurred. If one looks at Figure 6.1 again, the way to look at the supply/value chain is not so much in terms of the various component parts but by looking at the relationships that exist. By working in this way, a new attitude can be fostered which is not so much an 'us and them', but more of an overall 'networked us'. This is the approach that was taken for the Boeing 777, which took an amazing four years from inception to delivery. The whole value chain, including customers, were formed into a unified team and the Four + Four principles put in place. Most planes take ten years or more from inception to delivery. The fact that it took four was amazing in itself. What was even more astonishing was that this was a two-engine plane for transatlantic use, when at that time twin-engine planes were not allowed to be used for transatlantic routes. So part of the process was to change the very safety parameters within which the plane was being designed.[24] Seeing boundaries beyond the organogram,

---

23 'Supply chain' suggests a chain of people supplying each other towards the end customer. The term does not capture the value added that each step brings and the fact that it all adds up to the 100 per cent that the customer pays for at the end. On the other hand the term 'value-chain' does not capture the activity that is going on throughout the chain.

24 The Boeing 777 design phase was different from the company's previous commercial jetliners. For the first time, eight major airlines, namely All Nippon Airways, American Airlines, British Airways, Cathay Pacific, Delta Air Lines, Japan Airlines, Qantas and United Airlines, had a role in the development of the airliner. The eight airlines that contributed to the 777 design process became known within Boeing as the 'Working Together' group. At the first group meeting in January 1990, a 23-page questionnaire was distributed to the airlines, asking each what it wanted in the new design. By March 1990, Boeing and the airlines had decided upon a basic design. By October 1990, United Airlines became the Boeing 777's launch customer when it placed an order for 34. By January 1993, Boeing had formally designated its new airliner as the 777, and a team of United 777 developers joined other airline teams and Boeing designers at the Boeing Everett factory in Washington. Divided into 240 design teams of up to 40 members, working on individual components of the aircraft, almost 1,500 design issues were addressed. The Boeing 777 was the first commercial aircraft to be designed entirely on computer. This allowed a virtual 777 to be assembled, in simulation, to check for interferences and to verify proper fit of the many thousands of parts, thus reducing costly rework. Boeing was initially not convinced of the programme's abilities

which is very internally focused, is a good way to understand the nature and foundation of the dynamics within a complex network of relationships.

DEFINED STRATEGY

Strategy can be seen as defining *what* is delivered to *whom* and *how* it is delivered.[25] In many ways once this is clear then self-organisation can operate. Without such clarity the chaos that then ensues will be without underlying order, and the organisation will quickly fail. The question arises how is strategy decided? How can it best be clarified? In an oligarchy, the top propose, the bottom dispose. Yet the assumption which underpins this is fast becoming strained (that is, that the top actually know the solutions – see Chapter 4). This may explain the growth of strategy consulting.[26] Another way that strategy can evolve in a more dynamic way is exemplified by the story Ricardo Semler tells.[27] Here all of the organisation is involved, in a complex and adaptive way, in defining and clarifying strategy. This is an example of emergence and shows how people within a wider boundary can forge new boundaries for themselves. It also lends more to the strategy tradition of Clausewitz than Jomini as explored in Chapter 3.

Whilst describing strategy in three dimensions of *what* is delivered to *whom* and *how*, the mix of these can be complex and gives much play for innovation, as Figure 7.6 suggests. There are a variety of dimensions along which one can move – for example taking new products to old customers in the same way is seen as expansion of current market.

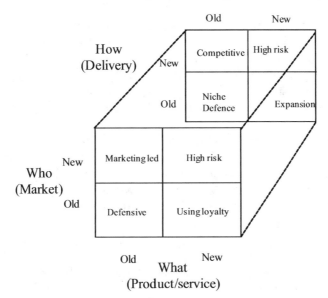

Figure 7.6   The what, who and how of strategy

and built a physical mock-up of the nose section to verify the results. The test was so successful that all further mock-ups were cancelled. The first Boeing 777 was delivered by April 1994, and the first commercial delivery was in January 1995.

25   I owe this simple but powerful way of seeing strategy to my colleague Professor Julian Birkinshaw at the London Business School.

26   Strategy Consulting has grown on average over 20 per cent a year during the 1980s and 1990s. shrinking by 12 per cent in the 2000s.

27   R. Semler, *How We Went Digital Without a Strategy.*

Strategy definition is becoming a wider dynamic involving more people than traditionally being confined to those at the 'top'. Mass intervention techniques such as Real Time Strategic Planning[28] allow a large number of participants to evolve strategy, and examples of this are given in Part III. Other techniques were explained in Chapter 3.

INVISIBLE BOUNDARIES

Larry Hirschhorn and Thomas Gilmore of Wharton stated: *'As organisations become more flexible, the boundaries that matter are in the minds of managers and employees ... The traditional organisational map describes a world that no longer exists.'*[29]

They proposed that the 'new' organisational boundaries which need to be managed are the Authority boundary, the Task boundary, the Political boundary and the Identity boundary. These four are well worth taking into account in any consideration of boundaries. An outline of each is as follows:

- **Authority boundary.** This answers who is in charge of what. The tension that Hirschorn and Gilmore identify is the classic one between oligarchy and polyarchy that has already been identified in the Preface. Again, a fractal pattern emerges. This is, in their words, about *'How to lead but remain open to criticism'* and *'How to follow but still challenge superiors.'* They further state *'In the new organisation subordinates must challenge in order to follow, while superiors must listen in order to lead.'* An example of the need for this was highlighted in a programme entitled 'Velocity' which was run across the top levels for thousands of executives in a Dutch multi-national bank in 2004/2005. This looked at new ways of leading, dealing with the polyarchic realities emerging in the organisation, focusing on coaching behaviours. This three-day leadership development workshop typically included participation from main board members – they were often asked *'What main change in behaviour would you like to see?'* The reply from the main board members was always the same: *'Challenge us more!'*

- **Task boundary.** As technology and market demands advance so too do the specialisms of knowledge needed and the fragmentation of work along knowledge lines. This is not really new as traditional task boundaries along knowledge have always been there. For example, the knowledge of marketing is different to finance. It was generally assumed that leaders had better knowledge than followers – but as Chapters 2 and 4 showed this is no longer necessarily true. So the 'task boundary' is becoming more complex. And as Chapter 3 showed, the traditional boundaries between these tasks/functions are becoming blurred with multi-skilled/functional teams. So there is a need to ensure that all are involved in understanding the overall task in hand, and their role in it, rather than simply the knowledge they bring or function they represent.

- **Political boundary.** Organisational politics is often a dirty phrase. It implies hidden agenda and factions competing internally for their own interests. However, the reality is that there *are* different interests and perspectives, and the multiplicity

---

28   See D. La Piana, *The Nonprofit Strategy Revolution: Real-Time Strategic Planning in a Rapid-Response World* for a practical example how of how RTSP can be used.

29   L. Hirschhorn and T. Gilmore, *The New Boundaries of the 'Boundaryless' Company.*

of these is vital. By asking 'what's in it for us?', solutions which have broader appeal can emerge. Also the vital skills of dialogue, negotiation and listening are enhanced.

- **Identity boundary.** This is linked to the Four + Four principle of Underlying Purpose. Identity gives a sense of belonging and fosters loyalty and motivation. It delineates 'who's in and who's out'. And it can serve as a fractal. In the British Army the backbone of the system is the 'Regimental System' – each regiment has its own unique identity and history. And within each regiment, each squadron/company does the same, as does each troop/platoon. There is a strong sense at all levels of belonging and identity which enables the soldiers to operate effectively in the most difficult and stressful environment.

Hirschhorn and Gilmore stress that these four 'invisible' boundaries are interactive rather than four stand-alone ones. As organisations become more complex these boundaries hold more meaning and power than the traditional organigram of old.

Skill/Will of People

If people do not have the skill or the will to do the job, then it will not be done to the best effect. Although this sounds very simple and common sense, it is far more complex to manage. The skill side of the equation is covered by reams of books on competency theory,[30] as is the will side by those on motivation theory.[31] It is not intended here to repeat or go into the detail of competency or motivation theory. What is necessary is to put a 'polyarchic' view on these areas.

SKILL

This falls into two broad areas – technical (that is, referring to the job in hand, such as finance) and operational (that is, referring to how the job gets done, such as interpersonal skills). As organisational complexity grows, so too is there a natural diffusion of technical skills due to increased cross-functional working and the sort of dynamic we saw in the buttons experiment of Chapter 5 (Figure 5.22). Examples of these skills are shown below in Figure 7.7.

As more followers are expected to take the lead, the importance of the diffusion of the operational skills grow. Multi-skilling needs to go beyond the traditional multi-skilling based on technical competence. Process skills are becoming increasingly important. Knowledge, which helps process go smoother, is becoming more valued. For example the MBTI (Myers Briggs Type Indicator) is now widely used across all levels in many

---

30   For a good overview see H. Azemikhah, *The 21st Century, the Competency Era and Competency Theory.*

31   The first motivation theory which was applied in business was formulated by Abraham Maslow in his paper 'A Theory of Human Motivation', which outlined his theory of hierarchy of needs. Since then a whole range of different theories have emerged, the most notable of which include Kurt Lewin's Force Field Theory, Edwin Locke's Goal Theory, Victor Vroom's Expectancy Theory (also known as the Valence-Instrumentality – Expectancy Theory) and David McCelland's Achievement Theory.

Technical (that is, Content) skills	Operational (that is, Process) skills
• Function skills (HR, IT, finance, marketing, procurement and so on).	• Interpersonal skills (for example, listening, psychological tools like MBTI, Belbin and so on).
• Industry skills (Retail, manufacturing, engineering accounting and so on).	• Role-specific skills (for example, project management, coaching, problem solving, facilitation and so on).

Figure 7.7   Examples of skills needed

organisations.[32] These skills are the oil of self-organisation and they are frequently overlooked in organisations which typically focus on technical skills.

WILL

The biggest barrier to people's motivation in an emerging polyarchy is the tendency for leaders/mangers to demotivate by using inappropriate oligarchic behaviours. This is important – in some cases by attempting to motivate others, the leader ends up demotivating. As will be seen in Chapter 9, using the incorrect leadership style is a frequent occurrence and can be very demotivating. The behaviour of leaders in an emerging polyarchy is vital for motivation. And that is not to say that leaders should motivate. It is to say that they need to think twice before acting and check that what they do is necessary. Chapter 10 gives some ideas about the types of behaviours and strategies which can be used, aligned to the skill and will of the individual. Another aspect to be taken into account when considering 'will', is where the person actually is. There are four zones that people can occupy: Performance, Parking, Stress and Depression, and each zone is a mix of states of being as shown below.[33]

People can flick between these zones very quickly and it is rather like being on a pinball table. Events, what people say, what one is doing – all these can affect the state one is in. And a mixture of challenge and support can be used to move people depending on where they are. Each state consists of two contradictions, and this again illustrates how paradox operates at deeper levels of truth.

- **Performance zone.** This is a curious and paradoxical mix of being relaxed but engaged at the same time – athletes call it being 'in the zone'. It is when a person is fully engaged in what is going on, but relaxed about it at the same time. It is not a place where people can stay for long. People thus typically flick between this zone and the next, the parking zone. In many ways this state is also described

---

32   See footnote 7, Chapter 2. It is estimated that since being developed, over 20 million people have taken the MBTI and currently some 2 million a year do it.

33   I am indebted to Didier Marlier and Chris Parker for this model, which has been adapted slightly, and which itself was based on Michael Apter's Reversal Theory. They have furthered their thinking and this can be found in their joint book *Engaging Leadership – Three Agendas for Sustaining Achievement*.

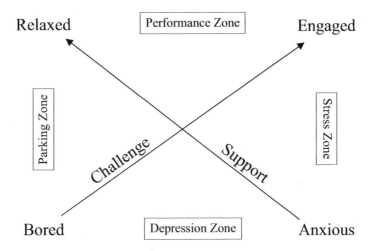

Figure 7.8   Motivational states of being

by Csikszentmihalyi in *Flow*[34] and Gladwell, *Blink*.[35] It should be noted that it is unusual (and unhealthy) for people to be in this zone for long, as they can become burned out. The flip is typically between Performance and Parking.

- **Parking zone.** Relaxed and bored, this is where people switch off and take a break. It is a natural, indeed necessary, place for people to be – but not for long! It can lead to depression if people remain bored but their relaxed state is replaced by anxiety. The best way to get people out of this zone and into the performance zone is to challenge them.
- **Stress zone.** This is where people are engaged but anxious about what is going on around them. Without support they will quickly go into the depression zone as they disengage, but their anxiety remains.
- **Depression zone.** This is where people are disengaged but anxious. It is a hard zone to move people out of, and depending on the individual a mix of challenge and support is needed. Support to get them into the parking zone and challenge to get them into the performance zone is one route. Another route is challenge to stress and then support to relax into the performance zone. Which one is better will depend on the person you are dealing with and the context.

---

34   See M. Csikszentmihalyi, *Flow: The Classic Work on How to Achieve Happiness*. Put simply, it's a state of mind you achieve when you're fully immersed in a task, forgetting about the outside world. When you're in the state of Flow, you:

-    are completely focused on the task at hand;
-    forget about yourself, about others, about the world around you;
-    lose track of time;
-    feel happy and in control; and
-    become creative and productive.

Flow takes the very Zen concept of being completely in the moment, and applies it to work tasks – being in the moment, focusing completely on a single task, and finding a sense of calm and happiness in the work. Flow is exactly that.

35   In *Blink*, Gladwell describes 'thin slicing' where the brain can function on little information but make rapid and accurate decisions.

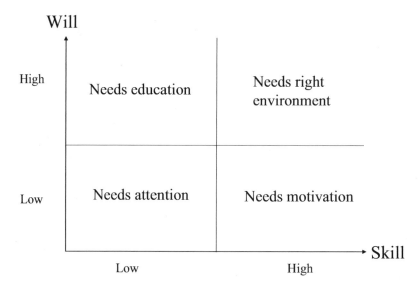

Figure 7.9   Skill/will matrix

The use of the states of being above, together with the leadership strategies explained in Chapter 10, gives a good roadmap of influencing people's will. Taken together the 'Skill/Will' matrix can explain where people can be at differing times.

The various strategies for moving people towards the High/High quadrant are explored in Chapters 9 and 10.

A Few Simple Rules

Relying on people's skill and will alone, without their having some guidance is a dangerous optimism. The few simple rules are the same as the 'few guiding principles' described by complexity scientists. They really cover two areas: Operational rules (that is, Standard Operational Procedures – 'SOPs') and Behavioural norms (that is, Core Values):

OPERATIONAL RULES

We saw briefly in Chapter 6 how Disney changed their approach to theme parks when they learned from the experience in France, and how they discovered that the myriad of rules and procedures began to constrain rather than enable. The evolution of an organisation having a myriad of rules and then jettisoning them for a few simple ones seems to be quite common. An example of one such journey is explained in Ricardo Semler's book *Maverick*.[36] This tightening and loosening seems to be a fractal of the 'freeze–unfreeze' of Richard Pascale.[37] SOPs allow people to get on with the work without any intervention –

---

36   R. Semler, *Maverick – The Success Story behind the World's Most Unusual Workplace.*

37   See R. Pascale, M. Milleman and L. Gioja, *Surfing on the Edge of Chaos – The Laws of Nature and the New Laws of Business.* The authors propose four key principles: 1. Equilibrium is a precursor to death; 2. Innovation increases near the edge of chaos; 3. Living systems self-organise under pressure; and 4. You can disturb a living system but you cannot direct it and unforeseen consequences are inevitable.

they are the glue for self-organisation, and without them the 'edge of chaos' can tip into pure chaos.

BEHAVIOURAL NORMS

The few simple rules that drive behavioural norms are often referred to as 'values' or 'core values'. Together with the underlying purpose, these values form the core ideology. In the *Built to Last* study, the existence of enduring core values is seen as a key feature of sustainable success. These are values which are endemic in the organisation and withstand the test of time. One of the companies in the *Built to Last* study which best exemplifies this is Hewlett Packard. The 'HP Way' represents the guiding values of the company, and helps sustain their performance.[38] Every organisation has implicit values, and some are even made explicit with a measurement process – but their sole existence does not guarantee sustainability. A very well respected, innovative and award winning company in Texas had 'Respect', 'Integrity', 'Communications' and 'Excellence' as their stated values. These values were shown on huge silk flags in their reception area in Houston. They had a measurement system and a well-designed 360 degree feedback process regarding these values right down to the individual level. There was even a process to base bonus compensation on how well the individual followed the values. The company was called Enron, which went bust in a spectacular way. Having values stated but not living them at all levels is a sure way to guarantee, sooner or later, disaster.[39]

These 'few simple rules' need to be fully understood by all involved and also need a feedback mechanism (explored under 'Unambiguous Feedback' below).

Tolerance of Ambiguity and Chaos

We do not like chaos and typically have a low tolerance of ambiguity. It seems that most, if not all, management thinking is aimed at clarifying and helping reduce ambiguity. This book is no different in that it suggests, like chaos theory and complexity science,

---

38   The 'HP Way' is based on the notion that an egalitarian, decentralised system is better and that employees' brainpower was the company's most important resource. For an outline of the history of the company see P. Burrows, *Hewlett & Packard: Architects of the Info Age: The Founding Fathers of Silicon Valley Steered Tech Away From Hierarchy*.

39   Enron grew wealthy due largely to marketing, promoting power and the fraudulently inflated stock price. Enron was named 'America's Most Innovative Company' by *Fortune* Magazine for six consecutive years, from 1996 to 2001. It was on the *Fortune* Magazine's list of '100 Best Companies to Work for in America' in 2000. Enron was hailed by many, including labour and the workforce, as an overall great company, praised for its large long-term pensions, benefits for its workers and extremely effective management until its exposure in corporate fraud. The first analyst to publicly disclose Enron's financial flaws was Daniel Scotto who in August 2001 issued a report entitled 'All Stressed Up and No Place to Go'. The values of Respect, Integrity, Communication and Excellence were emblazoned on large flags in the reception of their 40-storey headquarters in Houston. Their values were explained as follows:

- *Communication: We have an obligation to communicate. Here, we take the time to talk with one another and to listen. We believe that information is meant to move and that information moves people.*
- *Respect: We treat others as we would like to be treated ourselves. We do not tolerate abusive or disrespectful treatment.*
- *Integrity: We work with customers and prospects openly, honestly and sincerely. When we say we will do something, we will do it; when we say we cannot or will not do something, then we won't do it.*
- *Excellence: We are satisfied with nothing less than the very best in everything we do. We will continue to raise the bar for everyone. The great fun here will be for all of us to discover just how good we can really be.*

that there are underlying understandable dynamics at play. So to propose a tolerance of ambiguity and chaos is easier said than done!

There are various ways of looking at the tolerance of ambiguity and chaos: Scientifically, Psychologically, Philosophically and Empirically.

SCIENTIFICALLY

It is the knowledge that chaos theory offers that perhaps makes it easier to accept chaos itself. The areas described in Chapter 5 demonstrate this point. Chaos theory and complexity science are still in their infancy, so one can hope to expect more understanding and wisdom to emerge. It is easier to tolerate that which we understand, rather than that which we do not. And at the same time, we can understand that ambiguity and complexity are both natural and have some underlying laws. This makes it easier to embrace uncertainty.

PSYCHOLOGICALLY

There is a psychological aspect here, as some personalities have a higher tolerance for ambiguity than others. For example in MBTI (mentioned in Chapter 2 and under 'Skill/Will of People' above), those who have more of a 'Perceiving' tendency have a higher tolerance of ambiguity than those who have more of a 'Judging' tendency. Alpha types get stressed by chaos and ambiguity more than Beta types.[40] Understanding one's psychological type helps in terms of dealing personally with ambiguity.

PHILOSOPHICALLY

Taoism, explored in more detail in Appendix A, is one of the oldest philosophies which helps to develop a tolerance of ambiguity and chaos. This has already been highlighted by Figure 1.2 in Chapter 1. An understanding that chaos and order can co-exist as part of a wider dynamic can certainly help increase acceptance for ambiguity. A newer philosophy, one of 'flow', also lends some insight.

EMPIRICALLY

The experiences suggested by Peters, Pascale, Orf, Yorke et al., as well as some of the examples in this book, suggest that chaos and complexity do not mean disaster. Chaos theory and complexity science can be applied to good effect. However, this needs an

---

40   The use of psychological types is not new. Around 400 BC, Hippocrates, the Greek philosopher wrote of the Four Humours when describing human behavior: sanguine (strong willed), choleric (quick tempered), melancholic (gloomy) and phlegmatic (indifferent). The main four pioneers of modern psychology, Sigmund Freud, Carl Jung, Abraham Maslow and Roberto Assagioli, developed techniques into the causes of conflict and dysfunction in a rapidly changing world. Assagioli (inventor of Alpha and Beta typology) is the least known of the four, however he and Jung developed lines of reasoning that provide a basis for Differential Psychology (personality profiling). Jung wrote *Jung's Theory of Personality Types* in 1920, which was published by Princeton University as *Psychological Types* in 1971. Isabel Myers and Katherine Briggs later developed Jung's Typology into a widely used behaviour measuring tool, the Myers-Briggs Type Indicator (MBTI) – see footnote 7, Chapter 3. For more detail on Alpha and Beta see R. Assagioli, *Psychosynthesis*, for a description of Alpha and Beta typology. Psychosynthesis Typology (PST) mapping uses the same type of typology as the Complex Adaptive Leadership model using the two axis of people/relationship and goal/objective/purpose. The four 'types' of relationship Authoritarian, Participative, Facilitative and Permissive co-relate to the four leadership strategies of Tell, Sell, Involve, Devolve – see Chapter 9.

understanding of the underlying dynamics of chaos and complexity, as well as being able to know when to step in and, more importantly, when not to interfere!

So there are a variety of reasons and ways for people to become comfortable with ambiguity. The research done within chaos theory and complexity science gives a good solid foundation upon which to build such comfort. However, that does not mean that it should in its own right become a 'flavour of the month'. As Ian Stewart, Professor of Mathematics at Warwick University and leading chaos mathematician, warns: *'The danger is that chaos and complexity becomes the "Bible" – a new theory of everything … The real importance of chaos is as a new tool for problem solving, and a new way of thinking….'*[41]

Unambiguous Feedback

The paradoxical twin of tolerance for ambiguity and chaos is the need for clear and unambiguous feedback. There has been an explosion in the measurement business. This principle can be considered in two main ways: Operational/financial ('hard') feedback, and Behavioural feedback/'soft' feedback:

OPERATIONAL AND FINANCIAL FEEDBACK

These measures allow people to see how they are contributing to the whole and the extent to which they are achieving objectives. It also gives them a systemic view of how their team/department/unit is doing within the context of the whole organisation. These metrics need to be transparent and available to all. There is always a trade-off between the benefits of such transparency and the fear of allowing competitors to see what you are doing. For example, the most sensitive metric of a retailer is gross margin information. This shows the difference between what a retailer pays for its stock and what it charges. And yet in the UK gross margin information is regularly printed in the internal employee magazine of the John Lewis Partnership, one of the leading retailers in the UK.[42] Stuart Hampson, a past Chairman, said *'The potential loss of competitiveness we might suffer from publishing margin information is more than made up by the effectiveness of our people that we gain by keeping them fully informed.'*[43] It should be noted that John Lewis is a partnership where all employees are partners. Their approach to sharing information is also similar to that of Springfield Remanufacturing Corporation (SRC) in the USA. They practice what their CEO Jack Stack calls 'The Great Game of Business' (more commonly known as Open Book Management). This enables *all* workers to understand the finances and operational metrics

41   Ian Stewart quoted in Sardar and Abrams fun book *Introducing Chaos*. Ian Stewart has written several books, *Nature's Numbers* and *Does God Play Dice?* are recommended.

42   The John Lewis Partnership publishes a weekly in-house magazine, called *The Gazette*. It is the oldest in-house magazine currently still being published in the UK. Each John Lewis branch also has its own weekly magazine, called *The Chronicle*. Every employee is a partner in the John Lewis Partnership, and has a possibility to influence the business through branch forums, which discuss local issues at every store, and the divisional John Lewis and Waitrose Councils. Above all these is the Partnership Council, to which the partners elect at least 80 per cent of the 82 representatives, while the chairman appoints the remaining. The councils have the power to discuss 'any matter whatsoever', and are responsible for the non-commercial aspects of the business – the development of the social activities within the partnership and its charitable actions. The Partnership Council also elects five of the directors on the partnership board (which is responsible for the commercial activities), while the chairman appoints another five. The two remaining board members are the chairman and the deputy chairman. These routes ensure that every non-management partner has an open channel for expressing his/her views.

43   Sir Stuart Hampson, presentation to RSA Tomorrow's *Company Inquiry*, June 1994.

of the company and what part they play. Decisions can be made faster by those who will be ultimately responsible for implementing them.[44] Many fear such transparency as it diffuses power – but it is precisely because of this that such transparency is needed to avoid the tensions between oligarchy and polyarchy becoming critical. It should be noted that the way the John Lewis Partnership approaches this issue is very different to the way SRC does. Each organisation will have its own unique approach. Such is the way.

Another trend which is emerging in the area of financial feedback is the move away from budgeting.[45] Most would agree that the budgeting process is a waste of time and effort and typically involves:

- a yearly attempt to predict the future and a game between those 'leading' and those implementing;
- once finally done and dusted most budgets are shelved until the next round of yearly charades begins;
- the finance department is tasked with looking at variances to budget and reporting these to the top for action to be taken – this is like driving a car using the rear view mirror and steering wheel.

Budgeting has been replaced by some forward thinking organisations such as Maersk and Volvo with a rolling quarterly forecast.[46] This engages the finance department in a better dialogue about the future and what people see coming rather than a blamestorm about the past variances.

BEHAVIOURAL FEEDBACK

Giving and receiving personal feedback can be seen at two levels – organisationally and individually. From an organisational point of view the use of 360 degree feedback processes seem to be growing. The typical approach is that a manager receives aggregated and anonymous feedback from his subordinates and peers as well as the traditional feedback from his boss. Introducing subordinate feedback can be difficult, especially if the organisation has a strong hierarchy. It needs to be supported by training and the purpose of such feedback needs to be explained. The purpose should be to enable individual development. It is a big mistake to link such feedback, initially at least, to compensation. The flow of using 360 degree feedback seems to be one which takes around five years to become embedded in an organisation. This no doubt is due to the firm oligarchic assumptions (where feedback is what the boss gives subordinates and not the other way around).

---

44   In a 1995 BBC Radio 4 programme called 'Killing the Organisation', Jack Stack the CEO of SRC Inc. said that leaders should no longer know, or (more dangerous) think that they know, the answers to the problems facing the organisation. He stated that leaders should create an environment where the answers come up naturally from the bottom. This has a strong resonance with the issue identified in Chapter 4. In 1983 along with 12 other managers, Jack Stack scraped together $100,000 in cash, borrowed $8.9 million and transformed a failing division of International Harvester into one of the most successful and competitive companies in America. The Open-Book Management approach (later coined The Great Game of Business), has helped SRC Holdings Corporation become a thriving company of 1,200 engaged employees in 17 business units across a variety of industries producing $400 million in annual sales, increasing its stock price from 10 cents per share in 1983 to over $234 in 2008. The approach is based on a simple, yet powerful belief: '*When employees think, act and feel like owners ... everybody wins.*' This resonates very strongly with the concepts of polyarchy discussed in previous chapters. Complex Adaptive Leadership perhaps explains *why* this approach can work. For more details on Jack Stack's approach see http://www.greatgame.com/, accessed: 19 April 2010, and his book *The Great Game of Business*.

45   See for example Banham, R. (2012) 'Freed from the budget' September, *CFO Magazine*.

46   Such organisations are part of a new movement called the 'Beyond Budgeting Round Table' or BBRT.

The problem with the 360 degree feedback process at an organisational level is that it is only done yearly (or maybe twice a year). It can turn into rigmarole if it is not backed up by a culture of giving and receiving individual feedback. There is a need for giving and receiving behavioural feedback on a day-to-day basis. This needs training and an agreed process/methodology, many of which may already exist within the organisation. The key skill is to be able to separate behaviour from intention, be able to recognise what behaviour is in a non-judgemental way, and not to take things personally or become personal.[47]

In our research[48] this area is the one that typically scores the lowest. And yet it is vital if an organisation is to become adaptive and be able to meet the challenges of a fast moving context.

Need for 360 degree feedback sold to organisation backed by leadership effectiveness survey
▼
Process of 360 degree feedback designed plus back-up development process
▼
Details of what is included in the 360 degree feedback decided, involving those concerned
▼
Pilot to test the process and followup development courses
▼
Fine tune and roll out using those piloted to champion
▼
First few years link to development Allow to evolve towards compensation

Figure 7.10 Introduction of 360 degree feedback – possible steps

The Dynamic

The Four + Four principles have been shown above as discrete principles. However, their power is in their totality rather than individual parts and the multiplicity of relationships between them, of which there are 56 as shown in Figure 7.11.

A key issue is one of consistency and the reinforcing nature that each lends to each other. It should be stressed that every organisation finds their own way of expressing these principles, which can be seen in a fractal rather than rigorously applied rules. If any one of them is missing, then the tensions between oligarchic assumption and underlying polyarchy realities grow. So too do the risks identified in Chapter 2.

These principles are not only all inter-connected but can be put into sub-groups in a variety of possible ways. Thousands of possibilities exist. For example, Dan Pink in his book *Drive*[49] (explained in a wonderful RSAnimate Video[50]) links, in a fractal way, the 'will' part of the 'Skill/Will' principle to Skill (which he calls mastery), freedom (which he calls autonomy) and purpose. Pink shows, from a variety of independent research studies, that paying large rewards to gain motivation for tasks that require a degree of cognitive skill (rather than purely physical) gets the opposite effect – performance often suffers. Instead, people are motivated by having a mix of three key things:

1. a degree of freedom in how they work and being self-led (shades of polyarchy);

---

47   For a good overview of the differing ways of seeing feedback, see F. Nickols, *Feedback about Feedback*.

48   We have used the questionnaire and scorer with some 980 managers in over 30 organisations and from 40 countries. The average total score is 105.

49   Pink DH (2009) *Drive – The surprising truth about what motivates us*. Riverhead Books.

50   RSAnimate Video 'Drive – The surprising truth about what motivates us' http://www.thersa.org/events/rsaanimate/animate/rsa-animate-drive, accessed: March 2014.

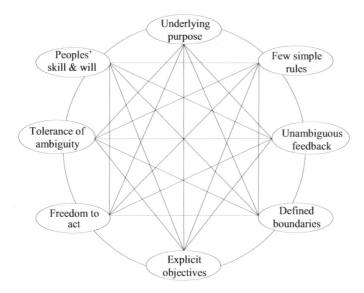

Figure 7.11 Four + Four dynamic

2. the possibility of developing themselves further and being better at what they do; and
3. a sense of higher organisational purpose which inspires.

So the 8 principles can be cut up and seen in isolation, as a whole or indeed in sub-groups. There is a 'yin/yang' element to these eight or 'Four + Four' principles. Having an inspiring purpose, giving people freedom to act whilst relying on their Skill/ Will and having a high tolerance for ambiguity is a very 'Yin' way of leading. Meanwhile, having clear objectives to hold people against, within clear boundaries and rules with feedback mechanisms to show people both how they are doing and what corrective action to take is a very 'Yang' way of leading. *Both* are needed.

An idea of how the possible interdependencies illustrated in Figure 7.12 can work between these principles can be found in Figure 7.13.

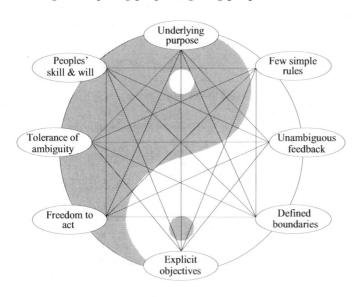

Figure 7.12 Yin/Yang of the Four + Four

	Underlying purpose	Explicit objectives	Few simple rules	Unambiguous feedback	Defined boundaries	People Skill/Will	Ambiguity tolerance	Freedom to act
Underlying purpose	A higher purpose which unites and inspires	Implicit purpose counter balance objectives to produce coherence	Allows purpose to be conserved and last – forms core ideology	Enables people to see if they are living up to purpose	Helps decide what is done and how, and gives strategy inspiration	Helps decide who belongs and who does not	Purpose is like a north star and allows ambiguity to be navigated	Purpose allows freedom to thrive with meaning
Explicit objectives	Explicit objectives counter balance implicit Purpose to become day to day	Objectives fully understood by those fulfilling them	Standard Operating Procedures (SOPs) which help	Operational metrics linked to the activities undertaken	Ensures level of responsibilities and authority are coherent and clear	Technical skill to do the job and learn from others	Flexibility for objectives to be changed and no loss of accountability	Individuals can decide how best to complete their objectives
A few simple rules	Purpose informs the few simple rules with a clear ethos	Objectives allows people to aim, rules gives the principles to use	Few rules of both what and how to guide and enable effective action	Rules and metrics linked to gauge organisational effectiveness	The rules help the action within the boundaries get desired results.	A few rules enable people to express their individuality to better effect	A few simple rules help people deal with ambiguity and uncertainty	A few rules act as counter balance for freedom to be exercised in a more focused way
Unambiguous feedback	General measures allow people to see that the purpose is being fulfilled	Feedback allows people to see, at any one time, how they are doing towards objectives	Feedback can enable metrics to allow the rules to have meaning and not be onerous	Feedback to cover both operational aspects and behaviour, linked to rules/ objectives	Feedback allows people to see how they can best interact with their boundaries	Feedback allows people to improve their skill and gain motivation when doing well	Feedback allows ambiguity to be better tolerated and is the counter-balance	Feedback enables freedom to operate without upsetting or interfering with others

Figure 7.13 Interdependencies of the Four + Four principle

	Underlying purpose	Explicit objectives	Few simple rules	Unambiguous feedback	Defined boundaries	People Skill/ Will	Ambiguity tolerance	Freedom to act
Defined boundaries	Strategy = who, what and how shows medium term fulfilment	Boundaries should support the objectives and clarify responsibility	Boundaries enable the few simple rules to operate with reason	Boundaries enable feedback to be more accurate and meaningful	Boundaries within which self-organisation can occur	Boundaries allow people to express their skills fully if they are wide enough	Uncertainty is contained in a managed way within boundaries	Boundaries allow freedom whilst ensuring less risk
People Skill/ Will	People who relate to the purpose are motivated (will)	Technical skill to achieve, and the will so to do	Will and skill enables and ensures compliance	Will to give and receive, skill to do so without emotion	Will to remain within the boundaries, skill to explore them	Skill to do the job and act in a polyarchic way, and will to do so	Skill to deal with ambiguity, will to embrace uncertainty	Skill to understand consequences, will to enable others freedom
Ambiguity tolerance	Ambiguity allows differing people to relate to purpose in differing ways	Allows discretion within objectives to be met in innovative ways	Enables the rules to be simple and a few rather than detailed and many	Counter-balances feedback to have impact and meaning	Enables boundaries to be recognised but also explored	Enables people to define skills further and use will deeper	Recognise the underlying 'flow' and embrace uncertainty	Enables freedom to move easily without too much constraint
Freedom to act	Each can relate to purpose in their own way for own meaning	Enables definition of how the objectives can be met	Provides a counter-balance for personal initiative	Risks are safeguarded through feedback and measures	Individuals are clear where their freedom extends and how far to go	Mistakes can be made without fear to enable further learning	Freedom gives a confidence which helps uncertainty to be embraced	Individuals encouraged to take initiative and act for greater good

Figure 7.13 Interdependencies of the Four + Four principle *concluded*

Do these principles make a difference to corporate performance? Some initial independent research was undertaken by Oliver Wyman in the USA under the auspices of the Centre for Aviation and Aerospace Leadership at Embry Riddle University. This showed that those companies which demonstrated high CAL principles achieved better revenue and EBITDA growth than those companies that did not – see Figure 7.14.

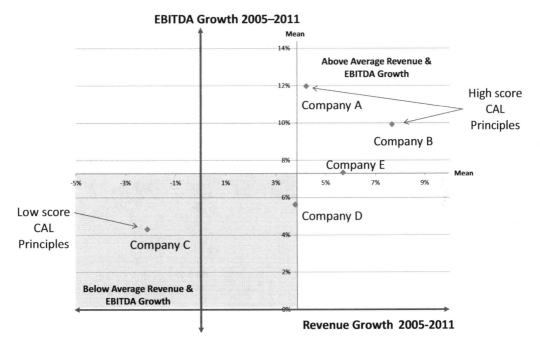

Figure 7.14 Companies with High CAL principles

Source: Bloomberg, Oliver Wyman proprietary analysis, 2009–2011 sponsored by Centre for Aviation and Aerospace Leadership at Embry Riddle Aeronautical University

Such a finding is hardly surprising as the 'Four + Four' principles are in many ways common sense. In today's dynamic markets those organisations which can adapt quickly with a well led and engaged workforce will do better than those that cannot adapt. Adapt or die. A similar research project was also undertaken in Tomsk in Russia looking at project teams working on complex software projects. Again the findings at this more operational level were similar to the more macro research undertaken by Oliver Wyman in the USA. In Russia the company Palex found that those project teams who had high scores regarding the CAL 'Four + Four' principles did far better in terms of process improvement, quality, motivation and knowledge base management than those teams with low scores.

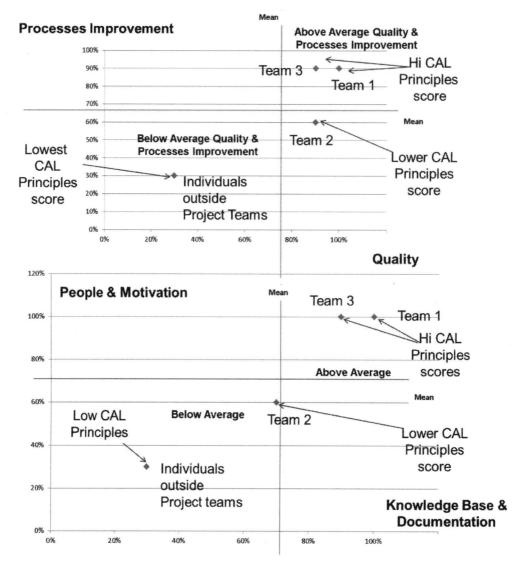

Figure 7.15 Research on project performance and CAL principles

Source: Original research Y. Sirazitdinova, Palex 2014 and ICCPM

Chapter Summary

So let's summarise this chapter, which looked at the Four + Four principles.

1.   Polyarchy can work well when eight principles are in place:

Implicit purpose	vs.	Explicit objectives
Freedom to act	vs.	Boundaries
Ambiguity and uncertainty	vs.	Unambiguous feedback
People's skill and will	vs.	A few simple rules

2. Examples of each principle abound, and there is a strong overlap with principles of success identified by earlier studies such as *Built to Last* and *Good to Great*, as well as by later research such as *Drive*.
3. These principles are inter-related and support each other. It is the dynamic which exists between these principles that is important, and enables each organisation to find its own unique way of applying them.
4. Initial research shows that companies which score highly in the 'Four + Four' principles do better in revenue as well as EBITDA growth compared to those which score poorly, as do project teams at an operational level.

A Quick Breather between Parts II and III

Let's take a quick breather and recap. In Part I we looked at the *context* of dynamic leadership and polyarchy. In Part II we looked at the dynamics of chaos and complexity. Here are the summaries from each chapter of Part II:

From Chapter 5

1. The trend in leadership practice from the traditional deterministic approach (for example, oligarchic) to a more non-deterministic approach (for example, polyarchic) is matched in the trend in science.
2. An understanding of this scientific evolution, as well as how chaos theory and complexity science can work, lays a good foundation for Complex Adaptive Leadership to be practised skilfully.
3. Relativity theory shows how deterministic rules which contradict each other can co-exist – it is not a case of 'Either/Or', but 'Both/And'.
4. Quantum mechanics shows how underlying reality is uncertain and non-deterministic – so reality is a paradoxical and seemingly chaotic dynamic between deterministic and non-deterministic forces.
5. Chaos mathematics shows how chaos has an underlying order and patterns which can be used to good effect. The key concepts include strange attractor (for example, butterfly effect), universality, fractals and bifurcations.
6. Complexity science shows that complexity has an inherent and underlying simplicity. The key concepts include: self-organisation (made up of far from equilibrium state, open feedback and complex connections), inter-relatedness, adaptiveness and emergence.
7. Post-normal science proposes that, when times are complex and decision stakes are high, a wider dialogue with key stakeholders is critical. Leaving decisions to a talented few is dangerous. And traditional charismatic leadership can kill innovation and is not required for a company to be visionary.

From Chapter 6

1. The more complex things are, the less traditional directional leadership one needs if certain principles are in place.
2. These principles form four paradoxical pairs which together allow complexity to work.

From Chapter 7

1. Polyarchy can work well when eight principles are in place:

Implicit purpose	←——→	Explicit objectives
Freedom to act	←——→	Boundaries to confine
Peoples' skill/will	←——→	Few simple rules
Ambiguity tolerance	←——→	Unambiguous feedback

Figure B2.1 Paradoxical principles of Four + Four model

2. Examples of each principle abound, and there is a strong overlap with principles of success identified by earlier studies such as *Built to Last* and *Good to Great*, as well as by later research such as *Drive*.
3. These principles are inter-related and support each other. It is the dynamic which exists between these principles that is important, and enables each organisation to find their own unique way of applying them.
4. Initial research shows that companies which score highly in the 4+4 principles do better in revenue as well as EBITDA growth compared to those which score poorly, as do project teams at an operational level.

So what? The key point is that an understanding of the dynamics of chaos mathematics and complexity science is a foundation upon which leaders can become more effective within their organisation, depending where the evolution towards polyarchy is. These dynamics include both the principles of chaos mathematics and complexity science, as well as the Four + Four principles for easing the tensions which arise between oligarchic assumptions and underlying polyarchic realties.

A key issue is exactly how, on a day-to-day basis, a leader in a hierarchic organisation, with firm oligarchic assumptions, can operate in a more effective way when faced with emergence of polyarchy. Since the publication of the First Edition of this book over 1,000 leaders around the world have been on programmes to teach the CAL approach and the good news is that the detail can be taught and it works. This is covered by Part III, to which we now turn.

PART III

The Leadership Angle

CHAPTER 8 *What is Leadership Anyway?*

A THOUGHT EXPERIMENT TO OPEN UP THE MIND ABOUT LEADERSHIP

There is a traditional view that leadership and management are different things.[1] As a point of departure, this way of looking at leadership can help (although, as will be seen, it is an arguable distinction). So below is the start of a list which makes such a distinction – please think about words which seem to capture the essence of each and add to complete the list as far as you can!

Please note that each word has a counterpart (for example, strategy vs. tactics, long term vs. short term and so on).

See how many pairs you can think of (bonus points if they rhyme!).

'Leadership'	vs.	'Management'
Vision		Budget
Strategy		Tactics
Long term		Short term
Inspiration		Perspiration

An example of such a list showing the distinction between 'leadership' and 'management' is in Figure 8.1 below.

'Leadership'	vs.	'Management'
Vision		Budget
Strategy		Tactics
Long term		Short term
Charisma		Phlegmatic
Inspiration		Perspiration
Empowerment		Control
Coaching		Telling
Big picture		Details
Direction		Execution
Formulation		Implementation

Figure 8.1 Leadership vs. management – take 1

---

1   Many leadership experts differentiate between management and leadership. Examples include: R. Pascale, *'Managers Do Things Right, While Leaders Do the Right Things'* in *Managing on the Edge* (1989); W. Bennis, *'The Manager Asks How and When; the Leader Asks What and Why'* in *On Becoming a Leader* (1989).

This is a traditional view and seems to see leadership as something different, harder and 'higher' than management. It is hierarchic in its outlook (leaders are higher than managers) and owes much to oligarchic assumption (it assumes there are fewer people around who can 'do' the leadership list above!).

When one asks a group of middle managers, 'what does good leadership look like?' a typical list emerges. Leadership is typically attributed to what leaders do. Leadership is something done by a few leaders to many followers. And the examples of 'good leadership' based on this assumption, typically returns a list as follows[2]:

1. enables a high degree of trust and followership;
2. has a charismatic vision for what needs to be done;
3. understand the issues and forms winning strategies;
4. has the power to get things done and exercises it;
5. has charisma and is seen as a hero, someone to follow in a crisis.

This is the leadership we *like*. But is it the leadership we *need* in such complex times?

Recent research has called into question some of the typical views above, some of which have been mentioned in other parts of this book. Let's summarise some of it here in light of the above list:

1. As far as evoking trust and followership are concerned: *'Subordinates need to challenge in order to follow, and superiors must listen in order to lead.' The Boundary-less Organisation*, Hirschhorn et al. (1992).
2. As far as charismatic vision are concerned: *'A charismatic visionary leader is absolutely not required for a visionary company, and in fact can be detrimental...' Built to Last*, Collins and Porras (1997).
3. As far as understanding and forming strategies is concerned: *'Leading from Good to Great does not mean coming up with the answers ... It means having the humility to grasp the fact that you do not yet understand ... and then to ask the right questions...' Good to Great*, Collins (2001).
4. As far as power is concerned: *'The more power you give a single individual in the face of complexity and uncertainty, the more likely it is that bad decisions will be made.' Wisdom of Crowds*, Surowiecki (2004).
5. As far as charisma and heroic leadership is concerned: *'Complexity science shows how the typical focus on 'heroic' and charismatic leaders can result in a lack of innovation in modern organisations.' Complexity and the Nexus of Leadership*, Goldstein et al. (2010).

This does not mean that the list of 'good leadership' is wrong. In certain circumstances it is needed. But is there more to leadership? Do we need to extend our horizons? And is the leadership we all *like* really the leadership we *need*? The problem with the typical distinction between 'leadership' and 'management' is that it can become very stereotypical. It also begs the question whether each on its own is sustainable. For example imagine a leader who had lots of vision and charisma but had no idea about details, implementation and day-to-day 'getting things done'. Sooner or later that leader is going

---

2   This list is a summary of some 20 lists drawn up from workshops with over 600 middle to senior managers in 20 different countries around the world during CAL workshops in the period 2011–2013.

to become unstuck. On the other hand imagine a manager who was great at control and details, but could not see the big picture and had no idea about how to empower others. Again, sooner or later that manager is going to have some problems.

One way around such a possible pitfall is to rely on team work, and thus have the visionary charismatic type surrounded by those who know how to get things done. Whilst such an approach is fine for an oligarchy, and indeed is very common, it begins to crack and strain within a polyarchy. And besides, it is a bit of a cop out – it assumes that a leader cannot do the detail, and that a manager cannot do the vision thing. However, another view is to say that both lists are vital for leadership. So we could promote 'Leadership' to cover both lists, and say that leadership is the successful delivery, and balance, of each. There is a Yin/Yang element to each side.

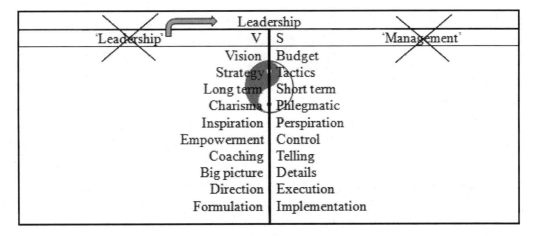

Figure 8.2   Leadership vs. management – take 2

However, the two lists and distinctions still remain. One needs to define what they stand for, as together they give a holistic view of leadership (or at least what it is supposed to deliver). Whereas before one stood for 'leadership' and the other stood for 'management', now that 'leadership' has been promoted to be over both, what are these two sub-categories? One way to answer this is to consider what each list is actually for. What is the underlying need? Why do we need vision and charisma? Who or what needs empowerment? Why do we need short term control? What's it for? There are no doubt a variety of different answers to such questions – but they often boil down to two basic needs. These are the needs of the people involved and the needs of the goal that needs to be achieved.

People need long term direction. They like to feel there is a direction and that what they are doing fits into something meaningful and bigger. They like to feel empowered and they like charisma. At the same time the needs of the goal achievement demand implementation and details. So if we took 'People' and 'Goal' those two headings could form the sub-categories of our lists as shown in Figure 8.3.

Leadership		
'People need'	**vs.**	**'Goal needs'**
Vision		Budget
Strategy		Tactics
Long term		Short term
Charisma		Phlegmatic
Inspiration		Perspiration
Empowerment		Control
Coaching		Telling
Big picture		Details
Direction		Execution
Formulation		Implementation

Figure 8.3   Leadership vs. management – take 3

This approach is similar to the conclusions of the research done by Paul Hersey and Ken Blanchard from Ohio State University in the 1960s. They studied leaders' behaviour and identified two main types of behaviour:

- structuring behaviour which relates more to the need of the *task* in hand; and
- developing behaviour which relates more to the needs of the *relationship* with the people.

The type of leadership behaviour demonstrated depended on the situation (whether tense or not), and also the level of 'readiness' (ability to do the work independently) of the follower.

Their conclusion gave rise to their Situational Leadership model, as illustrated in Figure 8.4. In outline there are four styles of leadership which, according to Hersey and Blanchard, need to be exercised depending on the situation:

- Style 1 (S1) Telling (high structuring, low developing). This is when people need a lot of guidance and/or there is a crisis which needs quick action. The reason followers may need guidance is that they simply do not know what needs to be done or are unwilling, or both. According to the model this would indicate a low level of 'readiness'. Another situation when the S1 style is apposite is an emergency, when there is no time for explanations and action is needed quickly. The S1 'Telling' style is typified by the 'Heroic/Strong'[3] leader approach – taking firm control, telling people what to do and ensuring they do it. It is reminiscent of Frederick Winslow Taylor's approach.[4]

---

3   For a good example of the type of leadership here, see C. Lowney, *Heroic Leadership – Best Practices from a 450-Year-Old Company that Changed the World*. In *Heroic Leadership*, Jesuit-seminarian-turned-investment-banker Chris Lowney examines organisational principles of effective leadership derived from the history and teachings of the Jesuits and applies them to modern corporate culture. Based on the four core values of self-awareness, ingenuity, love and heroism, this book identifies practices that sixteenth-century priests developed to foster dynamic, effective leaders.

4   It should be reiterated that Taylor for his day was probably correct in his assertion that workers should simply do what they are told. The effects of the bifurcation highlighted in Chapter 2 had yet to take full effect, and thus workers in those days expected to be told what to do by leaders they saw as more knowledgeable, educated and capable. And generally speaking, leaders in those days *were* more knowledgeable, educated and capable! The fact that Taylor's approach today is often seen as anathema is perhaps another indication that there is an evolution from oligarchy into polyarchy.

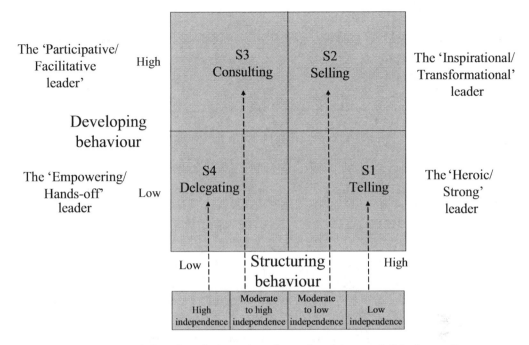

Figure 8.4   Hersey/Blanchard Situational Leadership model (adapted)

- Style 2 (S2), Selling (high structuring, high developing). This style is used when both the task side of the equation (needing structuring behaviour) and the relationship side (needing developing behaviour) requires attention. It assumes there is more time to deal with the issue, and that the leader needs 'buy in' to what he thinks need to be done (hence the term 'Selling'). This style is exemplified by the 'Inspirational/ Transformational'[5] leadership type.
- Style 3 (S3), Consulting (low structuring, high developing). This style assumes that followers have an input and thus are in a higher degree of readiness. The leader would 'consult' with followers and then make a decision what to do. Note that the leader is still 'in the lead'. This style is exemplified by the 'Participative/Facilitative'[6] leadership type.

---

5   J.M. Burns (in his book *Leadership*) first introduced the concepts of transformational leadership in his descriptive research on political leaders, but this term is now used in organisational psychology as well. According to Burns, transformational leadership is a process in which 'leaders and followers make each other advance to a higher level of moral and motivation'. Burns related to the difficulty in differentiation between management and leadership and claimed that the differences are in characteristics and behaviours. According to Burns, the transformational style creates significant change in the life of people and organisations. It redesigns perceptions and values, changes expectations and aspirations of employees. Unlike the transactional style, it is not based on a 'give and take' relationship, but on the leader's personality, traits and ability to make a change through vision and goals. See also his later book *Transforming Leaders* as well as B.M. Bass and B.J. Avolio (eds), *Improving Organizational Effectiveness Through Transformational Leadership*.

6   The most comprehensive exposition of participative leadership theory was proposed by Victor Vroom and various colleagues. The original work was done while Vroom was on the faculty at Carnegie-Mellon University (V. Vroom and P. Yetton, *Leadership and Decision-Making*); it was then expanded upon after Vroom moved to Yale University – see V.H. Vroom and A.G. Jago, *The New Leadership: Managing Participation in Organizations*. Over much the same time period, starting in the late 1960s, another theoretical framework emerged with a similar orientation. This is Frank Heller's influence-power continuum theory, which began while Heller was on a visiting appointment at the University of California at Berkeley and continued after he moved to the Tavistock Institute in Great Britain. In 1998 Frank Heller, with three of his closest

- Style 4 (S4), Delegating (low developing, low structuring). This assumes followers are fully capable to do the task and that they can just get on with it. Here the leader simply delegates and takes no further interest or action. This style is typified by the 'Empowering/Hands-off'[7] leadership type.

One could argue that some of the terms used in the model have changed their meaning since the 1960s, and that some of the formulaic approach suggested by the model is questionable, but as a basic model it is still used widely today.[8] It also serves as a foundation upon which the Complex Adaptive Leadership model is based, which is explored in more detail in Chapter 10.

Another leadership model which can be overlaid onto the Situational Leadership model is the one by Daniel Goleman. This builds on his 'Emotional Intelligence' work and is based on research done by Hay Consulting. This identified six styles of leadership (the original order of these styles differed to the order shown below):[9]

- **Coercive.** This is where the leader tells, and if necessary coerces people into doing what is needed. The research by Goleman suggests that this has an overall negative effect.
- **Authoritative.** This is leadership by example. It assumes the leader knows what to be done and communicates this by showing the example. It can be seen as the 'soft tell', and is aligned to the 'Transformational Leadership' style.
- **Pace Setting.** This is leadership by inspiring, driving, get-up-and-go. The data suggests this is the favourite style of executives, but can lead to stress, burn out and poor follower morale.

---

long-term colleagues and friends, G. Strauss, E. Pusic and B. Wilpert, published *Organizational Participation: Myth and Reality*. This was a rigorous summing up of their decades of research.

7   As footnote 13 to Chapter 7 shows, empowerment is not new. However, there has been much research linking this to the concept of self-leadership – see, for example, C.M. Manz and H.P. Sims, *The New Super Leadership – Leading Others to Lead Themselves*. Self-leadership has often been presented as a primary mechanism for facilitating empowerment and is defined as a systematic set of strategies through which individuals influence themselves towards higher levels of performance and effectiveness without needing leadership by a leader over them. In recent years self-leadership concepts have gained considerable popularity, as evidenced by the large number of practitioner-oriented books and articles on the subject. For a good overview of this literature see S. Yoho, 'Toward a Contingency Model of Leadership and Psychological Empowerment: When Should Self-leadership Be Encouraged?' *Journal of Leadership & Organizational Studies*.

8   There are some key differences between the Situational Leadership (SL) model, and the Complex Adaptive Leadership (CAL) roadmap as described in Chapter 9. In outline the key differences are:

- The (SL) model talks about styles – this assumes personality preferences which are fine as far as it goes. The CAL model focuses on strategy and choice of behaviour (and possible actions) which can be undertaken, regardless of style preference or personality. Changing 'style' or 'personality' is difficult – being mindful and choosing behaviour is easier.
- The application of the S1 'Telling' style to those followers who are of low readiness (low skill and low will) may have worked in the 1960s, and seems to resonate more with Taylorism (see footnote 15 to Chapter 3). It assumes that 'Telling' will improve the skill, and thus the will can improve once the skill is applied. An approach today would not get good results. The CAL model assumes 'Sell' is the best strategy for this situation.
- There is a skew towards S2 and S3 in the more detailed scoring compared to the CAL approach.
- There is more to the needs of people than 'relationship'. For example coaching is critical and the expectation for people to develop themselves is more important now than the mid-twentieth century.
- There is more to the needs of getting things done than just 'task'. This is only part of the goal and seems more centred on 'content' rather than 'process'.

9   For an overview of this method see D. Goleman, 'Leadership That Gets Results', *Harvard Business Review*.

- **Coaching.** Whilst the first three styles are 'push' (by telling, setting an example, or inspiring) this style tends more towards a 'pull' approach. It assumes the follower can do what is needed and coaching is employed to encourage.
- **Democratic.** This style is a participative and involving style, and is very much a 'pull' style.
- **Affiliative.** This assumes that the people are fully capable from a skill point of view and do not need input from the leader, but benefit from moral support and recognition.

The six styles can be placed onto the Situational Leadership model as shown in Figure 8.5. The point here is that there seems to be an underlying flow in both models towards the S4 style (although interestingly Goleman's approach does not get there). The S4 style is the 'point attractor' of Complex Adaptive Leadership and this will be explored more in Chapter 10. At this stage it is enough to see that differing choices exist, and they do give an indication of how leadership can be seen as behaviour or styles and that it is important to be able to exercise them all in an adaptive way to suit the circumstances.

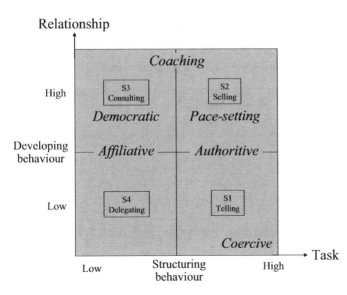

Figure 8.5   Situational Leadership (adapted) with Goleman's approach

How does this relate to Complex Adaptive Leadership? The use of the Situational Leadership model uncovers a typical trend. The model includes a self-assessment questionnaire, which has the 'ideal' score where each style receives 25 per cent of the answers. So the 'ideal' leader would be able to recognise the situation and which style is needed. However there is a trend of scores which a typical group of executives would show. This average score is shown in Figure 8.6.[10] As can be seen the lowest number is the S4 response, and the highest is the S2 response.

Our own more recent research seems to mirror those of the Situational Leadership research. We looked at the results from a broad range of executives around the world and found some interesting trends:

1. Firstly, there was a marked move from 'Selling' transformational choices seen in the earlier Situational Leadership research, towards the 'Involve' strategy. This may be due to the difference in the questionnaires or, more likely, the fact that the tendency to see 'transformational', 'inspirational', 'heroic' leadership (more attuned to the S3

---

10   This is drawn from the scores of some 1,000 executives as part of the research group described in footnote 1 to Chapter 2.

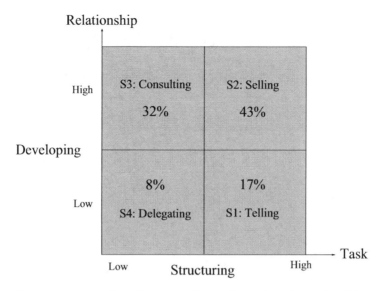

Figure 8.6   Average score distribution of the Situational Leadership model (adapted)

behaviour) as less relevant today than in the 1980s and 1990s and a trend towards more involving leadership (as things become more complex).

2. Secondly, similar to the earlier research, the S4 'Devolve' strategy was the least used – 30 per cent did not use it at all, and 70 per cent did not use it enough.

The findings of this research are below (Figure 8.7) (n = 1439). Again the ideal score is 25 per cent for each strategy.

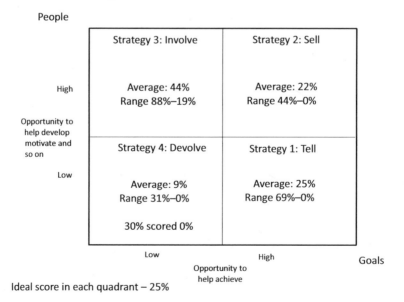

Figure 8.7   CAL Leadership Strategies

These trends, in the light of a consideration of polyarchy, generate a lot of debate. It is generally agreed that the S1 and S2 styles (of 'telling' and 'selling' – that is, 'PUSH' leadership) owe more to an oligarchic assumption of traditional leadership, and the S3 and S4 styles owe more to a polyarchic assumption (that is, 'PULL' leadership). It is also generally agreed that when the principles detailed in the previous chapter are in place, the S4 style is appropriate. Three main challenges are typically highlighted by executives when discussing their scores in the light of the lessons of Complex Adaptive Leadership:

1. **Executives need to let go more.** The low S4 score indicates that executives typically have a fear of letting go. Given that S4 is one of the 'point attractors' for Complex Adaptive Leadership, the low score seems to indicate leaders are tied to the oligarchic assumptions of the past rather than being comfortable with the underlying polyarchic realities which surround them. The issue of fear of letting go was covered in Chapter 7, under 'Discretion and Freedom to Act'.

2. **Executives are demonstrating the 'Red Queen effect',** running hard but getting nowhere fast. The hardest thing to do in the Situational Leadership model in terms of effort is S2 as it needs both high structuring and developing behaviours at the same time. Yet this is the typically highest score. Executives are working too hard, and possibly demotivate followers. This was highlighted in Chapter 2.

3. **A lot of executives are spending their time on unimportant things.** The S1 and S2 scores added together are higher than S3 and S4 score. This would suggest that most of the time executives think they know the solutions (to either sell or tell them). Yet this is out of sync with the numbers in Chapter 4, Figure 4.5 (which suggests that executives know solutions only 10 per cent of the time). This may explain why much of executive time is spent on unimportant activities (which may seem important but are not – see Figure 8.7 below). In addition to this, many executives seem to have a fear of separation and are too concerned about what people think of them – the S2 and S3 scores added together are far higher than the S1 and S4 scores (which involve an element of risk of separation). It seems that they are playing the charade pointed out in Chapter 4.

Research was undertaken by the author with some of the groups described in Chapter 2 using the Eisenhower Matrix.[11] (Urgent/Not Urgent vs. Important/Not Important), sometimes called the Covey Model. The research showed that on average typical leaders/ top executives of large multi-national organisations spend around 60 per cent of their time on unimportant issues, mainly due to delusion (either self-delusion or unintentionally by others). Similar research by the European Foundation for Quality Management (EFQM) found the same. The conclusion of the author is that this is largely due to leaders existing within an oligarchic assumption whilst the underlying realities are polyarchic, and the inability of leaders to let go. Put another way, using the insights from the Cynefin Model looked at in Chapter 5 – leaders are trying to solve problems from 'The Complex' using techniques from 'The Complicated' and/or 'The Simple'.

---

11   The Eisenhower Matrix (as it is still known in Germany today) was used by Eisenhower in prioritising action for the reconstruction of Germany. It has been asserted that he learned this idea from his mentor, Fox Connor. The matrix was popularised by S.R. Covey in his book, *The 7 Habits of Highly Effective People*.

	Urgent	Not urgent
Important	25% 'Crisis'	15% 'Quality'
Not Important	55% 'Delusion'	5% 'Waste'

Figure 8.8   Eisenhower matrix (adapted) – typical time profile for executives

The trade-off between these numbers is interesting. High performance executives typically score 15 per cent delusion and 55 per cent quality. Paradoxical as it may sound, the key to letting go is holding back and being able to say 'no' to those activities which press in but are essentially unimportant. This frees up time for more important things which may not look so pressing.

So the key challenges are a fear of letting go, working too hard and playing the leadership charade. These overlap and produce unnecessary leadership stress.

The approach of Complex Adaptive Leadership, and the typical scores from the Situational Leadership model when considered in the light of polyarchy, engenders much debate. What is interesting is that in over 200 groups of executives who have discussed

Figure 8.9   The stress of leadership

these issues, very few disagree with the three issues which emerge and are highlighted above. It seems that executives intuitively recognise the issues of not letting go, working too hard and playing a bit of a charade. The debate which typically ensues is how to address them. The following are typical conclusions:

1. The emergence of polyarchy should be seen as a positive force as it gives leaders less pressure to be worried continually that they should know everything.
2. Leaders need to *listen* well, to be able to spot the solutions and to support those who propose them. In so doing, they need to recognise that their job is no longer to know the solutions and pass them on, but to enable them to flow in a natural way.
3. The ability to follow, and know when to do so, is as important as the ability to lead.
4. To let go, leaders need to hold themselves back – knowing when *not* to act is thus as important as knowing *when* to act.

Whilst the Situational Leadership model is fairly neutral in its judgement of each style, Goleman's is more judgemental. His research indicates that the 'best' styles are coaching and authoritative and 'worst' styles are coercion and pace setting. The Complex Adaptive Leadership model tends to take both a judgemental and non-judgemental approach. It is judgemental in that it advocates that the 'point attractor' of leadership should be the S4 style. It is non-judgemental in that it recognises that a leader needs to be able to enact all styles given the demands of the context, in order to be able to practice the dynamics of Complex Adaptive Leadership (explored more in Chapter 10).

Chapter Summary

The chapter started with an exercise where 'leadership' was considered as something different from 'management'.

1. The distinction between 'leadership' and 'management' owes more to oligarchic assumption than to current polyarchic realities. But the distinction can serve a useful purpose, as each without the other is unsustainable. So one could say that 'leadership' and 'management' are on the same continuum, and it is all about leadership.
2. However, whilst we could roll 'management' into being part of 'leadership' the distinctions that each category previously assumed still exist. They can be re-categorised to action/focus needed for the people, and action/focus needed for the goal. Under this assumption, leadership is about developing people and ensuring goals are achieved.
3. This conclusion is similar to the Situational Leadership model, which sees leadership behaviour consisting of structuring and developing action aimed at task and relationship. A study of the results of the Situational Leadership questionnaire shows that leaders today are less than effective. Too much emphasis seems to be on 'Selling', and not enough on 'Delegating'.

The flipside of leadership is followership. It is to this we now turn, before, in Chapter 10, putting the two sides together in a new and powerful way.

9 *What About the Followers?*

A QUICK TEST TO OPEN UP THE MIND/SEE WHERE FOLLOWERSHIP IS IN YOUR ORGANISATION

Look at your organisation. Consider the questions below and select one category (for example, 'Neutral') and then one number within that category (for example, 5 or 6).

1. People get on with their work without having to be told what to do.

Strongly Disagree	Disagree	Neutral	Agree	Strongly Agree
1 or 2	3 or 4	5 or 6	7 or 8	9 or 10

2. People are expected to take the initiative when faced with uncertainty.

Strongly Disagree	Disagree	Neutral	Agree	Strongly Agree
1 or 2	3 or 4	5 or 6	7 or 8	9 or 10

3. There is a high performance culture in the organisation.

Strongly Disagree	Disagree	Neutral	Agree	Strongly Agree
1 or 2	3 or 4	5 or 6	7 or 8	9 or 10

4. Subordinates give upward feedback to their bosses.

Strongly Disagree	Disagree	Neutral	Agree	Strongly Agree
1 or 2	3 or 4	5 or 6	7 or 8	9 or 10

5. If a job is finished, people move onto what is needed next without being asked.

Strongly Disagree	Disagree	Neutral	Agree	Strongly Agree
1 or 2	3 or 4	5 or 6	7 or 8	9 or 10

6. Once a barrier to performance is identified it is quickly removed with minimum fuss.

Strongly Disagree	Disagree	Neutral	Agree	Strongly Agree
1 or 2	3 or 4	5 or 6	7 or 8	9 or 10

7.   People have a high degree of autonomy in how they do their job.

Strongly Disagree	Disagree	Neutral	Agree	Strongly Agree
1 or 2	3 or 4	5 or 6	7 or 8	9 or 10

8.   Results are more important than attendance – working hours are flexible.

Strongly Disagree	Disagree	Neutral	Agree	Strongly Agree
1 or 2	3 or 4	5 or 6	7 or 8	9 or 10

9.   When mistakes are made lessons are quickly learnt and blame not attached.

Strongly Disagree	Disagree	Neutral	Agree	Strongly Agree
1 or 2	3 or 4	5 or 6	7 or 8	9 or 10

10.   If someone is underperforming it is likely that peers will point it out and take action.

Strongly Disagree	Disagree	Neutral	Agree	Strongly Agree
1 or 2	3 or 4	5 or 6	7 or 8	9 or 10

11.   People have input into the strategy, understand it and their role in it.

Strongly Disagree	Disagree	Neutral	Agree	Strongly Agree
1 or 2	3 or 4	5 or 6	7 or 8	9 or 10

12.   360 degree feedback is an important part of the culture in the organisation.

Strongly Disagree	Disagree	Neutral	Agree	Strongly Agree
1 or 2	3 or 4	5 or 6	7 or 8	9 or 10

Add up the scores. The following should be a guide:

More than 100 = Excellent score – There is a high level of active followership prepared to take the lead. If polyarchy is not apparent then individual leaders may need some development work – Chapter 7 should help, whilst this chapter should reinforce what is already there.

80–100 = Good – some individual areas may need attention and this chapter may give some ideas.

60–80 = Danger zone – assuming many of the Four + Four principles are in place then followers and leaders need guidance;

40–60 = Severe danger – urgent action needs to be taken if individual and organisational effectiveness are to be safeguarded;

Less than 40 – Still existing?

So far we have looked mainly at the leadership side of the equation. The flipside of leadership is followership. This chapter looks at some aspects of followership. It builds on the idea of Hersey/Blanchard that followers are in a state of 'readiness' or have a level of independence which, depending on what that level is, will dictate to some degree what the leader should do. This could be described as followership 'maturity' – the extent to which they are capable of taking the lead themselves and getting on with what needs to be done with minimum input needed from an ascribed leader. There are various ways of looking at this, a couple of which are:

- Skill/will. This builds on the points made in Chapter 7, under 'Skill/will of People'. It assumes that a follower will be at any point in time in four possible states: high skill/high will; high skill/low will; low skill/high will or low skill/low will.
- Level 5 followership. This looks at how followers relate to the issue of leadership and to what extent they are ready to take the lead themselves.

Skill/will can be considered in a simple two by two matrix as shown in Figure 9.1 below.[1]

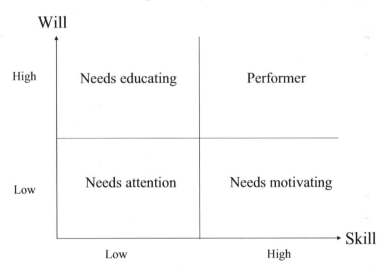

Figure 9.1   Skill/will matrix

- Will is about the willingness to do the job. This will depend on the self-motivation of the individual and the extent to which motivation is supported. Elements such as the underlying purpose of the work, as well as the extent of feedback, all play a part.

  The way a leader exercises his leadership also plays a key role, as there is nothing more demotivating than a leader exercising the wrong style. This is considered more in the next chapter.

---

1   A number of people have been involved in developing the Skill/will matrix. It has been used by Max Landsberg in his book, *The Tao of Coaching*. In his book he applies the older 1960s approach of the Situational Leadership model of low skill/low will needing the directive style, which would not work today (and which this book updates). Since then it has been widely adopted and is a useful method of ensuring that a coach's style of interaction is matched to a coachee's readiness for a particular task.

- Skill is about the capability and knowledge to get the job done. This is not just the technical skills needed to do the actual work ('content' skills) but also the skills to follow the way the job is done ('process' skills). All need knowledge. So whilst a newly joined team member may have the technical skills to do the work, s/he may not yet have the in-house knowledge to get the job done (for example, on a mundane level, knowing where the photocopier is).

The matrix suggests four states. It should be noted that this does not mean that these are 'types' of people. It implies that the situation can change where in one moment a person is highly motivated and capable, and in the next due to a change of situation one or other of Skill/Will can decrease. There is a point attractor element of the matrix where the aim is for the individual to be in the top right hand of the quadrant. This is explored more in Chapter 10. Meanwhile each of the four states is considered briefly below:

- High Skill/High Will. On its own this does not mean much. For example, there is not much chance of getting results with a highly skilled and motivated person when the objectives are unclear, the purpose is dubious and the boundaries are non-existent. In other words the other elements of the Four + Four principles need to be in place. If they are not, willpower soon suffers! But assuming that they are in place then, when a person has a high level of skill and will to get on with the work, leadership can be devolved.
- High Will/Low Skill. This would be typical, for example, of a newly joined team member who has not yet the full skills to do the job. There is a willingness to do the job but the knowledge and/or capability are not there yet. Training/education is the typical strategy needed here.
- High Skill/Low Will. This is where the individual has the skills and knowledge but the motivation to perform is lacking. The loss of motivation could be due to a variety of factors, and such a state could be hard to change (due to, for example, depression) or easy (due to a temporary mood swing).
- Low Skill/Low Will. This is where the individual does not know how to do the work, and even if such knowledge was there, does not want to. People do not like to be in this state for long, as no one wants to be a persistent underperformer. It is not in human nature so to be. However, situations can occur where people find themselves temporarily in this place.

Another way to look at followership is the extent to which followers are prepared to take the lead. Such a situation is vital for polyarchy to thrive. In this respect the work done by Oncken and Wass can be of help.[2] They identified five states or levels where a follower can be, as shown in Figure 9.2.

Again it should be noted that this does not assume 'types' of people but states that individuals can be in (although some people may have a preference for certain states). There is obviously a link to skill/will, as it can be assumed that an individual would find it hard

---

2   W. Oncken Jnr and D.L. Wass, in 'Management Time: Who's Got the Monkey?' describe these five levels as levels of initiative. They also use a good metaphor of ownership of problems as 'monkeys'. The original article appeared in 1974, and the 1999 article has a commentary from Stephen Covey which resonates with the research findings described in Chapter 8 about how executives typically spend their time.

Level 5 Followership	
1	Wait to be told
2	Ask to be told
3	Seek approval for a recommendation
4	Seek approval for action undertaken
5	Get on and inform in a routine way

Figure 9.2 'Level 5' followership

to be at level 5 if the skill and will to be there was absent. Let's look at each of the five levels in a bit more detail:

- **Level 1: Wait to be told.** This is the lowest level and an unacceptable state of affairs. It assumes the individual will just sit and wait to be told what to do. This puts a large and unsustainable strain on leadership.
- **Level 2: Ask to be told.** At this level, the individual would come to the leader and ask to be told what to do next. Whilst a little bit more pro-active than level 1, it is still at a low state and assumes a low level of skill and will.

The first two levels should be unacceptable – the lowest acceptable level should be level 3.

- **Level 3: Seek approval for a recommendation.** This is where the individual is unsure what to do, has an idea, but comes and seeks approval before acting. It may display a lack of confidence or just an honest appreciation that the situation is slightly more difficult than one which the individual is used to.
- **Level 4: Seek approval for action undertaken.** In this situation the individual has taken action but is unsure if it is right, so seeks confirmation from the leader. It may be a lack of confidence, or seeking to communicate action.
- **Level 5: Get on and inform in a routine way.** This is the best that should be aimed for. The key point here is 'routine' – there must be a routine for reporting to ensure accountability. Such a routine could include a weekly update meeting, a routine report, routine measurement etc.

Beware of the 'Monty Python' trap from *The Life of Brian* where Brian tries to get all his followers, who are at level 2 asking to be told, to level 5. He does that by telling them to go straight to level 5 to amusing, and hopelessly ineffective, effect! When he implores them that they need to think for themselves and they are all individuals, they all shout in unison 'We are all individuals' and 'Tell us more!'.

Leadership and Followership Behaviour

To consider 'Skill/Will' and 'Level 5 followership' in isolation to leadership behaviour would be a serious omission as the one will, to some extent drive the other, and vice versa.

Level 5 followership, and to a lesser degree Skill/Will, depends almost entirely on leadership behaviour. We are programmed to see leadership in a hierarchic way and,

```
Leaders get the followers they deserve

Followers get the leaders they deserve
```

Figure 9.3   Behaviour breeds behaviour

as transactional analysis[3] suggests, the way a leader acts will programme the way that followers operate. And vice versa. A couple of anecdotes help to demonstrate the point.

The first story concerns the head of an investment bank. He suffered from cancer and had to be away for long periods of time. After a particularly long absence, he came back to work and found a crowd of people outside his office. They had heard that he was coming back in that day. He asked what they were doing and they said that there were many things that needed to be discussed with him. He said initially '*OK, see my secretary, sort out a time to come and ...*' He then stopped and asked '*What would you have done if I had not been coming back in today?*' They replied that they would just have got on with things – so he said '*Just get on with it then!*'. The two people remaining were the two he really needed to see. It then hit him that he had spent his whole time programming his followers to be level 3 or 4 – always coming to inform him and check if what they were doing was OK. He had told them his door was always open and he expected them to check with him and keep him fully informed. He had told them he was always ready, in fact eager, to help them. And at the same time he had always struggled with the fact that he often felt that his team did not take the initiative and sometimes lacked drive.

Another example is an anecdote about a CEO I sat next to on a long haul flight. He ran a large subsidiary which belonged to a major multi-national group of companies. He had explained to me that he was a bit stressed as he had been out of touch for a week due to a problem with the internet connection, and had not been able to pick up emails. Just before boarding his flight he had managed to connect to the internet and downloaded some 200 emails. Whilst sitting next to me he started going through them and after a while, laughed, and shut the laptop. I asked what was up. He explained he had

---

3   Transactional Analysis, commonly known as TA, was developed by Canadian-born US psychiatrist Eric Berne during the late 1950s. according to TA, there are three ego-states (Parent, Adult, Child – PAC) that people consistently use:

- Parent ('exteropsyche'): a state in which people behave, feel and think in response to an unconscious mimicking of how their parents (or other parental figures) acted, or how they interpreted their parent's actions. For example, a person may shout at someone out of frustration because they learned from an influential figure in childhood the lesson that this seemed to be a way of relating that worked.
- Adult ('neopsyche'): a state of the ego which is most like a computer processing information and making predictions absent of major emotions that cloud its operation. Learning to strengthen the Adult is a goal of TA. While a person is in the Adult ego state, he/she is directed towards an objective appraisal of reality.
- Child ('archaeopsyche'): a state in which people behave, feel and think similarly to how they did in childhood. For example, a person who receives a poor evaluation at work may respond by looking at the floor, and crying or pouting, as they used to when scolded as a child. Conversely, a person who receives a good evaluation may respond with a broad smile and a joyful gesture of thanks. The Child is the source of emotions, creation, recreation, spontaneity and intimacy.

These states combine in relationships with, for example in leadership dynamics, Adult-Adult being productive, egalitarian and mature, and Parent-Child being domineering and immature. See Berne's original book *Transactional Analysis in Psychotherapy: A Systematic Individual and Social Psychiatry* and for an updated view: *Transactional Analysis in Psychotherapy: The Classic Handbook to its Principles*.

sorted the emails according to who had sent them, and had spotted a pattern. The first email invariably told him of some impending disaster and asked for advice. The next few repeated the request for advice, and then this was followed by one or two asking why he had not replied. These were then followed by an email saying they had not heard from him, had gone ahead and sorted the problem out and therefore did not need to bother him ... the CEO suddenly realised that for years he had answered the first few emails, and had unwittingly programmed his followers to act in a certain way towards him, and that he had wasted much time and effort on top of the unwitting damage he had done. This behaviour is classic of the delusional behaviour identified in Chapter 8, Figure 8.8.

This story always gets strong recognition from the many managers and executives who have been trained in Complex Adaptive Leadership. A good example is the country manager of a large multi-national. After hearing the story on a CAL course, he decided to turn his mobile phone and laptop off and ignore all emails and texts for a day during the rest of the CAL programme to see what would happen. Sure enough the emergency which cropped up, and which his subordinate sent frantic messages for guidance on, was worked out without him having to provide a lead. A good example of how followers need to learn to take the lead – otherwise they will just keep asking for leadership that they like, but do not necessarily need. As stated before but worth repeating, the leadership we all *like* is often not the leadership we *need*.

So how a leader behaves will dictate to some degree the level of followership maturity. Behaviour breeds behaviour. There are many strategies to move people towards level 5. Obviously skill/will is key and this is considered more in the next chapter. There are also other strategies that can be employed, examples of which are in Figure 9.4 below. The key point is to start where the observed behaviour is (rather than where you want to see it) and go step by step. So if someone is at level 1, move them to level 2 rather than straight to level 5! In that way the self-confidence of the individual concerned can be built up over time and become sustainable.

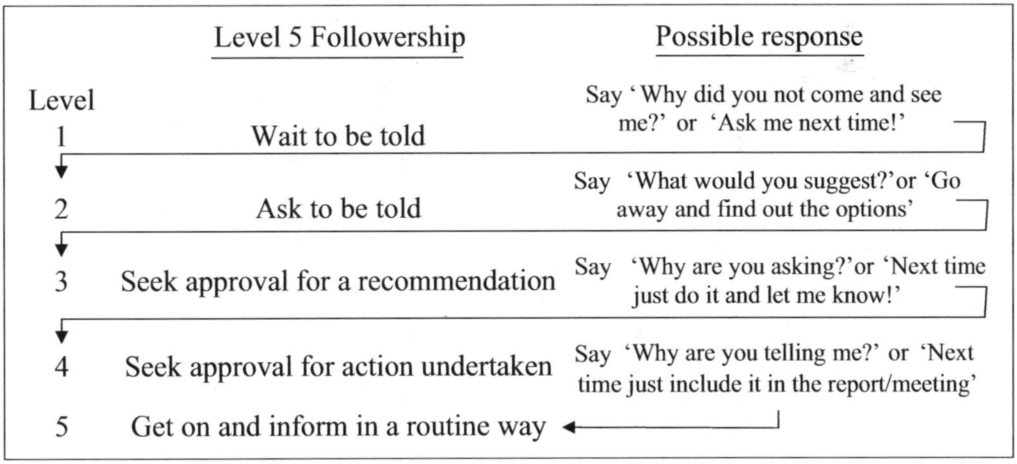

	Level 5 Followership	Possible response
Level 1	Wait to be told	Say 'Why did you not come and see me?' or 'Ask me next time!'
2	Ask to be told	Say 'What would you suggest?' or 'Go away and find out the options'
3	Seek approval for a recommendation	Say 'Why are you asking?' or 'Next time just do it and let me know!'
4	Seek approval for action undertaken	Say 'Why are you telling me?' or 'Next time just include it in the report/meeting'
5	Get on and inform in a routine way	

Figure 9.4 Moving people towards level 5

This does take time, but in the long run saves time, as followers take more of the initiative. At each stage you need to allow time for the follower to become comfortable with their new level (in other words if a follower is at level 2 you would not say 'Go away and find out the options' and then say when that is done 'Why are you asking?'! – give them time to adapt to each level before gently moving them on).

The flipside is that how a follower behaves will dictate the type of leadership that is shown in response. If, for example, a follower is continually checking what he does with the leader, then the confidence in the follower will be low, and a more hands-on approach will be taken. This itself drives the behaviour of the follower and a vicious cycle is entered into, an example of which is shown below.

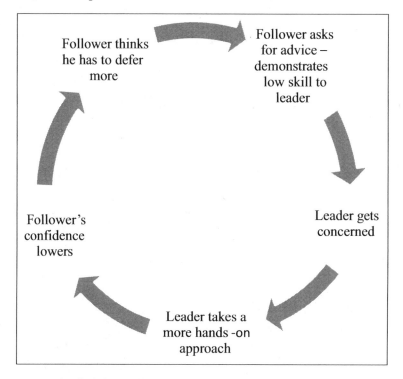

Figure 9.5   A typical vicious circle for leaders

In many ways this reinforces the leadership and followership charade highlighted in Chapter 4.

Chapter Summary

In this chapter we looked at the follower side of the equation in terms of Skill/Will and level 5 followership. The following are the key points:

1. Followership maturity can be defined as the extent to which a follower is prepared to take the lead and get on with what needs to be done without leadership provided by an ascribed leader.
2. A follower needs a high degree of skill and will in order for this to happen. Skill is the knowledge needed to do the job (technical content) as well as how to go about it (operational process). Will is the motivation to do the work, as well as the motivation to do it without supervision.

3. Followers will move between different states of skill and will. This demands a different approach by the leader to move them back towards high skill and high will.

4. Skill/Will should not be seen in isolation of the other Four + Four principles – a high degree of skill and will is not much use if the objectives are unclear.

5. Maturity can also be seen in terms of the levels of followership at which an individual is. The best level, the 'point attractor', is level 5 and high skill/high will.

We can see the followership side of the equation is as important as the leadership side. The two combine into a dynamic which can get better results in a more sustained way than the typical oligarchic approach. The next chapter looks at a roadmap which combines the key lessons from the previous two chapters. It takes the complex subject of leadership and shows a few simple rules that can be used to good effect.

10 *Complex Adaptive Leadership in Action*

A QUICK TEST TO OPEN YOUR MIND – WHERE ARE YOU ON THE MAP?

This should not take long. Assume you are the leader of a team of followers. It does not necessarily have to be the team you are currently in, if you have one. Imagine you are in the circumstances described. Read the possible responses. Do not think too long about which one you would choose. Circle/tick one of the responses that you think you most likely *would* do (as opposed to could or should!). Use the scoring table at the end to identify your scores.

1. **Your team is faced with a change of circumstance for which they are poorly experienced and unprepared. They don't want to adapt to the new context.**

    a. Tell them that they must adapt and show them clearly what needs to be done.

    b. Inform them about the benefits that the change will bring (including the new skills they will gain from the training arranged), and point out the cost of not adapting.

    c. Ask them how they propose to deal with the new situation and give what they say serious thought.

    d. Keep an eye on the situation, but do not interfere.

2. **A subordinate of yours is keen to move ahead. However, he does not know how to implement the new procedures put in place. He is concerned as performance might suffer.**

    a. Point out how the new procedures will improve both the situation and the team's environment, and how he will benefit.

    b. Seek his views as to how the new procedures should be implemented and consider his recommendations.

    c. Do not get involved yet, and wait and see what happens.

    d. Show him clearly how the new procedures can be followed and ensure more detailed training is done if he needs it.

3. **A difficult state of affairs has occurred, but despite him having the ability you have detected a distinct lack of willingness by one of your subordinates to deal with it.**

    a. Ask him what the problems/barriers are and seek his recommendations for solutions.

    b. Let him work it out for himself and do not interfere unless performance suffers.

    c. Inform him that you have detected his lack of willingness and that this is unacceptable and he must deal with the situation.

    d. Point out penalties for failure and offer him a small bonus to ensure success.

4. **New changes are underway. Your motivated team is coping well, but you are concerned that performance may suffer without further guidance.**

   a.   Do nothing yet – monitor the situation and be prepared to step in if performance or motivation begins to decline.

   b.   Remind them of what the new changes are and the expectations of how the team should act.

   c.   Reiterate how the new changes will benefit all concerned and what the penalties of failure could be.

   d.   Arrange a team meeting to voice your concerns and ask them how they can sustain their current performance.

5. **Morale is high despite a rapid change of direction. However your team does not yet have the new skills they will need and performance is starting to suffer.**

   a.   Show them how things have got better since the change of direction.

   b.   Ask them how they propose to deal with the change of direction.

   c.   Do not get involved, but wait for the training programme for the team to deliver.

   d.   Take action to let them know precisely how they need to change working practices and quickly bring forward the training course.

6. **A new change is needed and one of your subordinates is depressed about it – he does not want to change or upgrade his skills to do the new work. You have already arranged a training course to deliver the new skills that the team will need.**

   a.   Ask him to identify what the barriers are and how he proposes to overcome them.

   b.   Be careful not to do anything unless the situation gets worse.

   c.   Reiterate what the new changes are, that there are no other options, and that training is arranged for him.

   d.   Stress the benefits of the new training course and how the changes will improve the situation and help avoid a worsening situation.

7. **A change in procedures needs your team to adapt. They have the skills to deal with the new system but one of your subordinates is resisting the need to change.**

   a.   Avoid confrontation and see if she changes her attitude.

   b.   Take firm and swift action to tell her what is needed in clear terms.

   c.   Demonstrate how the new procedures have simplified her work and indicate the down side of non-compliance.

   d.   Ask what the barriers to change are and how she can overcome them.

8. **Challenging targets are being met with hard work and morale is high. Your team seem happy but you are worried that one of your subordinates might need more help.**

   a.   Tell her how she can best meet the targets and how to improve.

b. Remind her of the benefits that will accrue when the targets are met, and suggest further improvements.

c. Ask her how performance can be improved further and what needs to be put in place.

d. Leave her to continue her good work and relax a bit more.

9. **Your highly skilled team have been efficient and performed well, but you have seen signs that motivation is beginning to drop and this will soon affect performance.**

a. Arrange a fun offsite which includes a workshop to identify problems and opportunities to improve the situation.

b. Tell them they need to improve motivation and in clear terms what the expectations are.

c. Do nothing yet – monitor the situation and be prepared to step in if performance is affected.

d. Point out the benefits currently achieved as well as the penalties which may ensue if performance suffers.

10. **Your team are doing well and seem happy to meet the stretch targets that you have set them. However, you are worried that one of your subordinate's performance might suffer without further motivation because of a recent family bereavement.**

a. Keep an eye on him but do not interfere yet and be less worried.

b. Remind him of the consequence of failure and negative outcomes which may arise as well as the benefits which will accrue if he succeeds.

c. Tell him of your concerns and inform him again of what needs to be done.

d. Ask him how motivation can further be improved and consider his recommendations.

11. **Your team is highly motivated, but a rapid introduction of new systems has seen their productivity suffer and this will soon affect morale.**

a. Get an expert to show them how to use the system in a customised training session, and identify further training needs.

b. Seek their recommendations for how better to use the system.

c. Reiterate how damaging it is not to use the system in the correct way, point out the benefits and arrange a training session.

d. Let them work it out and do not get involved.

12. **There is a pressing need for the team to change to a new system and the change management team has arranged a training course for them. However, one of your subordinates does not want to change nor attend the course.**

a. Inform her of the benefits of change and the training she will soon receive, as well as the cost of not changing.

b. Wait until her performance is affected further before taking action.

c. Arrange a longer meeting with her to work out solutions to her problems.

d. Tell her she has to change and that she will do the training course.

13. Performance is good and your team have continued to show their usual high motivation. You feel that you are not contributing enough as their leader.

    a.   Introduce a new bonus scheme to improve morale and demonstrate your involvement.

    b.   Do nothing and be careful not to interfere.

    c.   Tell them that you wish to play a more active role and increase the frequency of their reporting to you.

    d.   Arrange a team off-site to have some fun but also to identify improvements and how to achieve them.

14. An older subordinate of yours wants to embrace the changes which are planned, but she feels daunted by the demands for the new skills which will be needed.

    a.   Reiterate how the new changes will improve things, and how the changes will help avoid the downward trend leading to job cuts.

    b.   Don't intervene yet and wait to see how she will really cope.

    c.   Tell her about the new skills needed and say she will be trained quickly if she needs it.

    d.   Ask her how she proposes to overcome the barriers to the new changes.

15. The external situation has changed rapidly and your team have been left behind, unable to cope. They feel they should quit.

    a.   Wait until someone actually quits before taking action.

    b.   Inform them of the dire consequences of quitting and that training support is available for those that need it.

    c.   Make everyone feel involved and seek their recommendations.

    d.   Act quickly and firmly by saying quitting is not an option, and show them in detail what needs to be done.

16. Your subordinates are highly qualified and are well capable of doing a good job. But they have not performed as well as they could and do not seem keen to do so.

    a.   Tell them clearly what the targets are and how they can best achieve them.

    b.   Ask them why performance is not as good as it can be, and seek their recommendations for how to improve the situation.

    c.   Do nothing yet – monitor the situation and be prepared to step in if performance is further adversely affected.

    d.   Remind them of the benefits if targets are met.

Scoring Sheet

Go back over your answers and circle the relevant response letter you chose in the table below. Then add up the number of responses in each column. The total responses should number 16 (assuming you answered all questions).

Strategy Question	Strategy 1	Strategy 2	Strategy 3	Strategy 4
1	a	b	c	d
2	d	a	b	c
3	c	d	a	b
4	b	c	d	a
5	d	a	b	c
6	c	d	a	b
7	b	c	d	a
8	a	b	c	d
9	b	d	a	c
10	c	b	d	a
11	a	c	b	d
12	d	a	c	b
13	c	a	d	b
14	c	a	d	b
15	d	b	c	a
16	a	d	b	c
Totals				

A customised report to support this questionnaire is available at:
http://www.complexadaptiveleadership.com.

Chapter 8 gave a view of leadership and suggested the basis of a possible model or roadmap. Chapter 9 gave a view of followership. The two can be combined to provide some powerful and simple strategies to enable polyarchy to thrive, and to lessen the tension that exists when oligarchic assumptions hold sway whilst polyarchic realities are emerging. The key elements of chaos theory and complexity science that are used in this chapter are the use of phase space (which lays down a roadmap for leadership and four basic strategies), a few simple rules (which lay a basis of how the strategies can be applied) and attractors (which shows some examples of how the basic strategies can be combined). This is one of the key differences that the CAL model has over other leadership models. Whilst other models speak of styles, the CAL model shows how differing behaviours can be blended. Whilst at times the approaches below may look very formulaic it should be noted that they are general approaches which should work most of the time. Given the complex nature of what is involved (human dynamics in often fast changing circumstance) the outcome is probabilistic rather than deterministic.

Phase Space Roadmap

In Chapter 9 we saw that leadership can be broken down into people and goal focused behaviour or strategies. If we created a phase space diagram (see Chapter 5 under 'Chaos Theory – Underlying Order; Attractors') to represent this, it could look like Figure 10.1.

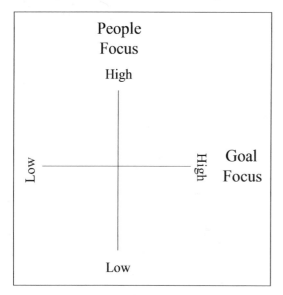

Figure 10.1 Complex Adaptive Leadership model – basis

Let's explain what we mean by 'People Focus' and 'Goal Focus'. For both axes, focus occurs because there is a need or opportunity for a leader or individual to make a difference, or to contribute through others.

- **People Focus.** This means there is an opportunity or need to develop people both in terms of their ability (skill and will) as well as in terms of the relationship with them. The aim is to leave them, or your relationship, in a better position, either from a motivation, capability or just basic human emotion point of view. It needs an open, fundamental and honest concern for the individual(s) concerned. An open heart is needed.
- **Goal Focus.** This means there is a need or opportunity to make a difference to the achievement of the goal through other people. This does not mean rolling up one's sleeves, elbowing people aside and doing the work oneself. That is not leadership (unless as a means to show an example for others in order to develop them).

Building on the lessons from Situational Leadership we can add in each quadrant the strategies (not styles) that a leader could employ:

- **Strategy 1 (S1): Tell.** (Low People, High Goal). This does not have to mean being dictatorial or in any way unpleasant. And sometimes it is needed – one hardly tells a new employee where the coffee machine is by saying 'Well, where do you think it could be?' Showing someone how to do something is a 'Tell'. Telling them the information they need so as to get on better is also a 'Tell'. Training people is also a 'Tell'. Tell can include either the what, the how and/or the why. As a general rule if you are having to 'tell' someone both the what, and the how and the why then something is amiss. The 'Why' is always best used as a 'Sell' (see next bullet point). So that leaves the 'What' and the 'How'. Again telling someone both is not as good as telling one of them. If they know the what, but do not know how to achieve it, then telling the how is natural. However, one needs to be aware of the level that the person is at in relation to level 5 followership (see Figure 9.2 in Chapter 9). The 'What' is more about 'content', and the 'How' is more about process. The accent of leadership is moving more towards process.

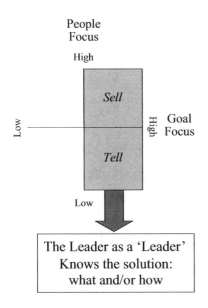

People
Focus

High

Sell

Low | High | Goal
Focus

Tell

Low

The Leader as a 'Leader'
Knows the solution:
what and/or how

Figure 10.2 Leader as a traditional leader – either tells or sells

- **S2: Sell.** (High People, High Goal). Here too the leader needs to know, but there is a need for the people to own the solution, rather than just accept and follow it. The term 'buy in' is often used. For 'buy-in' to occur, a 'Sell' needs to happen first. Selling involves ensuring that the buyer is aware of the benefits, and these match the underlying needs of the individual. Thus it is more about asking questions and listening carefully before aligning a proposed solution than doing inspirational speeches! There are a variety of approaches to selling. Perhaps the most useful for leadership purposes is that of the Huthway Research Group and SPIN.[1] This is a questioning technique which asks a series of questions that uncover the Situation, then the commensurate Problem, then the Implications of the problem (thus building up the desire to solve it) and then the underlying Need and how whatever is being sold can meet the need.

Taken together S1 and S2 are typical strategies when the leader knows the solution and either needs or chooses to 'Tell' it or 'Sell' it.

---

1   Huthway Research Group followed thousands of salesmen and analysed their behaviour. They found the more successful ones were those who asked questions. They then analysed the questions and found that they could be broken down into four basic types: Questions that clarified the *Situation*, then those that identified specific *Problems*, then uncovered the full *Implications* of the problems, and then the underlying *Need* of the potential customer, and how those needs could be met. Hence SPIN. See N. Rackham, *SPIN Selling*.

- **S3: Involve.** (High People, Low Goal). This is used either when the leader does not know or chooses to hold back to allow others to discover the solution. A variety of involve strategies exist ranging from asking an individual 'What do you think?', to running small teams focused on problems, to large scale mass intervention techniques.[2] The strategy is good for when either the time is not pressing and/or there is a good opportunity to educate and develop people's knowledge and skills further. It is more of a 'pull' strategy.
- **S4: Devolve.** (Low People, Low Goal). When the Four + Four principles are in place, which includes the follower having the skill and will to do the job, this is the strategy for leaders. It does not mean abdication as the role for a leader in a hierarchy or oligarchy would be to keep the finger on the pulse. This would include watching out for the Four + Four principles ready to sell or involve followers when the need for change arises. S4 is equal to the concept of 'wu wei' – the art of inaction – and inaction here does not mean doing nothing! Someone needs to keep an eye across the boundaries and into the future, and in an oligarchic assumed organisation (as most are) the leaders are in the best place for this role. Meanwhile they need to support and follow the people whilst they get on with achieving the goal. According to the Tao and ancient Chinese wisdom, as well as modern CAL approaches, it is the highest form of leadership. It is the point of leadership and in today's complex times it may explain the plethora of approaches which seem to go against hierarchy and management[3].

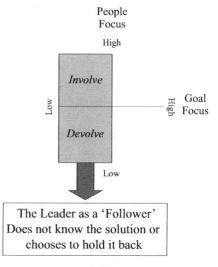

Figure 10.3 The leader as a 'follower'

Taken together S3 and S4 are typical strategies when the leader does not know the solution (or chooses to hold back) and follows/supports.

This leadership approach can also be applied to upward leadership and in today's complex world, where solutions are more at the bottom than the top, upward leadership (sometimes called active followership) is becoming increasingly more important.

You can also look at the top and bottom pairs in the phase space as requiring two differing levels of effort.

There is a Yin/Yang element to the phase space roadmap. Considered as pairs, the approach of S1 and S2 is more Yang than Yin – it assumes a male type leadership 'pushing' solutions. Meanwhile, S3 and S4 assume a more Yin type approach, more female and 'pull'. Considered individually, S1 is very Yang whilst S3 is very Yin. S2 has a mix of

---

2   Small group interventions are exemplified by the workout teams in GE, introduced by Jack Welch. Mass interventions techniques have been discussed (see footnotes 10, 11 and 12 to Chapter 3).

3   Perhaps the most radical article is by Gary Hamel called 'First Let's Fire all the Managers' in *Harvard Business Review*'s December edition in 2011. Robin Ryder's book *Never Mind the Boss – Hastening the Death of Deference for Business Success* is also instructive.

each (for example, typical sales process of pull to find out the needs, push to match the solution). S4 has a mix of each as well (for example, Yin for being able to be passive and let things flow, and Yang for having the courage and determination to hold back).

So far so good – however the phase space diagram is not just about four basic and individual strategies that can be employed. It is how these can be *combined* that is the powerful and fun bit. However before we get to that we need to lay down some simple rules for when each of the four strategies should be applied.

People Focus

High

Involve	*Sell*
Devolve	*Tell*

Low ← → High Goal Focus

High physical effort
Low emotional effort

Low physical effort
High emotional effort

Low

Figure 10.4 Differing types of effort for the strategies

A Few Simple Rules

This builds on the skill/will matrix identified in Chapter 7, and explored in Chapter 9. The question is if one has an individual who is in the low skill/low will quadrant where does one start? According to the Situational Leadership model one starts by telling the person what to do and then presumably by doing, he learns and his motivation increases. This was based on 1960s norms and probably would not work so well nowadays. In the Complex Adaptive

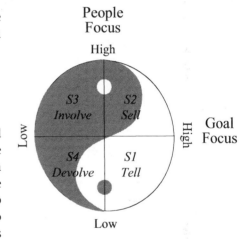

Figure 10.5 Leadership roadmap and Yin/Yang

Leadership model the strategy is to work on the will – motivate the person to want to do it, so they will be ready to be shown/trained/told to improve the skill. A possible way is shown below. The aim is to help the person to achieve the high skill and high will quadrant.

The Skill/Will matrix is one way of looking at followership. Followership is the flip side of leadership. If we flip the scales of the skill/will matrix (put low where high is and vice versa), then we can overlay the leadership roadmap strategies to show what should be done. In other words, we can get a suggested few simple rules, and the process in the figure above is linked to the strategies to show there is an underlying (one of many) dynamics.

A possible 'flow' of the strategies is considered under attractors below. The key point is that a crucial skill is to be able to move effortlessly between each leadership strategy. It is not about which style is better or worse. It is about which strategy has the best chance for success. There are no magic bullets and guarantees. The above should not be surprising and should be common sense. For example, if someone has high will (that is, really wants to do something) but low skill (that is, does not know how to) they will want to be shown (that is, told) how to do it!

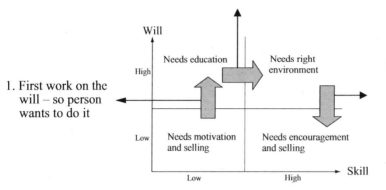

Figure 10.6 Skill/will possible strategy

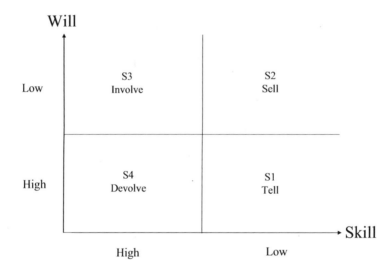

Figure 10.7 Skill/will and leadership strategies

So how well do you currently follow these simple rules? The questionnaire at the start of this chapter is for indicative use only, but may give some insights. Look at your scores from the questionnaire – you should ideally have scored 4 in each column. If not, you might be too attached to one particular strategy and need to work out why that is. It could be that you were simply unaware of the simple rules that have been described above!

In that case do the questionnaire again and note the score (and more importantly, do something different at work!). Or there could be something deeper. Here are some possible ideas gleaned from numerous discussions with the research group:

1. If your S2 score is the highest, and S4 the lowest, then you are faced by a typical challenge. You need to let go more, and have more faith in your subordinates (as the S2 style is used for low skill and low will individuals!).

2. If the sum of your S1 and S2 scores is higher than the sum of your S3 and S4 scores then you may be overestimating your own impact, and demotivating your subordinates. After all, according to the research in Chapter 4 you should employing S1 and S2 a fraction of the time!

3. If the sum of your S2 and S3 scores is higher than the sum of your S1 and S4 scores, then you might be working too hard! This also demonstrates someone who finds it hard to let go and be separated (either emotionally via low S1 score, or physically via low S4 score).

4. If the sum of S1 and S3 is greater than the sum of S2 and S4 then you may be taking too direct an approach. S2 and S4 require some subtlety.

So far we have looked at four basic strategies that can be applied and a few simple rules on how they can be applied. One needs to be able to move between each style effortlessly and the S4 strategy is the one that should be aimed for (by ensuring the Four + Four principles are in place and that includes people having a high skill and will level, as well as working at a level 5 followership). It is the way that these strategies can be combined which lends power to the model, and it is to this we now turn.

Attractors

To remind you from the chapter on chaos theory, an attractor is a plot of action on a phase space diagram (see Figure 5.9, Chapter 5 for examples). There are three basic types of attractors:

- **Point attractors.** This is where the action gravitates to a particular point of a phase space diagram.
- **Period attractors.** This is where the action revolves around a specific part of a phase space diagram.
- **Strange attractors.** This is where the action describes a pattern which does not gravitate to a particular point or revolve around any specific point.

These three basic types of attractor are also visible in leadership. If we use our 'People/ Goal' phase space/roadmap we can plot various combinations of strategies to useful effect. Attractor theory gives us another way of looking at leadership than just the usual strategy approach. Rather than just having a particular strategy to consider, attractor theory gives us a flow or dynamic that combines these strategies in a powerful way.

BASIC POINT AND PERIODIC ATTRACTORS

If we look at the flow described in the Skill/Will model in Figure 10.5, and consider the combination of leadership strategies in the Skill/Will model in Figure 10.6, we could describe a common flow as follows:

You have an individual who has low will and low skill when facing a situation that needs to be dealt with. The first step is to sell the idea to the individual of the need for change. This could include additional compensation, but also the fact that there would be personal benefit. It should also include a hint of the downside of NOT doing something. This would need an understanding of the individual's aspirations, and how the task in hand can be matched to them. An indication of the will increasing is the complaint, 'I'd accept the need for change, but I don't know what should be done about it.' The individual is then ready for the next step, and for you to tell them what needs to be done. Having been given some basic skill, the third step is to involve in fine tuning the action and the how that needs to be done (that is, 'pull' some of the solution from his ideas, for more ownership). Once the individual is operating fully and effectively within the task, the final stage is to let go and devolve completely. So in summary one simple and common blend of the four strategies are:

Sell the WHY

Tell the WHAT

Involve for the HOW

Devolve once execution begins – let them get on with it.

This approach can be applied to individuals as well as play a part of a change management strategy for organisations. This blend is based on a variety of case studies[4] including that of Jack Stack, the CEO of SRC Inc. (who we mentioned in Chapter 7, under 'Unambiguous Feedback'). In a BBC Radio 4 programme entitled 'Killing the Organisation'[5] Jack needed to get on board a worker called Denise Redfeld with his new approach of Open Book Management. At first she thought it was, in her own words, a load of bunkum. Jack first sold the idea to her by asking her if she thought her product line was making money. Challenging questions are a typical part of a sales process. (Step 1 – Sell). She of course answered yes, so Jack then told her to prove it by doing a profitability study. She had no idea how to do that so Jack showed her (Step 2 – Tell). He asked her to come up with a recommendation. So she went away and did the profitability study. She found that she was losing the company money and so she recommended for her line to be closed down (Step 3 – Involve). In her own words she made her job redundant. The next step was to move her to a more profitable line, where she could also apply her newly learned skills (Step 4 – devolve). At the time of the interview Denise was managing a new line of products. Needless to say such leadership does not operate in a culture of fear. So had Denise felt she would have been sacked if she came up with the outcome, she would have resisted. There has to be an underlying honesty and willingness to employ people elsewhere, if possible.

If we were to plot the above example it would look like Figure 10.8 opposite. The point attractor for leadership here is the S4 style. This is not a new concept, but has been around thousands of years. This is 'wu wei' where the leader devolves fully and in many ways then follows the followers. This perhaps explains the quote of Lau Tzu in Chapter 1 where

---

4   Having told the story of Jack Stack to hundreds of executives and discussed the case, in a typical group of 20 people, often several similar examples arise. When I break out groups into table discussions of five to six people, it is very rare that a table does not have the combined experience to come up with some identical examples of such a flow (Sell–Tell–Involve–Devolve).

5   See footnote 40 to Chapter 7.

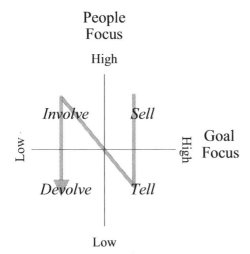

Figure 10.8 Point attractor towards self-organisation

he said '... *the best leader is one whom the people hardly know exists, leaving them happy to say, once the aim is achieved, "We did it ourselves".'* This is similar to General Lafayette's *'I am their leader, therefore I must follow them'*[6] or Ghandi's *'I must follow my people, for I am their leader.'*[7] Although not new, this concept has been largely philosophical, but the point attractor gives us a more scientific way of seeing it. And given the contextual changes outlined in Chapter 2, the time for a point attractor for leadership is more relevant than ever before.

So again the flow here is:

- sell the why;
- tell the what (or how);
- involve for the how (or what); and
- devolve for the details (for example, when, where, who and so on).

This particular point attractor best summarises the aim for Complex Adaptive Leadership – which is to move towards self-organisation allowing polyarchy to thrive, and remove the strains and stresses when underlying polyarchic realities clash with all pervading oligarchic assumptions. The example above may not be so complicated. It may well be that after selling and telling, one can devolve and let go. What happens here is that the leader sells then tells, and then can devolve straight away. Motivation slips more easily than memory, so as suggested in the flow in Figure 10.6, the leader's next intervention with the individual is to help him maintain motivation by involving himself in improving things. What typically happens is that the person is happy to get on with things in a self-organised way. Meanwhile the leader is looking further ahead and sees the need for change, so the next stage is to sell the need for major change. And so the cycle begins again. This would look like the periodic attractor shown in Figure 10.9:

So the flow here is:

- sell the why;
- tell the how/what;
- devolve for the how/what;
- involve to improve/keep motivation; and
- move back to sell the why if major change needed.

---

6   General Lafayette was a General of the Continental Army in America during the war of independence, 1777–1781. It was 80 years later that the French politician Alexandre Ledru-Rollin also exclaimed upon seeing a crowd marching through Paris: *'There go my people, I must find out where they are going so I can lead them.'*

7   Attribution to Gandhi made by L. Howell, *Freedom City: The Substance of Things Hoped For.*

This cycle can be repeated many times. In reality the effort of focus to 'Sell', 'Tell' and so on decreases each time as the leader and follower quickly understand each other. So in some ways the dynamic between the two transcends the typical leader/follower relationship. Each leads and follows, they operate more like a team than a typical boss/subordinate. Another way of looking at that is as another point attractor. Each time around the loop in Figure 10.8, the effort needed is less and less.

So the flow here is:

- sell the why;
- tell the how/what;
- devolve for the what/how;
- involve to improve/keep motivation;
- move back to sell the why if major change needed – but does not need as much effort as before; and
- continue around until the distinctions become blurred.

This may sound a little philosophical but is based on the reported observations of special forces patrols operating in jungles for long periods of time. Such a dynamic may not occur in typical organisations, although many will recognise that the effort to lead some subordinates who are well established is a lot less than newer ones.

The periodic attractor is common in most organisations who go through change, and the starting point will depend on the state of the change, and to what extent it is anticipatory, reactive or crisis.

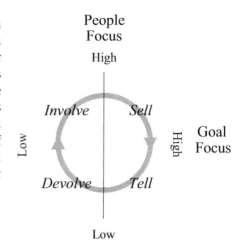

Figure 10.9 Periodic attractor for improvement

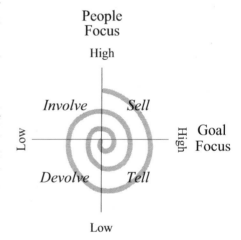

Figure 10.10 Point attractor towards transcended state

It should be noted that the attractors in Figures 10.9 and 10.10 are remarkably similar to those highlighted in Figure 5.9. This is another example of the link of chaos theory to leadership.

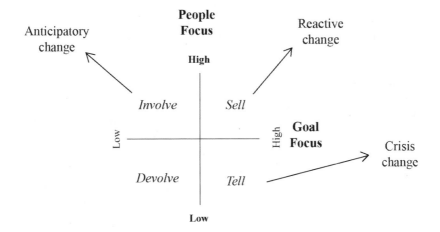

Figure 10.11 Periodic attractor within state of change

PAIRED PERIODIC ATTRACTORS

The examples above show how all the strategies of Sell–Tell–Involve–Devolve can be combined. However, other powerful flows exist when the strategies are paired. The four most common of these are considered below. They are:

- coaching attractor – Paired strategy of Sell–Involve (S2/S3);
- directive attractor – Paired strategy of Tell–Sell (S2/S1);
- development attractor – Paired strategy of Involve–Devolve (S3/S4); and
- reminder attractor – Paired strategy of Devolve–Tell (S1/S4).

Coaching attractor. Of all the periodic attractors on paired strategies, this is the most powerful and also demands the greatest skill. As Figures 10.2, 10.3 and 10.4 suggest there is a large divide between S1/2 (Sell–Tell) and S3/4 (Involve–Devolve). On the one side of the divide (Tell–Sell), the leader acts as the leader. On the other (Involve–Devolve) the leader encourages the follower to take the lead. Coaching is a good technique to bridge the divide, as well as move an individual towards level 5 followership (gets on with things without supervision and reports in a routine way). There are many different coaching approaches and methodologies. The most effective one for Complex Adaptive Leadership is the GROW model coupled with a questioning technique which makes use of a mix of open/closed and suggestive/non-suggestive questions. Let's look at how this works. In phase space the action is a mix of Selling (using suggestive questions) and Involving (using non-suggestive questions). So the plot would look like Figure 10.12.

The GROW model is a questioning technique.[8] GROW stands for the questions asked: Goal, Reality, Options, Will. It is a coaching questioning technique designed to enable the person being coached to find a way through a problem. It assumes a level of knowledge

---

8   No one person can be identified as the originator of the GROW model. It was conceived by Graham Alexander and Alan Fine who built on the work of the Inner Game theory developed by Timothy Gallwey, a tennis coach. It was brought to the fore by Sir John Whitmore who made his name in the field of high performance coaching in the sporting and business arenas. The technique is flexible enough to be applied virtually anywhere. Like most coaching models it provides a structure for conversation that is designed to ensure outcome whilst overcoming internal difficulties. Max Landsberg

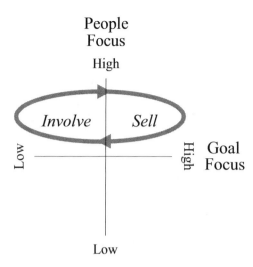

People
Focus

High

Involve *Sell*

Low | High Goal
Focus

Low

Figure 10.12   Coaching attractor of Sell and Involve

Goal

What would you like to achieve?
What benefit would you gain?
What would happen if you failed?

Reality

How far are you from your goal?
What are the barriers that you face?
Who could help you?

Options

How could you achieve your goal?
If that approach failed, what then?
How could you ask for help?

Will

What is the very first step?
When will you take it?
Do you really want to do this?

Figure 10.13   GROW model example questions

by the person answering the questions and is very much a 'pull' technique. As such, it would belong as part of the S3 (involve) strategy. The GROW model assumes open questions some examples of which are shown in Figure 10.13. The line of questioning follows a natural flow, although in reality one would jump about a bit. For example, having identified the goal and why the person wishes to achieve it, the options may indicate that the goal stated is in fact an option of a deeper goal – one would need then to cycle back and clarify the goal again. As can be seen in the example in Figure 10.13, the questions are open and non-suggestive. Open questions cannot be answered by 'yes/no' and non-suggestive questions do not imply an answer in any way. This is an important distinction.

If questions were suggestive (for example, 'Would such-and-such a solution work?'), and the person took the approach suggested it would not be wholly owned. Non-suggestive questions mean that any answer or solution which emerges is wholly made by the individual and so is more easily owned. If there is success, the sense of achievement is enhanced. If there is failure, the accountability is clear. However, the GROW approach does assume the individual has the tacit knowledge to uncover the solution or the way forward. If that tacit knowledge is incomplete, then the leader will need to suggest solutions. So questioning can be suggestive and non-suggestive. When coupled with open/closed questioning technique, four basic types of questions can be employed during the GROW process.

Let's look at each in a little more detail:

• **Get Out/Lifeline.** This is when the person says 'I don't know'. Examples of such helpful questions include 'Would such-and-such a solution work?' or 'I know of a person in a similar situation. He did x. Would that work for you?' This

also describes GROW in his book *The Tao of Coaching*. This book builds on the model by showing *how* (that is, four types of questions) to do the *what* (that is, four themes of GROW questions).

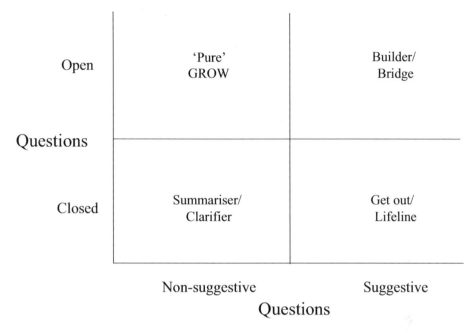

Figure 10.14 Types of questions that can be used with GROW coaching

type of question could also be used to pull someone back from a solution they think would work, but in fact would be a disaster. An example could be 'Someone did that last year and x happened. Do you think that could happen here?' This type of questioning should be used sparingly.

- **Builder/Bridge.** This is often used to follow a Get Out/Lifeline question (such as 'Would this solution work for you?') – if the answer is 'Yes' then an example Builder/Bridge question could be 'In what way would this solution work for you.' If the answer is 'No' then 'Why not?' could follow. The idea is to be able to Bridge across to a 'Pure' GROW question.
- **'Pure' GROW.** These are the best to ensure full ownership. It is where one needs to be most of the time. Examples are in Figure 10.13.
- **Summariser/Clarifier.** These questions are key. They should be used every few minutes to summarise what has been said. It is also useful to remind oneself where one is in the GROW process. An example includes 'So I understand you wish to achieve x goal for y reasons – is that correct?' or 'I understand that you consider x approach is best and you said you would do y next – am I correct?'

In terms of time, best practice suggests 80 per cent of the time on non-suggestive questioning and 20 per cent of the time on suggestive questioning.[9]

The questioning flows between suggestive and non-suggestive, selling ideas and involving the individual's own ideas. The dynamic looks like Figure 10.15.

The overall direction of questioning is to lead the individual from what needs to be achieved (Goal), through the existing factors which affect performance (Reality),

---

9   These percentages are based on a study of the technique being put to use by 400 of the research group mentioned in footnote 1 of Chapter 2.

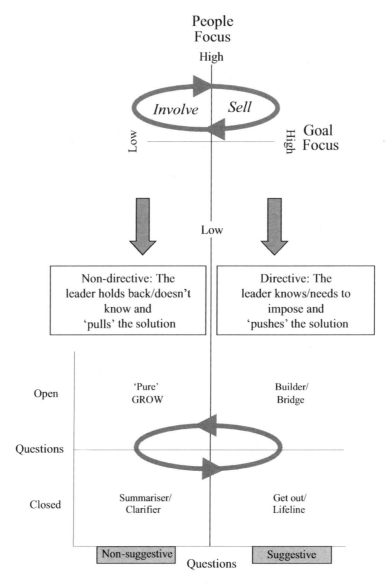

Figure 10.15   Coaching attractor linked to questioning technique

through the various options which exist and an estimation of the up- and downsides of each of them (Options) to what the individual is actually going to do (Will). The majority of questions will be non-suggestive to ensure ownership, whilst the leader's own ideas can be expressed via some suggestive questions. It is a sophisticated approach, and increasing sophistication can be added by forming the questions according to the MBTI psychological type of the person being coached.

Directive attractor. This pairs the Tell and SI strategies together. It is the skill or art of persuasion. We have looked at the SPIN and GROW models as questioning techniques. They can be used with the Tell approach. For example one could tell an individual the situation and problem and, using questioning techniques, explore the implications and what needs to be done. Or one could explain what the goal and current realities are and,

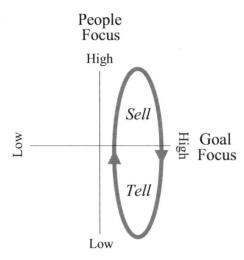

Figure 10.16 Directive attractor of Tell and Sell

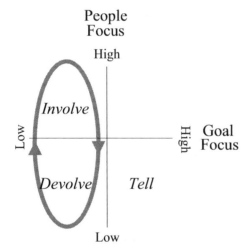

Figure 10.17 Development attractor of Involve and Devolve

using questioning, explore the options and agree what the individual will do.

Development attractor. We have seen in the skill/will model (see Figures 10.6 and 10.7) that when an individual is working with a high degree of skill and will, it is the will that can be more variable. It is common sense that motivation can drop faster than memory. So once an individual is working in a self-organised way, the leader will need to be ready to intervene to improve motivation when needed. The best way to do this is to involve the individual and show appreciation for such involvement. Once the will is improved, then the devolve approach can be then re-employed.

Reminder attractor. Although the typical slip from high will/high skill is towards high skill/low will, occasionally the skill slips whilst the will remains. In other words the individual temporarily forgets, or discipline slips, or the context changes. This is typical in the situation when working habits have been recently changed, but sometimes the individual needs a nudge as a reminder. This is a gentle reminder, with the leader using a Tell before the individual can resume self-organised working and the leader can resume Devolve.

The paired periodic attractors can be summed up as shown in Figure 10.19. It should be noted that there are four dynamics at play, but that one can switch between them as the context (or even conversation) changes. The linking of such periodic attractors tends towards a strange attractor.

STRANGE ATTRACTOR

This is a mix of the basic point and periodic attractors shown in 10.8 and 10.9 above. It can be exemplified by the case study of Ken Sinfield and National Vulcan in the mid-1990s.[10] National Vulcan was an engineering and insurance subsidiary of Sun Alliance insurance group. Their business was split into making engineering safety inspections and providing engineering insurance. Clients ranged from corner garages to nuclear power stations. The company was struggling and was firmly rooted in the past. It was slow, very hierarchic and uncompetitive. Ken Sinfield was put in to turn their fortunes around. He

---

10   N. Obolensky, *Practical Business Re-engineering – Tools and Techniques for Achieving Effective Change* has the case study of National Vulcan's turnaround. It describes the first phases of change – the 'sell' and 'tell' phases.

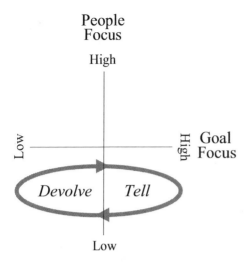

Figure 10.18   Reminder attractor using Tell and Devolve strategies

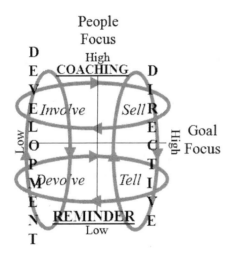

Figure 10.19   Summary of paired periodic attractors

turned around the company by first selling (S2 Sell) the need for change. Although most inside knew that there was a need for change, many found it hard to accept. He also had to sell the idea to the parent company that his change strategy could work. When the need for change was accepted, and support gained, he then spent the first year directing (S1 Tell) what needed to be done. This included moving some processes from three months to 24 hours. At the same time he formed cross-functional self-managed groups to design how the new targets were to be met (S3 Involve). By the end of the first phase of change the new targets had been achieved, and the company had been turned around leaving Ken Sinfield free to take a longer term view of the future (S4 Devolve).

What he saw was disturbing – National Vulcan had merely caught up with competitors, but would soon slip as the market become more demanding. The days of being a simple engineering and insurance company were numbered as clients were looking for more sophisticated risk management approaches. He then cycled through the process again. He formed a small team to look at the future and then present to his board what would happen if they did not change again (S3 Sell). This was hard to sell as the company had just been through two years of change and was successful again. However the long term analysis of the team was clear – it would not last. Once the need for change had been accepted, he formed a small team called the 2001 Team with consulting support and told them to design a process which would deliver a new strategy (S1 Tell). The Team acted as a facilitator which oversaw a process which involved all the workforce (S3 Involve). Having redesigned the strategy, Ken moved on to head up European Operations and handed over his role having achieved a major turnaround (S4 Devolve). This process of first selling why, then telling what and when, then involving for how, and then delegating for the implementation is a common 'strange attractor' for change management. The leader sells the why for change, tells the process, involves for the details and then devolves for the implementation whilst he looks ahead to spot the next change that comes along. When he sees it, he will invariably need to sell the need for change again. This is a cycle of continual innovation and evolution, and will help improve an organisation's chances of survival.

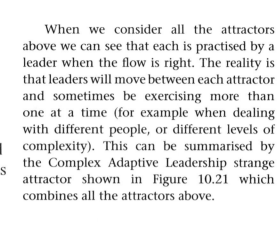

People
Focus
High

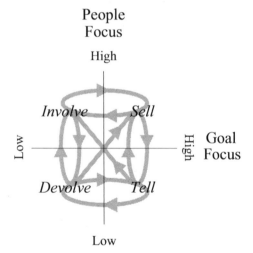

Figure 10.20 Typical change management strange attractor

People
Focus
High

Figure 10.21 Complex Adaptive Leadership summary strange attractor

When we consider all the attractors above we can see that each is practised by a leader when the flow is right. The reality is that leaders will move between each attractor and sometimes be exercising more than one at a time (for example when dealing with different people, or different levels of complexity). This can be summarised by the Complex Adaptive Leadership strange attractor shown in Figure 10.21 which combines all the attractors above.

Chapter Summary

This chapter has shown how Complex Adaptive Leadership works. In summary:

1. A roadmap for leadership can be drawn using the axes of People Focus and Goal Focus.
2. These two axes, when drawn as a phase space diagram, indicate four possible strategies that can be employed – Sell, Tell, Involve, Devolve.
3. The aim of Complex Adaptive Leadership is to enable the devolve style as much as possible.
4. A few simple rules matching people's (or indeed an organisation's) skill and will to the four possible strategies help lay a foundation of how to move followers to take the lead, and enable polyarchy to thrive.
5. The four basic strategies can be combined in numerous dynamic ways which can be illustrated by a variety of different attractors. This dynamic approach is the core to Complex Adaptive Leadership.

A Final Breather between Parts III and IV

Before we suggest a way to put these theories into day-to-day practice, let's just take a summary overview of Part III.

Here are the summaries from each of the chapters:

From Chapter 8

1. The distinction between 'leadership' and 'management' owes more to oligarchic assumption than to current polyarchic realities. But the distinction can serve a useful purpose, as each without the other is unsustainable. So one could say that 'leadership' and 'management' are on the same continuum, and it is all about leadership.
2. However, whilst we could roll 'management' into being part of 'leadership' the distinctions that each category assumed still exist. They can be re-categorised to action/focus needed for the people, and action/focus needed for the goal. Under this assumption, leadership is about developing people and ensuring goals are achieved.
3. This conclusion is similar to the Situational Leadership model, which sees leadership behaviour consisting of structuring and developing action aimed at task and relationship. A study of the results of the Situational Leadership questionnaire shows that leaders today are less than effective. Too much emphasis seems to be on 'Selling', and not enough on 'Delegating'.

From Chapter 9

1. Followership maturity can be defined as the extent to which a follower is prepared to take the lead and get on with what needs to be done without leadership provided by an ascribed leader.
2. A follower needs a high degree of skill and will in order for this to happen. Skill is the knowledge needed to do the job (technical content) as well as how to go about it (operational process). Will is the motivation to do the work, as well as the motivation to do it without supervision.
3. Followers will move between different states of skill and will. This demands a different approach by the leader to move them back towards high skill and high will.
4. Skill/will should not be seen in isolation of the other Four + Four principles – a high degree of skill and will is not much use if the objectives are unclear.

5. Maturity can also be seen in terms of the levels of followership an individual is. The best level, the 'point attractor', is level 5 and high skill/high will.

From Chapter 10

1. A roadmap for leadership can be drawn using the axes of People Focus and Goal Focus.
2. These two axes, when drawn as a phase space diagram, indicates four possible strategies that can be employed – Sell, Tell, Involve, Devolve.
3. The aim of Complex Adaptive Leadership is to enable the devolve style as much as possible.
4. A few simple rules matching people's (or indeed an organisation's) skill and will to the four possible strategies helps lay a foundation of how to move followers to take the lead, and enable polyarchy to thrive.
5. The four basic strategies can be combined in numerous dynamic ways which can be illustrated by a variety of different attractors. This dynamic approach is the core to Complex Adaptive Leadership.

So what? The approach of Complex Adaptive Leadership is to recognise that complexity has an underlying order which can be harnessed. So whilst self-organisation and polyarchy may look chaotic they are in fact not. However, to ensure that the chaos follows the scientific and mathematical definition, rather than the common one (that is, complete disorder), there are some simple approaches which can be undertaken. These include recognising the interplay between some basic strategies and the maturity of the followers and organisations that one leads. It also means that in order for polyarchy to thrive, the leader needs to aim at a devolved style. In reality this style is only ever temporarily achieved and so a dynamic between the four strategies occurs. Hopefully this makes clearer the point made way back in the Preface that polyarchy is not about getting rid of oligarchy, but is a paradoxical mix of oligarchy (traditional leadership) and anarchy (chaos).

PART IV

Looking Forward and Other Interests

CHAPTER 11

Beyond This Book – the Choices You Have ...

This chapter does not have an introductory exercise, quick test or thought experiment as it is an exercise! There are two parts:

- Transition from Ha-Ha through Ah-Ha to Yee-Ha!
- KISS.

'Ha-Ha' Through 'Ah-Ha' to 'Yee-Ha'

Reading this book may have been interesting and even fun. Let's hope it was, as every author would like to think, an engaging and interesting read. But if that is all it has done for you it has been at the 'Ha-Ha' level – intellectually useful but not much more. A bit of entertainment. Ha-Ha. Not to say that this is unimportant – having a laugh or an entertaining read is a good foundation of the next step! After all if something is dull and no fun it is unlikely to engage.

The next level is that you may have recognised some things, or been excited by some of the concepts. You may have found some insights, or been struck by others. 'Ah-Ha' you think and feel. These are the insights that can make a difference to you. There are no right or wrongs – the insights you have are the ones that you have! But you need to make a note of them and recognise something that might lead to action...

The next stage is to move towards action. You have generally been intellectually stimulated (Ha-Ha – Mind, Intellect). You see an exciting insight ('Ah-Ha!' – Heart, Emotion), and think 'I need to *do* something about this.' You want to charge over the hill and do something with what insights you have gained. 'Yee-Ha' – Hands, Behaviour.

So the choice you have, having read this book, is to stick at any of those three levels:

- Ha-Ha – a good read – perhaps it helped pass the time on a (very) long flight; this is engaging the mind – the intellect.
- Ah-Ha – some good insights that made an emotional connection; this is having a feeling/emotion about it, and the heart begins to be engaged.
- Yee-Ha – a desire actually to do something about some of the things you have picked up in this book. This is what leads to the hands doing something, actual behaviour. Here the heart is engaged and new knowledge becomes belief.

Assuming the choice is 'Yee-Ha', the question then is: How to go about this? That leads us to KISS – Keep, Increase, Start, Stop.

KISS

KISS will be a familiar mnemonic to many. It often stands for 'Keep It Short and Simple', or 'Keep It Simple, Stupid'. Hopefully this book has shown that one should embrace complexity and chaos rather than avoid it by trying to keep things simple! So I propose a new version of KISS.

There are things that you have probably recognised in this book. Maybe stuff that you have read and you have thought: 'Ha! I always thought I was doing that right – and now I know why.' This book must have reinforced some things that you are already doing. These are your 'Keep' actions. Keep doing them!

There are some things that you have read that you are doing, but perhaps you recognise that you are not doing enough. For example, you could be using some of the questioning approach suggested in Chapter 4, but now you recognise that you are not doing enough of it. These are the things you should 'Increase'.

There could be things that you have come across for the first time. Or perhaps some of your insights have led you to think that you should do something that you have not done before. These are the things you could 'Start'.

And finally, there may be some things you are doing, but you now realise that in fact you should not. Perhaps this could include the idea of always answering subordinates' questions with straight answers when they ask what to do (rather than moving them to level 5 followership, explained in Chapter 9). Or it could be that you always thought leaders should 'lead'. These are things that you can 'Stop'.

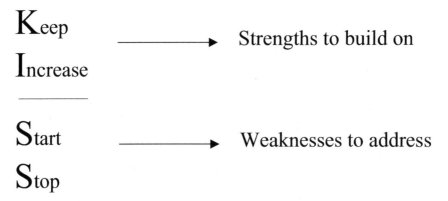

Figure 11.1 KISS: Keep, Increase, Start and Stop

As can be seen from Figure 11.1, the first two parts of KISS are about strengths – these are things that you do well or can do well but need to do more of. The Stop/Starts are about weaknesses or opportunities to improve what you already do. You need to have as many stop/starts as keep/increases. And you need more stops than starts – specific actions rather than aspirations.

Previous chapters started with an exercise. This one ends with one:

> Consider the key insights you have gained from this book. Reflect on them or jot them down. Now answer the following four questions:
>
> - In relation to Complex Adaptive Leadership what are you already doing well that you should **K**eep up?
> - What can you do well but are not doing enough so you should **I**ncrease?
> - What are you not doing but you could, so you should **S**tart doing?
> - What are you doing that is not actually needed, or does not help so should **S**top?

The answers to the four questions above are the *most* important things from this book. And the most important of the four is the final one 'Stop'.[1] In handling complexity, leaders tend to grip more and try to get more control which leads to a huge amount of waste. The average executive can save one to two days a week for more valuable things if the lessons in this book are taken on board fully. Compared to these identified actions all the rest of the book is grapes or froth, but the answers to the above is the wine or beer. I wish you the best of luck! There is a mobile phone app ('ComplexAdaptiveLeadership') available for free where you can share with others your experience of using the approaches in this book, and what does and does not work. I hope you will add your experience and views.

---

1   See how powerful the 'Stop' approach can be in the book by Mathew May (2013) and many others called *The Laws of Subtraction – Six Simple Rules for Winning*, McGraw-Hill.

Appendix A:
The Insights of Tao and Buffalo Maps

The Taoist Yin/Yang symbol has been used a few times throughout this book. Chapter 1 has also given some outline of Taoism. This appendix is intended to build on the points already made, as well as lift out of the *Tao Te Ching* some parts of the ancient text which seem relevant.

As has been seen in the main body of this book, the Yin/Yang model shows how the concepts of 'complementary opposites' and 'Both/And' work. They demonstrate how paradox can work, and how opposites can co-exist to produce deeper meaning. This has been shown in the figures earlier in this book:

- Figure 1.2   The power of Yin/Yang opposites.
- Figure 3.3   Possible evolution of personal feedback within an organisation.
- Figure 4.3   Breaking the charade via challenge and support.
- Figure 5.3   Yin/Yang – chaos and order.
- Figure 6.2   Yin/Yang and the Four + Four model for leading complexity.
- Figure 7.12   Yin/Yang of the Four + Four.
- Figure 8.2   Leadership vs. management – Take 2.
- Figure 10.5   Leadership roadmap and Yin/Yang.

As Figure A.1 shows below, the symbol has two sides – a dark side (Yin) and a light side (Yang). Each side also has an element (small circle) of the other. This is to accentuate the fact that these two opposites both co-exist and have within themselves an element of their opposite. How many times has one seen leaders grappling with dilemmas? Perhaps it would help them if they realised that a dilemma can often be a sign of a complementary opposite in action. So within the two opposites there is the potential of a deeper and more powerful truth. A metaphorical example of this is a light bulb – do we argue and debate about which charge, positive or negative, is better? No, we just turn on the light!

Figure A.1   The Yin/Yang model of Tao

In verse 28 of the *Tao Te Ching*, Lau Tzu advises one to: *'Understand the thrust of the Yang, but be more like the Yin in your being.'*[1]

---

1   L. Tsu, *Tao Te Ching*, trans. M.H. Kwok, eds M. Palmer and J. Rosemary.

He seems to suggest that whilst the Yang approach is needed and needs to be fully understood, implementation lies in the Yin. This certainly accords with Complex Adaptive Leadership which sees the 'S4 Devolve' strategy (more Yin than Yang) as the one to aim for (as a point attractor), but tough action may be needed along the way. It also accords with the underlying dynamic of polyarchy being one of self-organisation and seemingly chaotic action (Yin). Tough knowledge and intention, gentle with people and action.

So the yin/yang symbol has some use when grappling with the paradox of chaotic order. But Taoism also offers some insights into leadership itself. When one reads the *Tao Te Ching*,[2] there is much advice relevant to polyarchy. It is almost as if the writer saw that the role of the leader is to enable others to take the lead, while doing little but going with the flow, and being part of the flow. Many may think that this is a sort of minimalist approach of 'laissez faire' leadership. That would be a mistake. The quotation in Chapter 1 perhaps is the best one from the *Tao Te Ching* on leadership: it certainly is the most relevant for polyarchy. *'The worst leader is one that lies and is despised; Not much better is one that leads using oppression and fear; A little better is the leader who is visible, loved and respected; However, the best leader is one whom the people hardly knows exists, leaving them happy to say, once the aim is achieved, "We did it ourselves"'.*

Figure A.2　Emperor Kangxi's throne and 'wu wei'

This approach of 'wu wei', or 'wu wei ar zhe' – which can be translated as 'Effortless Leadership', runs deep in Chinese wisdom. Many Chinese entrepreneurs have it inscribed in gold on red in their office.[3] If you go to the Forbidden City in Peking, in the Inner Court in the Jiao Tai Dan (the Hall of Union and Peace) you will see the throne of the one of the most successful Emperors, Kangxi, above which is inscribed in large ancient Chinese characters in gold 'wu wei'. It should be noted that Emperor Kangxi was one of the most diligent and

2　　See footnote 1 above and also footnote 6 from Chapter 1.

3　　I am grateful to the Chinese venture capitalist Allan Liu of PAG Capital in Hong Kong for telling me this during a CAL seminar for CEOs that was run in Singapore in 2013.

hardest working – so 'wu wei' is not so much about doing nothing, but knowing when to act and when not to act, and how to go with the flow, or when to swim against it.

The approach was also used by the Tang dynasty as a way of ruling China, during which time China saw the largest growth and expansion in terms of trade.

So the movement towards Devolve as being the highest form of leadership is not new – what is new is that complexity science explains WHY and WHEN it can work and CAL shows HOW it can be done. The highest form of leadership does not need to be a mystery or shrouded in ancient Chinese wisdom which for many is impenetrable..

In addition to linking to 'wu wei', the *Tao Te Ching* has much else to offer on leadership and what it takes to enable polyarchy to thrive. Below are 14 similar quotations with a brief commentary.

The wise leader has no attachment to anything and therefore does what is right without speaking by simply being in the Tao. (verse 2)

This seems to suggest the need to 'let go' and not be attached. Perhaps in so doing the leader sets a powerful example where others might say: '*Your actions are so loud I don't need to hear what you say.*' Letting go is hard to do, as was discussed in Chapters 4 and 7. It is a crucial skill. It is not about 'not caring', it is about not being driven and choosing instead when to act with wisdom.

The wise leader's greatness lies in taking no credit. (verse 2)

This seems to echo the findings in Collins' study *Good to Great* where he found leaders of great companies would often ascribe success to others, whilst taking the blame for any shortcomings.

The wise leader restrains himself by not being greedy, by not dominating, and by keeping himself healthy and fit. (verse 3)

It seems the first two aspects, greed and domination, are all too common and even encouraged. Indeed some leaders see the acquisition of more wealth, and being seen as a driver of events, as something to be lauded. In a typical oligarchy this is understandable, but anathema to polyarchy. The final point of fitness is important – taking time to keep fit is important 'Mens sana, in corpore sano'.[4]

The wise leader guides his people by putting himself last. (verse 7)

Selflessness is hard to do as we are essentially selfish beings, driven by self-interest. However, putting others ahead of oneself is not necessarily to deny oneself and indeed can be aligned to self-interest as it is often rewarding. This is not about altruism or being a martyr but is about how leadership is about putting others ahead to get the best. Self-fulfilment through the service of others is well appreciated. It is not for nothing that the

---

4   Full quote from Juvenile Satires, no. 10, 1.356 '*Orandum est sit mens sana in corpore sano*' – You should pray to have a sound mind in a sound body.

motto of the Royal Academy Sandhurst is 'Serve to lead' – and every cadet will tell you it is the service of those who follow which is critical.

> *Like water, the wise leader waits for the moment to ripen and be right; water never fights, it flows around without harm. (verse 8)*

This is similar to the concept of 'wu wei' – the art of inaction, and right action at the right time and not before. Going around obstacles and not attacking head on also seems to resonate with Badaracco's 'Quiet Leadership'. Wu wei does not mean 'checking out' – one is still very much present and ready to act when needed.

> *If you follow Tao without pretension, you will never burn yourself out. (verse 15)*

Executive stress and burnout is all too common. However, much of it seems self-driven by a mistaken assumption that a leader needs to lead all the time, be in the know and know the solutions. Understanding the wider context and underlying dynamics helps an individual to 'go with the flow'.

> *The wise leader has the purest motives, and relies wholly on quiet and inner peace. (verse 16)*

Again this resonates with Collins' 'humility' and Badaracco's 'quietness'. The 'purest motives' are hard to tie down in a typical business as it begs the question what is a business for? The narrow definition of providing a return to shareholders can often lead to short-sighted and disastrous decisions. Perhaps a wider definition is to create value – for shareholders but also for employees, suppliers, customers and the wider community. And this needs a sense of higher purpose and a more inclusive approach. Such an approach was propagated by the RSA Tomorrow's Company inquiry in the UK, as well as the US study *Built to Last* and the Caux Roundtable in France. This provides insight into what a pure motive may look like, and resonates with Greenleaf's *Servant Leadership* approach.

> *Be true to yourself and all will go well with you. (verse 22)*

Moral integrity and staying true to one's deeper and better self is easier said than done, yet such a position seems to reflect the wisdom of many other philosophies. It takes great self-confidence as well, especially when it comes to admitting that perhaps one does not know the solutions to the problems one faces! This ancient wisdom has been echoed by many others, including Shakespeare's *Hamlet* '*This above all: to thine own self be true, And it must follow as night follows day, Thou canst not then be false to any man*' (Act 1, Sc 3, 1.68).

> *If a leader behaves as if he's invented the world, he will do no good at all … A wise leader abandons greed, false charm and every last iota of pride. (verse 29)*

Again this echoes verses 2 and 3 above, and reinforces the need to abandon ego. As was identified in Chapter 7, 'letting go' is a huge barrier. A key issue about letting go is the issue of ego and how that underpins the symptoms of fear, intention and unawareness.

> *Wu wei – this is the way to get things done. The best way to run the world is to let it take its course, and to get yourself out of the way of it. (verse 48)*

This is a key quotation and reinforces the concept of the 'S4' devolve strategy as being a natural point attractor for leadership. At first it is very counter-intuitive, as leadership supposes that a leader takes action to change the world, not be rolled over by it! But the subtlety is that a leader arranges the context so that things will run themselves, so that he can practise 'wu wei'. It also suggests that wisdom is not so much knowing when to act, but when not to act. The story of the CEO dealing with his myriad of e mails in Chapter 9 is a case in point!

The wise leader is never opinionated – he listens to the mind of the people. (verse 49)

This seems to echo the point made by Collins in his study *Good to Great* as well as the underlying logic shown by Surowiecki in his study *The Wisdom of Crowds*. Perhaps this point is more important than ever before. It echoes the point made in Chapter 4 (that the leader no longer knows the solutions, but his people often will). Hence the need to listen, and hold back one's own opinion until its needed.

The more rules you have, the more unhappy people will be. (verse 50)

This echoes the Four + Four principle of a 'few simple rules' highlighted in Chapter 7. Rules *are* necessary but the minimum should always be sought and planned with some intelligent thinking so that they can get the effect needed.

Ruling a big country is like cooking a small fish – you have to do it with care. (verse 60)

This seems to reflect the underlying law of complexity that a complex situation or organisation can be easily changed by a small input. This 'sensitivity to initial conditions' (as it is called, and explored in Chapter 7) means that one needs to be careful and think through the consequence of taking any given action.

A journey of a thousand miles starts with the first step. To act as if you know it all is catastrophic; and if you try to control it, you will stare into your empty hand. (verse 64)

This seems to emphasise the journey nature of leadership – and there is a healthy paradox. To take a step one needs to decide which way is best, but if one thinks one always knows what is best, that can lead to catastrophe. Perhaps the answer is to take a step and then be open enough to be ready to change direction.

Buffalo Maps

It might be a mistake to see the verses above, indeed the whole of this book, as a possible failsafe recipe, THE answer, an absolute way forward. The terrain is not the map and, although perhaps out of place from a cultural point of view re Taoism, a story from the Cheyenne Indians of North America may hold some wisdom. The story is called 'Buffalo maps' and is useful when faced with those seeking an actual answer and ultimate model.

The North American Indians depended on buffalo for their survival. They used the meat to eat, the skins to build their tepees and the fur to keep themselves warm. The system of survival was fairly simple. They would set up camp and then hunt for buffalo.

The buffalo were not stupid – when the Cheyenne moved in, they tended to move out. So the Cheyenne had to hunt from their camp and then it was a simple trade-off – how far did they need to go in order to find buffalos with how much energy expended, vs. how much energy would they expend to move the camp closer to the buffalo herds. A 'key success factor' was to find and kill buffalo, and to move camp in the right direction (when the buffalos were too far away). The initiation of young men into the tribe included the test for them to go and find a buffalo, kill it and bring it back. Such a day was full of great excitement, when the young men would have their faces and horses painted and, with loud whoops, they would canter off across the plain. But the further they got from camp, the more uncomfortable they became and the lower their spirits and bravery sank. For many, if not all of them, this was the first time they had left the safety of the camp, and as the tepees got lower and lower on the horizon behind them, so too often did their courage. When the tepees were low on the horizon, more often than not the young men would pull their horses into a turn and ride a wide and long circle around the camp, looking far onto the horizon and yet keeping the tepees just within sight. They would come back late that day to tell the chief that the buffalo were no longer in range so he had to move the camp. But the chief would send them to the Medicine Man saying there was a 'magic' buffalo map that would help them. So they went to the Medicine Man and he pulled out of his tepee a crinkled piece of buffalo skin with strange markings. He smoothed the 'map' out on the ground and said:

Pay attention. This map will help you find the buffalo. You see this mark here – this is where we are now. You see this ridge here – this is that line of hills low on the horizon over here. This mark here is the mountain you can see way over there. You will need water for your hunt, and you will find it at this point here. And you will find the buffalo in this region here…

With that he gave the map to the young men, who with renewed courage and much whooping would gallop off and disappear over the horizon. One or two days later they would reappear with a buffalo. And there would be great celebration and recounting of deeds and adventures they had along the way. The old Medicine Man would come and say 'Can I have my buffalo map back please…?' and more often than not the reply would be 'I do not have it, Running Bear had it last I think … But anyway, did you hear how we …'; and he would then ask Running Bear 'Do you have my buffalo map please …?' And the reply would be, 'No, I gave it to Stalking Wolf, but did you hear about the adventure we had on the way ….'. And the old Medicine Man would finally track the map down and the person giving it back would say 'Many thanks! Oh, by the way, the water was not here, it was there, and the buffalo were not where you said they would be, but we found them over here ….'

The moral? Much of what is written in this book, as in many others, can be simply seen as a buffalo map. It is not so much the truth it proposes that is important as the encouragement it can give to venture beyond a horizon, and to go further than one would normally feel comfortable … and when you cross that horizon you will be in a new place and see things differently and further than you have ever before. And with that journey I wish you luck!

Appendix B:
Polyarchy and Leadership Models[1]

Most leadership models have the assumption of oligarchy – leadership is done by a few leaders over many followers. In other words, leadership is done by leaders who are in a position of authority. It is a positional view of leadership which then assumes that, in order for them to acquit their role, leaders need special attributes and competencies. Nothing wrong with that – it has served us well and, more or less, continues widely. However as things become more complex there is a need for a wider view of leadership which engages many more in the endeavour of leadership. If polyarchy is fast replacing the old oligarchic assumptions, does this make these old leadership models redundant? In other words, can traditional leadership models be used under a completely different assumption to that upon which they were based? Many such models exist. Older and more traditional models such as Greenleaf's *Servant Leadership*, Hersey/Blanchard's 'Situational Leadership' and John Adair's 'Task–Team–Individual' models are well known and seem to have withstood the test of time. Newer models such as Collins' 'Level 5 Leadership'[2] and Badaracco's 'Quiet Leadership'[3] are beginning to show that a different type of leadership is needed. We have already seen in Chapter 8 how polyarchy can add a further dimension to the Situational Leadership model. And frequent reference has been made to the work of Collins. This appendix will consider John Adair's model[4] using a polyarchic assumption. This will show how in detail another traditional leadership model can be seen in a new light using a different assumption. It may also explain why new ways of looking at leadership, such as Collins' 'Level 5 Leadership' and Badaracco's 'Quiet Leadership', are beginning to emerge.

John Adair's model suggests that the role of the leader is to attend to the needs of the Task, Team and Individual. The leader is at the centre, holding the strands of these sometimes conflicting interests. The leader's role is to ensure these needs are balanced and aligned – no easy feat (see Figure B.1).

To do this the leader needs a variety of skills, attributes and competencies:

- **Task.** He needs to have a technical knowledge of the task in hand. Such technical knowledge can be specific professional knowledge for the task in hand (for example, legal, engineering, manufacturing, retailing and so on), as well as more general knowledge for his own leadership development. For example, in business much value is placed on having an MBA, and it seems to have become a Sine Qua Non for those wishing to progress.

---

1   This Appendix was originally prepared for a series edited by Professor Jonathan Gosling at the Centre for Leadership Studies University of Exeter. I would like to acknowledge the advice of anonymous reviewers in that process, who have contributed to whatever is of merit here.

2   J. Collins, 'Level 5 Leadership'.

3   J.L. Badaracco, *Leading Quietly: An Unorthodox Guide to Doing the Right Thing*.

4   See J. Adair, *The Action Centred Leader*.

- **Team.** An understanding of team dynamics and how the whole can be greater than the sum of the parts.
- **Individual.** An ability to connect and motivate differing people and how each person can best achieve.

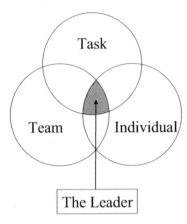

Figure B.1   John Adair's Leadership model (adapted)

So far, so oligarchic. If we applied a polyarchic view then a complementary picture could emerge as seen by the possible model below. Instead of the leader acting as a bridge and vital link between task–team–individual, leadership as a dynamic can be the concern for all. This demands new skills and knowledge of *all* the players. The skills and knowledge that hitherto were the concern and, to some extent, privilege of the leader need now to be widened to be the concern of all. That might sound ideal but it is a common factor in many organisations that are more polyarchic in their approach. Springfield Remanufacturing Corporation (SRC Inc.) in the USA was mentioned in Chapter 7 as practising 'open book management' – people in that company understand the numbers and what they mean. Figure B.2 shows how other possible (and by no means exhaustive) areas of knowledge used by all the players can be overlaid onto John Adair's model. The role of the leader, given the co-existence of oligarchic assumption and polyarchic realities, is perhaps to enable this knowledge to become widely held and day-to-day practice.

When such knowledge becomes more widely known the strains between the assumption of oligarchy and reality of polyarchy become eased, and leadership can be exercised in a more effective way. In such an organisation a person may be leading one

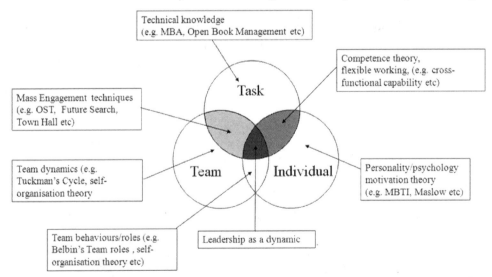

Figure B.2   After John Adair's model (adapted) – a possible extension and example of skills

day, and following those he leads the next without any strain or effort. This may sound idealistic but in Oticon Headquarters in Copenhagen it is every day practice. A person could be leading a project team on one day, leading and guiding a project team member who, on the next day, is leading him in another project.[5]

This widening of knowledge is evidenced by the growth of self-managed teams, and the distribution of power where teams sometimes do not have a boss (for example, Cygnet, in Scotland), can select their own bosses (as happens in Oticon in Denmark) or, more radically, 'sack' their boss (as we saw happens in Chapter 5 and W.L. Gore & Associates in the UK). Even those organisations who do not have such a thing as 'self-managed' teams often do off-site team building (to enhance team skills using instruments such as Belbin) or off-site workshops (to enhance technical understanding and decision making).

John Adair's model also includes seven functions of leadership as shown in Figure B.3. One almost sees the implicit process which their order seems to imply within an oligarchy. The leader (no doubt informed by the vertical flows of information, as well as a horizontal appreciation of the context) defines the task that needs to be done. The next step will be for the leader to plan the action, and decide who will do what, when, where and if necessary, how. When that is decided, the next stage will be for the leader to brief the subordinates, ensuring each understands their role and how it fits within the overall context. Once the action starts, the leader controls by keeping a close eye on what is going on and stepping in to correct if needed. The leader is ready to issue any further corrective instructions. Although he may involve others, especially in the decision making, he is responsible for the provision of the necessary functional actions and therefore the meeting of the three overlapping areas.

Functions of Leadership
- Defining the task
- Planning
- Briefing
- Controlling
- Supporting
- Informing
- Reviewing

Figure B.3   John Adair's Functions of Leadership (1)

He supports his subordinates by, amongst other things, lending advice (as he is invariably more experienced and knowledgeable), and is kept informed (as well as informing upwards and if needed sideways in the organisation) of progress and problems. Once the task is achieved, he leads a review session to ensure task completion to original specifications, as well as to uncover any lessons learnt for continuous improvement. So far, so oligarchic.

How would these functions operate in a polyarchy? The key difference is that under a polyarchy the leader *ensures* the process rather than *doing* the process, which is implied under an oligarchic assumption.

So the leader moves away from content to process. Before one looks at how these functions would work in a polyarchy, one needs to reiterate that for the functions to work

---

5   N. Obolensky, *Practical Business Re-engineering.*

Oligarchy

Functions done
by the leader
Leader focused
on providing content

Functions of Leadership
• Defining the task
• Planning
• Briefing
• Controlling
• Supporting
• Informing
• Reviewing

Polyarchy

Functions done
by the individuals
Leader focused
on ensuring process

Figure B.4   John Adair's Functions of Leadership (2) (adapted)

well in that context, the other Four + Four principles described in Chapter 7 need to be in place. Assuming that they are, the functions of leadership could operate like this:

a) **Defining the task.** As Ricardo Semler points out in his article 'How We Went Digital Without a Strategy', once individuals fully understand the context within which they operate, the task which is needed to be done can be defined and clarified by those involved, rather than waiting for a leader to do so. There is often a resource issue, so the decision is really about which task has the priority. Task decisions are not only reactive to contextual needs but can also be proactive, allowing innovation to occur. Perhaps the most famous exemplar process of this is 3M's 'skunk works' which allows each employee 15 per cent of his time and available resources to be devoted to pet projects. Thus staff are encouraged to take the lead and define new products – the most well-known which resulted from this was the Post-it™ note.

b) **Planning.** Whilst planning in an oligarchy tends to be 'top down', in a polyarchy it is more bottom-up. An example of this is Nonaka's 'top-down-bottom-up management'.[6] Once the direction and task is clear, those responsible for execution need to be involved in the planning in a dynamic way. The detail of who, what, when, where and how need to be clear. In a polyarchy, planning might take a bit more time, and resemble at times a chaotic negotiation – but once the plan is set it will have a greater chance of success. Accountability will be sharper. After all, if a leader's plan fails, the followers can blame the leader – if a polyarchic plan fails, the individuals only have themselves to blame.

c) **Briefing.** This is mainly concurrent with planning as those involved are self-briefed. This function is less important in a polyarchy than in an oligarchy, save for the wider briefing across boundaries for those not involved but indirectly affected. The responsibility for this is best done by those actually doing the task (as they know the detail) and time needs to be set aside for communication activities. Practically, however, this role is more important for leaders in an oligarchy.

d) **Controlling and informing.** In a polyarchic system the functions of controlling and informing are almost hand-in-hand, as it is the free flow of information that

---

6   Nonaka and Takeuchi describe in their book *The Knowledge-Creating Company* many examples of planning processes which are much more dynamic than the traditional linear top down 'cascade' approach. The key is participation – for this to occur, leadership needs to be exercised at all levels.

provides the controls. In a polyarchy, horizontal peer pressure is more obvious and important than vertical pressure from superiors. If performance is lagging, rules broken, boundaries crossed, targets missed then corrective action is exercised by those 'around' the problem rather than by those 'above' it. Processes can be put in place to help this occur, an example being the team compensation-based policies at Nucor in the USA.[7] In SRC in the USA and Oticon in Denmark information is available, shared and transparent – for this to work, everyone needs to have the skills to be able to understand the information.

e) **Supporting and reviewing.** Again in a polyarchy these two functions tend to go hand-in-hand. As processes become more dynamic, 360 degree review and real-time feedback become a key function. However, those in a leadership role still have a part to play. Setting an example (what Daniel Goleman would call 'authoritative' leadership) and coaching are key roles. Indeed the research by Goleman and the Hay Consultancy shows that such leadership gets the best results.[8] Support via peers is very powerful. The process of peer review in BP for example was instrumental in its turnaround.[9]

So it can be seen that in a polyarchy the seven functions of John Adair operate in a more dynamic way than in an oligarchy, and that the functions *are still needed*. The loop is closed by the review process which should clarify the next task that is needed. This dynamic is illustrated in Figure B.5.

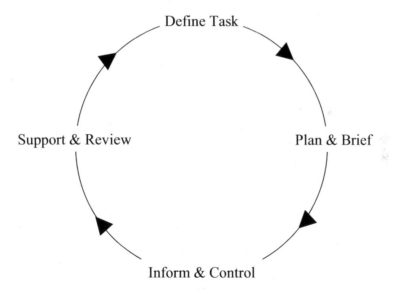

Figure B.5 John Adair's Functions of Leadership – polyarchic dynamic

---

7   Over 50 per cent of the compensation of the steel workers at Nucor is based on team performance. This helps support a team self-led culture. In one extreme example, team-mates chased a lazy member out of the plant with an angle iron!

8   See footnote 8 of Chapter 8.

9   At a seminar at London Business School in 2002, Rodney Chase (the then number two at BP) reported that the peer review process put into the company helped those business units that needed support to improve more than anything else. The process was so successful it was formalised further and units were organised into peer review groups where the compensation of the top performers is partly decided by the performance of those bottom performers that they are responsible for coaching.

For this to work it needs leaders who know how and when to follow as well as to lead, and followers who know how and when to lead as well as to follow. An understanding of how polyarchy can work will differ in each organisation as each one has its own experience and unique perspective. But as has been shown, traditional leadership models and practices can be seen in a new light. The key is to have the Four + Four principles in place, which includes the skill and the will of both leaders and followers to act in new ways. A possible way of seeing how these principles work together is shown by using the Task–Team–Individual model of John Adair in Figure B.6 below.

Adair's Principles: Four + Four	Task	Team	Individual
Underlying meaningful purpose	Each task supports purpose – consistent rationale	A unifying meaning which lends meaning and passion for the whole team to share	A compelling 'get out of bed' motivation which endures regardless of current task
Explicit simple objectives	Objectives support the task in hand and all involved understand how their part fits into greater task achievement	Inter-dependencies identified for all the team to understand how the individuals fit into the team success	Clear responsibility and accountability with individual having full authority for that which he/she is responsible for
Freedom to act	Ability for players to decide how the task is done with the what linked to the contextual need	Team to plan the action together allowing key decisions to be taken at team level, with full dialogue, debate and ensuing agreement	Individual allowed to express creativity and expected to take initiative if situation needs it
Boundaries to confine	The limit of the action with links to other upstream/downstream activities understood across the boundaries	Limit of team members – clarity with who is full and part time, and if part time exactly when. Inter-dependency with other teams (if applicable) understood	Individual role understood within limit of what is expected when to what quality, and interdependency of others understood
People's skill/will	Skill aligned to technical need of task and will aligned to underlying meaning and enjoyment	Team as a whole to have all the skills needed and ability to sustain their motivation and morale	Individual skill aligned to role and responsibility, as well as self-discipline and motivation
Organisation's few simple rules	Standard Operating Procedures to simplify repetitive task and understood process to manage exceptions with clear standards for what has to be achieved	Team ground rules and values fully understood for governing how the team work together	Blend of the rules of what and how as pertains for each individual, also depending on feedback (see below)

Figure B.6   Four + Four overlaid onto John Adair's model

Adair's Principles: Four + Four	Task	Team	Individual
Ambiguity/chaos	Enough flexibility in task to allow for fast moving and changing context	Team flexibility to allow changing roles and composition, as well as adaptability to let go when needed	Individual comfort with ambiguity and chaos, and ability to adapt, improvise and overcome
Unambiguous open feedback	Metrics and measuring process in place to allow progress to be understood for the what	Metrics and team feedback process for the how, including team dynamics and behaviours – use of 360 degree instruments	Blend of what is being achieved and how behaviours are seen by others clear to each individual

Figure B.6 Four + Four overlaid onto John Adair's model *concluded*

Appendix C:
Polyarchy and the Relevance to Modern Political Leadership

Introduction

The main focus of this book has been on the relevance of Complex Adaptive Leadership and polyarchy to the leadership of organisations. However, there is also a wider relevance to political leadership. After all, polyarchy's academic use has been mainly in the sphere of political philosophy. So a study of polyarchy without any political consideration would be barren, even if a study like this considers polyarchy in a different way. This appendix takes some of the conclusions of the book and considers their possible relevance to political leadership. The main conclusions brought into this appendix, and the potential questions raised, are as follows:

- **From Chapter 2.** Recent times have witnessed a divergence, or bifurcation, between the underlying assumptions of what leadership is and the reality of the radically changed context within which leadership is practised. Questions raised: *So does this mean the process of politicians being voted in every few years working in an oligarchic way (that is, 'leading' the country from the top) is actually the best way for a country to be 'led'? Is the periodic election of a representative oligarchy the best way for a democracy to uncover and implement the solutions it needs both to resolve the issues it faces and to advance society? Is elected representation the only route for people to govern themselves democratically?*
- **From Chapter 3.** Meanwhile, linked to this change of environment, organisations have become flatter, less hierarchic, and the 'death of deference' has occurred.[1] Questions raised: *Would this explain why in modern day democracies a significant number of voters do not bother to vote, whilst those who do vote seem to expect too much of their politicians? Are politicians and electorates becoming increasingly estranged, and, if so, is there any way such a divergent course can be reversed?*
- **From Chapter 4.** These changes have led to tensions. This is mainly due to leaders often no longer knowing the solutions to the problems faced by the organisations they lead. However, they frequently pretend to know because they (and others) think they should know. Meanwhile followers, who often know the solutions, typically wait/expect to be led. Such a charade is going on in most organisations. Questions raised: *Are we absolving ourselves from social responsibility, when we vote every few years and then not get involved except as on-lookers in the issues that really matter? Would this*

---

1   Ted Heath is reputed to have said that the programme 'That Was The Week That Was' caused the death of deference in British society. The death of deference certainly has been reported widely.

explain why the media often have a field day when politicians prove to be less than perfect? Could these tensions explain why the politicians seem driven more by media hype than by firm principles or the wider held views of the so called 'silent majority'?

- **From Chapter 5.** The traditional dynamic between leader and follower has changed, the leader needs to encourage the follower to take the lead. Followers need to learn how to lead, and leaders need to learn how to follow. Letting go is the biggest barrier. Questions raised: *Is there a way where instead of the politicians wishing the electorate would engage with politics, the politicians can engage more fully with the electorate? Is there a way politicians can work hard to enable the will of the people to be followed, rather than work hard to lead the people to follow their will?*

- **And from Part III.** This situation requires a dynamic and more complex, chaos-theory-based approach to leadership. Questions raised: *Are we at a crossroad where the very way a democracy is led and run is about to witness fundamental change? Is there a better, more engaging way for a democracy to self-organise in a complex adaptive way? Can the theories of Complex Adaptive Leadership considered earlier in this volume be applied to political leadership within a democracy?*

Some of these questions may seem provocative or unrealistic. But many have begun to question the efficacy of modern political systems. We saw in Chapter 2 how leadership assumptions have become static. As far as politics is concerned the situation seems to be the same. This is what a paper published by Domaine de Nianing said about current politics:

Cultural transformations and technical innovations are taking place at phenomenal pace. However, social and political thinking and acting has remained practically unchanged and is now so out of touch with reality as to be, like a broken machine, out of order, that is useless.[2]

This state of affairs may explain why some commentators have a less than optimistic outlook. For example, Patterson wrote in *The Vanishing Voter*:

What remains of democracy is largely the right to choose among commodities. Business leaders have long explained the need to impose on the population a 'philosophy of futility' and lack of purpose in life, to concentrate human attention on the more superficial things that comprise much of fashionable consumption.[3]

This is similar to what Chomsky wrote in his *Hegemony or Survival*:

Deluged by such propaganda from infancy, people may then accept their meaningless and subordinate lives and forget ridiculous ideas about managing their own affairs. They abandon their fate to corporate managers and the PR industry and, in the political realm, to the self-described 'intelligent minorities' who serve and administer power.[4]

---

2   'Polyarchy: A paradigm', published by Domaine de Nianing (Novara-Oxford-Bydgoszcz-Bern-Zürich) 2002–2005, <http://www.polyarchy.org>, accessed: 21 April 2010.

3   T. Patterson, *The Vanishing Voter*.

4   N. Chomsky, *Hegemony or Survival*.

Despite the misgivings above, this appendix assumes the best approach to leading nations is still democracy, and a snapshot will be taken of the state of democracy at the turn of the twenty-first century. The UK will be used as the primary example. Its movement towards democracy has, unlike other nations, been an evolutionary one, so it can serve as a founder example of parliamentary democracy.

When the conclusions outlined above are applied within the context of modern day politics, a picture emerges which shows how democracy has moved away from its foundations and has become corrupted. There is a need to revitalise and even redefine democracy and change how it is practised. This would include moving more towards polyarchy and the use of self-organisation. Norman Johnson from Los Alamos concluded:

> *Because our world is quickly becoming more complex, often changing faster than we can evaluate the changes let alone respond to them, the process of collective self-organisation may be the only option.*[5]

It is often said that democracy may not be perfect, but it is the best we have. That does not mean that it cannot be a lot better! Before this is fully considered, it is useful to look at polyarchy in a traditional political way.

'Traditional' Polyarchy

As was highlighted in Chapter 1, polyarchy is an old term but is not very much used or even recognised. Hitherto it has mainly been used in political science. The main proponent of polyarchy within modern political thought has been Robert Dahl, who did much work in the late 1960s/early 1970s.[6] His definition of polyarchy was a narrow one, and he saw it as a manifestation of an unrealised ideal of democracy. He saw polyarchy as made up of two aspects of democracy: opposition and participation.

- **Opposition.** This is defined as the extent to which opposition to those leading the country is tolerated, and the extent to which such opposition can be freely expressed. Dahl called this public contestation, which needs a commensurate level of liberalisation.
- **Participation.** This is defined as the extent to which people are free to participate in the political leadership of the country – this is measured by the extent to which people have the right to vote, and the possibility to stand (UK) or run (USA) for political office themselves. Dahl called this inclusiveness.

---

5   N.L. Johnson, 'Collective Problem Solving – Functionality beyond the Individual'.

6   Robert Alan Dahl (born 17 December 1915), is the Sterling Professor emeritus of political science at Yale University, where he earned his PhD in political science in 1940. He has often been described as 'the Dean' of American political scientists. He earned this title by his prolific writing output and the fact that scores of prominent political scientists studied under him. In *How Democratic is the American Constitution?* (2002) he argued that the constitution is much less democratic than it ought to be, given that its authors were operating from a position of 'profound ignorance' about the future. However, he adds that there is little or nothing that can be done about this 'short of some constitutional breakdown, which I neither foresee nor, certainly, wish for'. In some ways his observations reflect that gap which is becoming more apparent as polyarchic (my definition, not Dahl's!) realities impede oligarchical assumptions.

When these two aspects of political polyarchy are mapped, four broad types (or extremes) of regime emerge as shown in Figure C.1 below. These types are perhaps extremes, as many countries will fit somewhere in the middle ground. However, as a broad consideration of approaches to political leadership, it is a useful map.

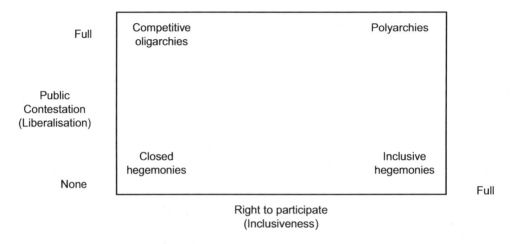

Figure C.1   Political definition of polyarchy[7]

With regards to Figure C.1 above, Dahl states:

Democracy might be conceived as lying at the upper right corner. But since democracy may involve more dimensions than the two in the Figure, and since (in my view) no large system in the real world is fully democratized, I prefer to call real world systems that are closest to the top right hand corner polyarchies ... (they) may be thought of as relatively (but incompletely) democratized regimes ... Some readers will doubtless resist the term polyarchy as an alternative to the word democracy, but it is important to maintain the distinction between democracy as an ideal system and the institutional arrangements that have come to be regarded as a kind of imperfect approximation of an ideal ...[7]

So, for Dahl, democracy is an as yet unrealised ideal and polyarchy is the actual 'imperfect' approximated reality which demonstrates the two aspects of opposition and participation. The four possible states, with examples, are as follows:

- **Closed hegemony.** Dahl uses the term hegemony as he sees it as 'more appropriate than terms such as hierarchic, absolutist, autocratic, despotic, authoritarian, totalitarian etc.'[8] His suggested synonyms show what he sees hegemony meaning. It essentially means a system where people do not have a say, and opposition is not tolerated. An example of this would be the Soviet Union under Stalin.
- **Competitive hegemony.** Although public debate and discord are accepted, the ability for people actually to change anything is limited. Those involved in 'running' the country and having political access are limited in number, and people do not

---

7   Ibid., pp. 8–9.

8   Ibid., p. 9, footnote 4.

have a vote. An example of this may be, for example, the Southern USA where Negroes did not have the vote until the late 1960s, even though in some states they constituted the majority.[9]

- **Inclusive hegemony.** This may include wide elections and yet the tolerance to public opposition and debate is low. An example of such a state could be post-Stalinist USSR or China towards the end of the twentieth century: elections were held for officials, yet there was effectively only one party and, as events in Tienneman Square showed, opposition was not tolerated.
- **Polyarchy.** This is described by Dahl above, who sees it as one would normally see a modern 'Western' democratic state.

So democracy and polyarchy are clearly linked within the political context. If one accepted polyarchy as an ideal (or, as proposed in Chapter 1, a Hegelian dialectic evolving out of anarchy and oligarchy) then democracy in the political sense could be seen in part as its actuality. In other words, Dahl's treatment can be turned on its head, even if this was on the face of it a purely semantic exercise. Polyarchy can be seen as an ideal which is emerging, whilst democracy can be seen as its imperfect current expression. Another possible way of looking at democracy is as a transitional device allowing the evolution between pure oligarchy (Dahl's closed hegemony) and pure polyarchy. After all, democracy has elements of an oligarchy, but it is one which is voted in by the people. Many democracies also have a mixed market economy of both a centralised public sector (mainly in health, education, law and order, defence, and so on) and a decentralised market-based private sector. It is interesting to note that the trend towards more dynamic private sector involvement has been increasing; many areas of state nationalised industries have been given over to the private sector. Some, however, would see this as merely a transition of power from one elite group to another. Be that as it may, the traditional view of the private sector being private, and the public sector being public, is also slowly being turned on its head. For example, most of the private sector companies quoted on the stock markets are owned in large part by the pension funds (who account certainly for the largest share) – and whose pensions are they anyway (that is, the people's)?[10] Sadly the way they are typically managed is hardly representative or effective.[11]

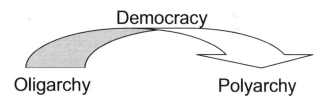

Figure C.2   Democracy as a bridge between oligarchy and polyarchy

---

9   For example, in the 1860s, the percentage of slaves in the southern states of the USA was high. In South Carolina they numbered 57 per cent and 55 per cent in Mississippi. Dahl, *Polyarchy: Participation and Opposition*, p. 93, footnote 5.

10   The hope that an increased ownership of equities by pension funds would herald a new form of economic liberalism has been questioned (see for example L. Cerri, 'Why the Emergence of Pension Funds in Europe Does Not Enhance Economic Democracy: The Question of Corporate Ownership and the Structural Contradictions of Liberalism'). Be that as it may, pension funds are the largest group owning equities and, for example, in the UK prior to 1997 owned 30 per cent of all UK equities although after 1997 this dropped a little (S.R. Bond, M.P. Devereux and A. Klemm, 'The Effects of Dividend Taxes on Equity Prices: A Re-examination of the 1997 UK Tax Reform').

11   See F.F. Reichheld and T. Teal, *The Loyalty Effect – The Hidden Force Beyond Growth, Profits and Lasting Value*: 'The biggest players in the growth of institutional stock ownership are the pension funds and most are managed in precisely the manner you find so destructive and destabilising. On any given day, pension funds account for half the trading on the New York stock exchange'.

This supposition is not beyond the realms of reasonableness and would broadly accord with Dahl's view. The argument would be that political leadership in the far past was typically exercised by the few (for example, in the UK, by the royal family and aristocracy). As time moved on past the Middle Ages, and as education and talent became more widely dispersed, this leadership was shared more widely (in the UK as an example) with parliament. As education and society evolved further, universal suffrage widened towards the modern day democracy, with full universal suffrage in the twentieth century in the UK. Such a 'journey' is shown schematically on Dahl's map in Figure C.3 below.[12]

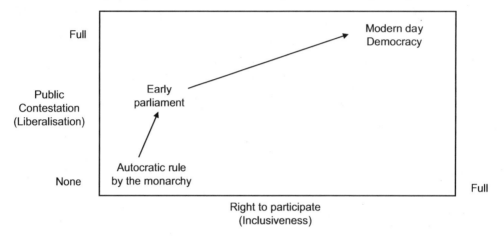

Figure C.3   Example of UK according to Dahl's theory

However, if one took the *reality* of participation and opposition, rather than their existence in theory, a disturbing picture emerges, posing clear challenges for modern day democracies ...

The Challenge

The underlying assumption regarding leadership for Dahl is still oligarchic, an assumption shared by modern day democracy. We still talk of the President of the USA as the 'most powerful man in the world', and of the Prime Minister 'running the country'. The 'running' of the country is oligarchic with a hierarchy of ministers/senators/senior politicians, senior civil servants, middle management and so on. The actual reality may be different, but the living assumption, symbols and structures remain

But what is the reality? Are so-called democracies 'run' by politicians? Or do modern states reflect, on a wider and greater scale, the same sort of tensions reflected in complex organisations? As seen in Chapter 3, power has diffused away from the state. That is not to say state organs lack power. The state in the UK has the power to do good (in terms

12   Dahl in fact identified five possible routes towards polyarchy/democracy. The UK route is an example of the evolutionary one. Other routes include: via revolution (such as France); imposition by an outside state (such as post-war Japan and Germany); evolution as a dependency of another state (such as Canada); and, finally, revolution by a dependency of another state (such as the USA). All of these countries are democracies (or polyarchies as Dahl would prefer to call them) but they have moved from closed hegemony in very different ways.

of education, health and security and so on) as well as harm (for example, by waging illegal war and eradicating centuries old civil liberties[13]). But if the engine of a modern democracy is its economy then this is driven by markets rather than political parties. So in a sense no one is 'running' the country, it is more of a complex web of interests and relationships. As the realities of a wider polyarchy become apparent, tensions occur within a political system still stuck on an oligarchic assumption. Although people can vote every few years, the 'running' of the country is still left to an oligarchy. The vote is seen by many as having very little effect in terms of directing the country. In one sense voting is nothing more than selecting one branded 'product' over another, with policies marketed like any other consumer item. At the end of the day it is an elite oligarchy who ends up in control. Or so it seems ...

Modern day political systems within a democracy are still stuck on the old leadership assumption of oligarchy. This is creating tensions. While political systems should become more enabling to allow wider participation and debate, the *opposite* is actually happening. In the UK there is an increasing tendency for the state to assert its power, as if it intuitively knows that power is slipping away. In the UK alone the following disturbing trends have emerged in the last 20 years:

- **Less participation in politics.** The actual level of voting has witnessed a sharp decline.[14] For example, voting in the 2005 UK election was 61 per cent of the total eligible to vote. Of that number, just over 36 per cent voted for Labour – in other words, some 22 per cent of the country actually voted for the Government. Many put the low number of those who vote down to apathy. But, as will be seen below, there may be other reasons. At the same time, and to exacerbate this trend, politics are becoming less transparent – for example in the six-month period after the new Freedom of Information Act came into force, the UK Government refused over 1,000 legitimate requests for information regarding their actions.[15] The membership of political parties has also seen a sharp decline. In the 1950s Conservative Party membership numbered over 2 million, and Labour over 800,000. In the 1990s the members of the Conservative Party numbered some 1 million, Labour over 200,000 and the LibDems over 90,000. By 2013 those numbers had declined to the extent that less than 1 per cent of the electorate belonged to a party, with Conservative membership less than 100,000, Labour less than 200,000 and the LibDems around 40,000[16].
- **Less toleration of opposition.** The eviction of Wolfgang Walter at the Labour Party political conference in 2005, and the following day when he tried to get back in, marked a shocking departure from a traditional tolerance towards the expression of oppositional views.[17] This issue was also highlighted by Jeremy Boden in early

---

13   This erosion of civil liberties in the UK is so alarming that MPs themselves are beginning to highlight the issue (see *The Guardian*, 'Davis warns MPs of erosion of civil liberties', 20 February 2009).

14   R. Niemi and H. Weisberg, *Controversies in Voting Behaviour*, shows a slow decline in many democracies – India seems to be the exception and has remained fairly flat at around 60 per cent participation.

15   See R. Verkaik, 'Central government "still obstructive" over FOI', *The Independent*, 17 June 2005.

16   'The decline of party membership' http://thebackbencher.co.uk/the-decline-of-party-membership/ and 'Can political parties be saved from extinction' http://www.bbc.co.uk/news/uk-politics-12934148, accessed: April 2014.

17   Wolfgang Walter, a pensioner aged 80 and party member, shouted 'Rubbish' during a speech by the Foreign Secretary at the Labour Party conference in 2005. He was forcibly evicted by heavy bouncers. When he tried to get back into the conference, he was arrested and held by the police using new draconian anti-terrorist legislation.

2007 on Andrew Marr's 'Sunday AM' programme, who stated the UK Government had been successful in eradicating debate about, and opposition to, its war in Iraq, seen as illegal by most people. Meanwhile the recent scandal of GCHQ and NSA intrusion into private communications and the subsequent destruction of computers in *The Guardian*'s head office[18] have only fuelled the feeling of the state being less tolerant of opposition.

- **More centralised control/observation.** The UK is one of the oldest democracies, and yet it has become subject to the most surveillance in the world. The average citizen is captured 300 times a day on CCTV.[19] There have even been desires expressed by politicians to widen powers of intrusive surveillance and monitoring of citizens even further.[20] It seems the politics of fear are holding more and more sway.

- **More draconian police/legal powers.** This includes the abandonment of habeas corpus, the attenuation of the right to silence, the disposal of the inadmissibility of hearsay evidence, the presumption of innocence turned towards presumption of guilt, 'beyond reasonable doubt' replaced by 'balance of probabilities', freedom of speech and right to demonstrate curbed and in some cases criminalised, powers of shoot-to-kill without warning by the police, stop and search powers, warrant to search from a judge replaced by warrant from police, re-imprisonment of hundreds every week by probation for little reason, and so on.[21] The police in the UK have been given a lot of power. All power corrupts. Recently widespread corruption and the cover up of mistakes has been uncovered and the reputation of the policeforce is in tatters. Over recent time they have covered up the deaths, due to their negligence, of dozens of football supporters in the Hillsborough tragedy; shot people unnecessarily and then covered up their negligence (Menezes case, amongst others); injured and killed innocent protesters and then covered up the killing (Tomlinson amongst others); conspired through false testimony to force the resignation of a cabinet minister who was supporting police budget cuts (Mitchell case); detained journalists doing their work to uncover the use of mass surveillance (Miranda case); and sought to block justice to a family whose son was cruelly murdered (Lawrence case). The old

---

18   http://www.theguardian.com/uk-news/2014/jan/31/footage-released-guardian-editors-snowden-hard-drives-gchq, accessed: April 2014.

19   This is an often quoted statistic – but it is unfounded – see *The Times*, 3 March 2009 'The strange case of the surveillance cameras – How often are we caught on CCTV? Three hundred times a day, we are told. In search of the truth about a much-cited statistic', by David Aaronovitch.

20   The current privacy picture in the UK is decidedly grim. The UK has been the world leader in adopting intrusive surveillance technologies such as biometrics, surveillance cameras, computer databases and DNA testing, largely implemented without debate. The Information Commissioner has warned that the UK is 'sleepwalking into a surveillance society.' A 2006 ranking of 37 countries by Privacy International found the UK level of surveillance was 'endemic', higher than any other EU country and at the same level as Russia, China and Singapore. For a comprehensive overview of developments in the deployment of surveillance technologies in the UK, see: FIPR, Technology development and its effect on privacy & law enforcement, February 2004.

21   The UK police have seen a rapid expansion of power, all of which are supposed to enable them to enhance 'public protection'. However, these powers are often abused by the police. For example Home Office statistics, which were released to the *Daily Mail* under Freedom of Information laws in May 2009, show a ten-fold use in the power since the introduction of laws which allowed police to stop and search people under anti-terrorist legislation. In 2000–2001, just 3,583 people were stopped under Section 44, and of these, only one was arrested for terrorism offences. In 2006–2007, over ten times this number were stopped and searched by officers (37,197 people). Only 28 were subsequently arrested for terrorism-related offences. Each search can take up to 20 minutes and individuals are searched and asked a series of personal questions by police. It is widely accepted that this policy drives a wedge between the police and the community they are meant to be protecting. Instead of protection they are seen as delivering persecution.

age of 'British justice', 'Fair play' and the honest "Dixon of Dock Green" Policemen are long, long dead. Where the system can get away with it, it will close ranks and the courts will now bow to the state (as has been seen in countless cases and only uncovered because the victims simply would not give up).

As politicians display an almost voracious appetite to extend their powers, voters seem to be getting more disinterested. Why is the actual participation in politics so low? Research would suggest a variety of reasons:

- **Apathy.** Voter apathy is the main reason quoted, especially by politicians. In other words they blame the electorate. Those voters who are apathetic would say there is little to distinguish political parties from each other, so voting is a waste of time. And to be fair it seems when one looks at the left and right of politics there has been a degree of convergence – it seems as much energy is spent by politicians debating *how* policies are carried out rather than *what* they are.
- **Relevance.** As power has become more diffused, most intuitively know politics has become less relevant. Governments do not 'run' countries as much as they used to, as the underlying reality of polyarchy emerges. Power has passed from the state, through corporations to the markets. And whenever governments try to take on the markets, they inevitably lose as they do not have enough power to beat the markets – witness, for example, the UK Government's hopeless attempt to control its own currency in the debacle of Black Wednesday.[22]
- **Trust.** With the seeming continuous run of scandals and exposés of corruption, politicians are held in increasingly low esteem. Scandals of self-interest and corruption do little to enhance trust within the electorate and so the politicians become even more distant. The pursuit of power and naked ambition have never been traits universally respected, and yet that is what politicians seem to exemplify.[23]

The charade highlighted in Chapter 4 also seems prevalent in modern day democracy. Every few years people vote in a new oligarchy in the hope those voted for will recognise and implement the solutions to the country's problems. It seems whenever our nation's leaders prove less than perfect we take great delight in lambasting them in the press. Meanwhile, as they struggle to fix problems they hardly understand themselves, they often make things worse. Witness, for example, the failed Middle East foreign policies (for example, US support of Israel against Palestine) which led to a rise of terror attacks (for example, New York's '9/11'), themselves fuelling further failed foreign policies (for example, Iraq), giving rise to yet more attacks (for example, Madrid and London's '7/7') – a cycle of destruction and incompetence no doubt history will look back on with incredulity. And meanwhile the more the government tries to fix problems, the less we take responsibility for them. We seem happy to put our head in the sand in the same way as our politicians (who, for example, stated categorically the war in Iraq had nothing to do with the London terror attacks even when the suicide bombers themselves left video tapes behind saying the illegal

---

22   W. Hassdorf, 'Emperor without Clothes: Financial Market Sentiment and the Limits of British Currency Machismo in the ERM Crisis'.

23   There is myriad research regarding the dwindling of trust of politicians. The main research often quoted was done by G.A. Almond and S. Verba, *The Civic Culture: Political Attitudes and Democracy in Five Nations*. This was updated by G.A. Almond and S. Verba, *The Civic Culture Revisited*. A more recent study is in B.G. Peters, *The Politics of Bureaucracy*.

war was their prime motivation). So our social responsibility has gradually diminished to the extent we are happy to blame the politicians for any ill the country faces. It is similar to the charade described in Chapter 4. We are the same as the workers standing around the water cooler complaining 'Management should ...', 'The company should ...', before going back to work, our consciences replete with comfortable self-righteousness.

Such criticism is perhaps unjustified as it seems the people themselves have little opportunity to actually make a difference, within the current way democracy is practised. To do anything about the problems we face would be a nice opportunity, but all there is (short of demonstrations nowadays more often ignored or made illegal[24]) is a vote every few years. In some ways, the charade is played out in Parliament itself with politicians seemingly more interested in scoring points off each other than actually fixing the challenges we face. To many it seems that politics have become confined to party dogma, with each party still needing 'whips' (an illuminating term) to ensure party line rules over individual conscience. Parliamentary sessions often resemble what has been called 'Punch and Judy' politics. When Paddy Ashdown was the leader of the Liberal Democrats he once described Parliament as 'the longest running farce in the West End'. Parliament may indeed not be perfect but at the moment it is the best we have. Could it better? It certainly seems to be getting worse ...[25]

While the relevance of state power is becoming less, it seems the state is trying to make up for it by extending its powers. They are being extended widely in the UK. This has allowed the state to do things 20 years previously many would have thought impossible. How else can one explain that a modern day democracy went to war in Iraq – a war which most people see as illegal?[26] How else can one justify the shooting of innocent people by the police with impunity?[27] How else can one rationalise the unjust imprisonment of thousands of people in the UK and the commensurate overcrowding of prisons?[28] Most would see this as an intolerable abuse of state power.

---

24   Demonstrations and agitation have historically resulted in significant change (for example, women's rights, Ghandi's India). However, the largest demonstration in the UK's history to stop the Iraq war was hardly reported and achieved little. Perhaps this is yet another sign of democracy becoming corrupted.

25   The expenses saga in 2009 in Parliament has not helped this situation.

26   The Secretary General himself, Kofe Annan, stated that the war was illegal and contravened the UN Charter as reported by the BBC on 16 September 2004.

27   See 'De Menezes jury damns police "cover-up": Officers' claims of shouting warning before gunning down innocent Brazilian rejected' by Charlotte Gill, *Daily Mail*, 13 December 2008. Despite the manifest failings no police have been in any way punished for the shooting of De Menezes in London in 2005 and the subsequent cover up. Similarly no sanction was taken against the police who shot Mohammed Abdulkahar, 23, at his home in Forest Gate, on 2 June 2006.

28   According to an official briefing by NAPO (Paper BRF 19-06 dated 25 October 2006 by Harry Fletcher, Assistant General Secretary) the number of individuals released from prison in the UK and then subsequently recalled quadrupled between 2000 and 2005. This occurred just after new legislation which removed the need for probation to take the case in front of a judge. Overall the work of the Parole Board during the same period increased by over 100 per cent. In 2000–2001, 2,457 prisoners who had been released on parole were recalled, and this had risen to 9,320 by 2004–2005. The number of long term prisoners recalled rose from 267 to 712 during the same period. The recall of lifers on licence rose from 30 in 2001 to 71 in 2004. The vast majority of short and medium term prisoners were recalled for technical breaches and not for further offending. The paper contains two dozen examples of people imprisoned for no good reason (including the case of William Rogers who was sentenced to three years for burglary in 2004. *'He served 18 months and was released in March 2006 to a bail hostel. He registered with the local drugs team and saw a doctor for depression. He did miss an appointment with the drugs dependency team but believes he was given the wrong date and time. He did turn up the following day but by that time he was given a final warning and was recalled back to prison. He was actually seeking work and had had several job interviews.'* This case is fairly typical, and explains why the prison population in the UK has soared). In addition to the widespread questionable practices of probation services, the regime of sentencing people using IPP (Indeterminate Sentence for Public Protection) has been described by one Lord Chancellor as the biggest stain in the history of UK criminal justice and by the European Courts as a breach of human rights. The establishment ignores this and despite the

The trends outlined above can be shown schematically, as in Figure C.4 below.

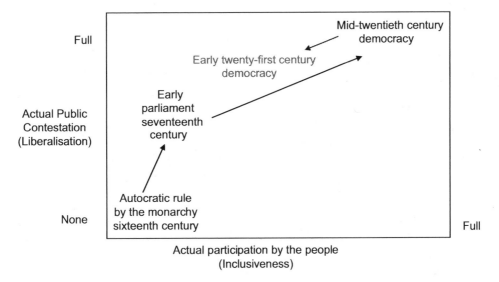

Figure C.4 UK example according to interpretation of modern reality

It shows how in modern times democracy has taken a backward step. Such a trend could be seen as a natural reaction of an oligarchy to secure its power when faced with an underlying pressure for more polyarchy. The challenge for modern day democracies is to enable a wider participation in politics, as well as a more engaged debate encompassing oppositional views. As the underlying trend towards polyarchy (in the sense expressed earlier in Chapter 1) continues, there is a collision waiting to happen as our political systems seem to become more and more oligarchic and centralised, out of date and unfit for purpose.

It seems politicians are becoming set on a divergent course away from those they purport to represent. Rather than asking how the electorate should become more engaged in politics, perhaps they should ask how the politicians and politics can become more engaged with the electorate ...

What Does the Future Hold?

We seem to be at a crossroad in modern politics, with the underlying tensions between an old assumption of oligarchy, struggling to stay alive through extending powers, and a new reality of underlying polyarchy where power is diffused. If these tensions are not addressed, there is a danger of them erupting into conflict. How can a modern day democracy begin to address this?

As was seen in Chapter 2, the reason for the bifurcation (between the context of leadership and the assumption of what it is) is mainly due to the rapid evolution of

---

regime being scrapped, thousands still languish in prison, far past their sentence end date, not knowing when or even if they will be released.

technology. And maybe technology has the answer. The *old* assumption of democracy was as follows:

> There is a need to involve more people in the running of the country as they have their views, and an increasing ability to discern what needs to be done. This has been fuelled by rising education and awareness, as well as expectations. However, the technology does not exist to allow them to participate in real time. Furthermore, people generally are not fully aware of all the ins and outs of the details of what needs to be done, so they can only express their opinion on broadly based party political lines (for example, 'for' nationalised industry or 'for' the free market). So we have an oligarchy of people elected on their perceived merit every few years to actually run the country, as they should know what best needs to be done on a detailed level. To ensure a degree of consistency politicians will be aided by a highly educated, politically neutral and professional Civil Service who also act as the executive to implement the laws passed by the elected politicians.

This assumption was reasonable only until relatively recently. However, technology has moved on a lot, as Chapter 2 showed. People can vote in real time for reality TV shows – why can they not be allowed to vote in real time for the stuff that actually matters? Part of the challenge is that the devil is in the detail, and so many would argue people generally lack the knowledge and intelligence to make detailed judgements. This certainly seems to be borne out by research. For example, Carl Sagan calculated 95 per cent of Americans are scientifically illiterate.[29] Surowiecki wrote in his *Wisdom of Crowds*[30] that at the height of the Cold War 50 per cent of Americans thought the USSR were members of NATO. So on the face of it, it may seem foolish to suggest that the population should be engaged in the wider political running of the country beyond their right to vote every few years or so. However, as the research from Surowiecki shows, such an idea is not without merit. He suggests the wisdom of a crowd will be better quality, and come up with better decisions than experts, if three things are in place:

- **Diversity.** The crowd needs to have a wide diversity of opinion, background and capability.
- **Independence.** It is important each person can voice their opinion in confidence and without being influenced unduly by the voiced opinion of others.
- **Method of aggregation.** There needs to be a confidential method to collect and aggregate the votes.

These things can surely exist in any modern society. So it follows that specific issues can be voted on. The issue being voted on has to be presented in a factual and unbiased way, with options and scenarios to choose from, rather than a straight 'yes or no'/'agree or disagree' vote. This would help avoid Arrow's 'Impossibility Theorem' which shows that an increasing number of voters, faced by an increasing number of choices, would be unable to come up with a rational resolution.[31] It is hard in such

---

29   As reported by C. Sagan, *The Demon-Haunted World – Science as a Candle in the Dark.*

30   J. Surowiecki, *The Wisdom of Crowds.*

31   Kenneth Arrow's 'Impossibility Theorem' demonstrates that no voting system can convert the ranked preferences of individuals into a community-wide ranking while also meeting a certain set of reasonable criteria with three or more

a media driven 'spin enriched' world to see how unbiased information and facts can be made available. However, this problem is not insurmountable. One wonders what would have happened if the objective and true facts had been presented to the American and British public for a vote prior to the Iraq war. It was clear, certainly to many British politicians, that the general public thought the invasion of Iraq was unwarranted and the arms inspectors should have been given more time to uncover the suspected weapons of mass destruction (which in fact were never found). Indeed Robin Cook, the then Foreign Secretary who resigned over the decision to go to war in Iraq, said in his resignation speech:

> *The longer that I have served in this place, the greater the respect I have for the good sense and collective wisdom of the British people ... They want inspections to be given a chance, and they suspect that they are being pushed too quickly into conflict by a US Administration with an agenda of its own.*[32]

In this sense the 'wisdom of crowds' was not used or even really listened to.

This 'wisdom of crowds' achieving better results in problem-solving is not a new idea. One of the classic expressions of a self-organising social/economic system was captured by Adam Smith's description in 1776 of the 'invisible hand' in a decentralised economy. Many other studies have come up with similar conclusions.[33] So if we assume such conclusions are correct, and Dahl's political map can be used to show what is actually happening, then there are some ways of seeing what the future holds. Two broad options or scenarios emerge:

- **Continued political divergence.** Should the state continue to diverge from the people, then history shows after a while conflict arises. This is a possibility but, given the availability of knowledge and information, such an outcome is unlikely. The only doubt is how much damage has to be suffered before democracy becomes realigned towards what needs to be done.
- **Democratic convergence.** In this scenario there is a realisation that the old ways of democracy do not work as well as they used to, and voting for an elitist oligarchy every few years is not the best way to do things, even at a local level. There is a convergence between the politicians and those they purport to represent. Such a convergence could result in some or all of the following possibilities:
  - Politics moving away more from 'policy' and 'content' to 'process' and 'procedure'. In a sense, as noted above, this is beginning to happen. Such a move is not always well managed – for example many see the trend towards 'targets' being at the expense of an effective holistic service delivery. There generally seems a convergence within policies of 'left' and 'right' – indeed many people see no difference and the joke of the UK's 1997 election was 'Tony Blair MP' was almost an anagram for 'Tory Plan B'. There certainly seem to be more debate about *how*

---

discrete options to choose from – see his original paper 'A Difficulty in the Concept of Social Welfare'.

32 Robin Cook, Foreign Secretary, resignation speech, House of Commons 17 March 2003.

33 For example see N.L. Johnson, 'Collective problem solving', research paper LA-UR-98-2227 which also references many other works.

policy is executed rather than policy itself. This is not to minimise the differences between different political parties, as they still exist at a philosophical level.

- Political ideology would emerge from the people rather than defined by a narrow group offered as a consumer choice. Thus ideology could be the basis of community which a person may belong to and which can be used (or not) to help decide how to vote on a particular issue.

- A concerted effort would be needed to 'clean up' legislation by removing laws which affect civil liberties and are not actually needed. This is happening in some democracies such as New Zealand.[34] Much legislation is out of date and based on assumptions which have been long overtaken. Such a clean-up would take an innovative approach, as government is used to introducing legislation, not removing it!

- A clear idea for each parliamentary sitting to identify what issues will be presented to the people for decisions to be made. This is linked to the move away from content (as highlighted in the first sub-bullet point above) and more of an issue of process rather than coming up with the right policies/answers.

- Civil Servants spending time to present the options and underlying facts in a balanced and unbiased way to enable people to vote on what they think needs to be done. This would assume a 'de-politicisation' of the civil service, and a wider and more engaged public debate, supported by unbiased factual information to inform debate. Again this would take some change, as it is rare to come across unbiased information. And the Civil Service has become increasingly politicised at best, and corrupt with too much power at worse.

- Politicians enabling people to decide what needs to be done and how, and working hard to follow the will of the people, rather than working hard to get people to follow their will.

- Technology used to enable people both to access relevant facts as well as vote/express opinion on issues. This is already in place – all that is needed is the political will to use it and set people free. There are some early signs this is happening. For example a political web site set up by the UK Prime Minister in 2006 allowed people to express their views. Over 1.5 million did so against road charging using satellite technology put into cars and this affected the debate considerably. Blog sites could be used to engender a wide debate enabling people to participate in debate rather than just watch it on TV. Mobile phone technology could be used to gather votes.

- Press spending more time on important issues that can make a difference to others, and much wider and engaged political debate.

- More accountability and transparency in running health, law and order, education and so on. More private sector ethos of delivery and service, rather than a fixation with targets for targets' sake and dogmatic policy freeing up control.

---

34   This is easier said than done. In the UK it was noted in a speech by Mr Norman: 'A final point about regulation that is often missed by Ministers is that it erodes the productivity of the public sector, which is the fastest growing employment sector in Britain today. It is also the sector with the lowest productivity growth ... We are creating layer on layer of overlapping regulation, and there is no process in the system for unpicking the history and removing legislation that is often completely out of date and no longer relevant to today's business environment. In addition, we are world beaters in enforcement in this country – we have thousands of enforcers. I challenge the Minister to name a single inspection or enforcement department that has diminished', Hansard, 30 June 2004, column 394.

If we mapped such a change, then the trend would show that the current tightening of state powers is like a step back in an advancing helix. It is similar to a strange attractor, with the evolution of political movement towards an increasingly polyarchic state, and commensurate increase of democracy (see Figure C.5).

The key point is that the changes outlined in Chapter 1 (advancement of technology and the increase of the general level of human awareness) allow/enable both a wider participation by people in the running of the country, as well as a wider public contestation. The only thing lacking is the political will and specified procedures to allow this to happen.

It may be easy in principle to say a wider referendum approach could be taken with democracy. It may be a way to ensure better decisions and to avoid mistakes such as the Iraq war. However, such a process would be as much subject to abuse as the current one. A light-hearted example of this can be provided by the UK comedy soap opera 'Yes Minister' which was described by Margaret Thatcher as reflecting reality more than most would like to admit.[35] In one particular episode the Minister Jim Hacker is discussing the merits of more open government with his senior adviser Sir Humphrey Appleby.[36] To the horror of his senior Civil Servant, the Minister has come up with the idea of a referendum on military service. To hold a referendum would detract from the power of the Civil Servants and so Sir Humphrey manages to convince the Minister against such an idea. He does so by saying referenda can be manipulated to get the answer one wants. For example, he argues, if one wanted a positive vote for national service one would ask a series of questions thus: 'Do you believe the youth of the day lacks discipline?' 'Do you feel young people today are not fit enough and do not take enough exercise?' 'Do you think young people today would benefit from some outdoor life, and good training to look after themselves?' 'Do you support National Service?' If, on the other hand, one would want a negative response the following could be asked: 'Do you favour young people being exposed to violence?' 'Do you think young people should be trained how to use guns?' 'Do you think killing other people is a good thing?' 'Do you support National Service?' With these arguments Sir Humphrey convinces the Minster to abandon the idea of a referendum and more 'open government'. It may be a light hearted example but it demonstrates a more serious point.

How could such a 'Sir Humphrey syndrome' be avoided? How could polyarchy be widened, with democracy becoming more inclusive and liberalised? Can such a change be enabled? One can begin to sketch out some possibilities by using the Four + Four principles outlined in Chapter 6. This could well employ further thinking and engender debate:

- **Underlying purpose.** The purpose of a wider engagement of the electorate would be to ensure wiser and more sustainable decisions to be made for the greater good. This needs to be clearly communicated. This approach builds on the assumption, explored in Chapter 3, that leaders no longer know the solutions to problems faced by the organisations they lead, and the assertion by Surowiecki that a crowd, given certain conditions, will together come up with better solutions

---

35 'Yes Minster' was Thatcher's favourite programme and she even wrote a small cameo part for herself in the show whilst Prime Minister herself, as reported by Robin Stringer, TV and Radio Correspondent of *The Daily Telegraph*, 21 January 1984.

36 The sketch itself is worth looking at in full from the episode YPM 1.2 The Ministerial Broadcast 16 January 1986 and can be seen at <http://www.yes-minister.com/ypmseas1a.htm>, accessed: 21 April 2010.

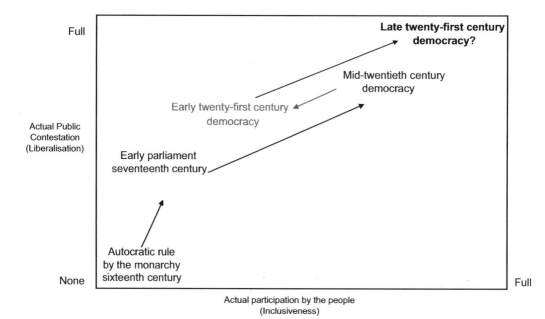

Figure C.5   UK possible long term trend

than experts. Again this also needs to be made publicly explicit, even though many will resist the idea. 'Power to the people' may be an attractive slogan, but with power comes responsibility and many find shirking responsibility more convenient for a comfortable life. A time sense of underlying purpose goes beyond the strictly utilitarian. It needs to extend to an underlying and sincere sense of social responsibility within each citizen to take an interest in issues which affect the wider good, as well as themselves.

- **Simple rules.** These would need to include some of the approaches described by Surowiecki in his *Wisdom of Crowds*: the ability to vote or express opinion independently; having the issue considered clearly and objectively presented, and the possible options, in an unbiased way (to avoid the 'Sir Humphrey syndrome' described above!); and having a process to aggregate the deliberations of a sufficiently diverse number of people. The latter point is an issue: how many people should vote in order to have a quorum? Is not the best route that of Australia, where to vote is deemed a civic duty and thus not to cast a vote is against the law?[37]

- **Unambiguous feedback.** During the discussion phase, the use of blog sites and feedback loops can help a wider engagement. Some may argue that a web enabled system would discriminate against those who have no internet access, but on the other hand it would be a lot more inclusive than it is currently. The result of the vote needs to be quickly published. The way forward also needs to be clear.

---

37   Similar laws are rare and exist in Belgium, Greece and Brazil. High turnouts occur in countries who do not have such a law. For example between 1960 and 1995 Malta had 96 per cent turnout and Austria had 93 per cent (with no such law) whilst Greece had 86 per cent turnout and Brazil had 83 per cent (with such a law).

- **Clear objective.** The clear objective of referenda is to ensure the best possible legislation with the backing of the majority.[38] The specific issue needs to be clear as well as the various options available to get to the required end state/result.
- **Defined boundary.** This can partly be applied to the content of the issue at hand and also the process. As far as the former is concerned, the issue and options need to be clearly defined. As far as the latter is concerned, the process of voting and timetables for debates and so on need to be clear as well.
- **Freedom to act/discretion.** This would imply that each individual has the opportunity of voting and having the vote done in a way which allows them full independence.
- **Tolerance of ambiguity.** Whilst there can be no ambiguity about the actual process of the vote, the issue at hand will be more ambiguous than not. So it is not the ambiguity of the process, rather than the ambiguity of the issue at hand that needs to be understood. Right vs. wrong decisions are easy to resolve; the right vs. right options are the hardest.
- **People's skill and will.** Of all the principles this one is the most relevant and controversial. For polyarchy to work in the political sphere it needs the will of the people to become engaged in the debate of issues which affect them, and also needs their ability to listen to and understand different points of view. There are many who might argue it is naïve to expect an electorate already apathetic to democracy to become more engaged in the habit of voting, when many do not even vote every five years. It might be argued that a generation brought up on soap operas, tabloid press and reality TV shows can hardly be expected to be able to make decisions on weighty and complex matters – better to leave such things in the hands of those who are educated enough to deal with them. Such arguments are reminiscent of those who argued against the extension of universal suffrage in the nineteenth century.[39] Then it was argued people did not have the ability to discern between the general choices posed by the various political parties. But they did – and it is too easy to underestimate the wisdom of the crowd.

Each Four + Four principle above has a varying degree of importance as far as the application of polyarchy to politics is concerned. This varying relevance is summarised in Figure C.6 (the more the shade, the higher the importance).

---

38 Referenda are criticised by many, best summarised by the then European Commissioner for External Affairs and British politician Chris Patten in an interview in 2003 when discussing the possibility of a referendum in the United Kingdom on the European Union Constitution: *'I think referendums are awful. They were the favourite form of plebiscitary democracy of Mussolini and Hitler. They undermine Westminster [parliament]. What they ensure, as we saw in the last election, is if you have a referendum on an issue politicians, during an election campaign, say oh we're not going to talk about that, we don't need to talk about that, that's all for the referendum. So during the last election campaign the Euro was hardly debated. I think referendums are fundamentally anti-democratic in our system and I wouldn't have anything to do with them. On the whole, governments only concede them when governments are weak.'* (BBC, 2004).

39 The more important legislation in the UK included the Reform Acts of 1832, 1867 and 1885. Over that 53-year period, suffrage moved from one in seven to broadly the whole male population. Full universal suffrage did not occur until the Reform Acts of 1917 and 1928.

Purpose	Objective	Discretion	Rules	Feedback	Ambiguity	Skill/will	Boundary
●	◑	◖	◑	◖	◔	●	◔

Figure C.6   Relevance of Four + Four principles to political polyarchy

Summary

This appendix has been a brief consideration of the conclusions of this book as applied to the field of politics. It seems that democracy has taken a backward step when we consider polyarchy as defined by Dahl. There is an increasing divergence between voter and politician, whilst at the same time the state seems to be widening its powers. This situation could result in conflict. There is a need for polyarchy to be enabled further with a wider participation by the people in politics. Possible actions could be considered under the Four + Four principles which this book has advocated.

Although the principles look like a prescribed list of actions, perhaps too simplistic, it should be stressed they are merely headings under which ideas can be grouped to engender a broader debate. The fact remains that a wider engagement in the running of the country and its foreign policy is now more possible than ever before. But for it to be an actuality, it needs more than just a prescribed application of principles! It does seem the political assumptions that define the way we currently run democracy are as anachronistic as the assumptions we hold about leadership.

There will be many powerful self-interested groups that will resist such a change. Politicians and governmental departments all crave power and do not lightly give it up. However, given the underlying reality of the emergence of polyarchy and the bifurcation against some old leadership assumptions, it is perhaps only a matter of time until political changes will come about. And it will take a bold and visionary political leader to enable such a change to happen ...

Appendix D:
Leadership Development

Can leadership be developed? This question is often asked – if one believes firmly in the old oligarchical model then the question is harder to answer. However, from a polyarchic complex adaptive point of view the answer is: *Very Much So*!

The question then remains: how?

This appendix is a quick summary of what works well, and is drawn from over 30 years' personal experience in leadership development. It looks at two areas:

1. Content – what curricular needs to be included in leadership development; and
2. Process – how can leadership development best be delivered?

Content

In the early 1990s a world-leading strategy consulting firm was engaged in the Netherlands with a small leadership development firm to design a leadership programme for some of its staff. As one can imagine they were demanding and rigorous in defining the content and how it could be best structured and used. The programme which emerged was called the LEAD (Learn, Exercise, Achieve and Define) Programme and was used to good effect in both subsequent in-company programmes for blue chip clients as well as open programmes at the Netherlands leading business school Nyenrode University.

The design team first had to define leadership and used much of the thinking in Part II. Leadership was seen on two axes, as per the model below. Each axis had the areas for development defined to support the need for 'Valuing differences in people', and for 'Getting things done'. Within each of these two key competencies exist three competencies for development (see Figure D.1).

Within each of these six areas is a whole range of academic content that can be used to develop knowledge and know-how. The research that was used to design the programme looked at over 50 leadership programmes and categorised the content – all of the content of these programmes fell into these six areas. The LEAD Programme evolved and Figure D.2 shows some of the content that was covered under the six areas .

The list is not exhaustive, nor is it intended to be applied in a global sense. Each group will need more or less of the above. However, it shows one way in which a leadership development programme can be constructed and the soft and hard skills that are needed to enhance capability for Complex Adaptive Leadership. It ties in fully with the leadership model in Parts II and III.

The subjects above could each have a book written about them. Each of them had at least half a day's delivery and many days of structured practice. It is outside the scope of this book to detail them. What is important to highlight here is that, within each area,

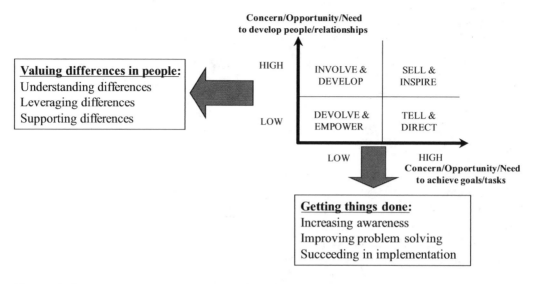

Figure D.1   LEAD Programme – two development areas and six key competencies

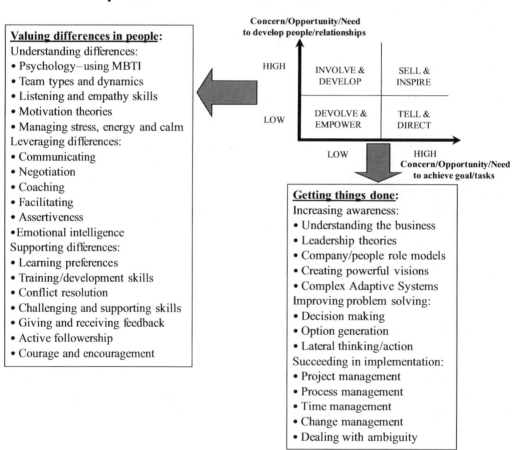

Figure D.2   LEAD Programme – 30+ key curricular subjects

the application of complex adaptive thinking and principles of polyarchy can be applied to enrich the subject matter. For example, in Figure D.2 opposite, the second bullet point in 'Increasing awareness' (under 'Getting things done') is 'Leadership theories'. Appendix B shows how new thinking can enrich insight into traditional models and learning when applied to older leadership models.

Process

More important than the knowledge (that is, the *what*) of leadership development is the process of delivery (that is, the *how* of leadership development).

Successful leadership development encapsulates three areas:

1. **Intellectual** – knowing what to do – leading edge thinking to enhance knowledge.
2. **Emotional** – believing why to do it – experiential learning to gain emotional understanding.
3. **Behavioural** – understanding how to do it – specific action and review to embed new skills.

Having a clear idea of how each of these areas will be addressed is vital to bridge the typical 'knowing–doing' gap. Too many leadership development programmes concentrate on the intellectual agenda at the expense of the emotional and behavioural.

1. **Intellectual** models to help enhance knowledge and also to give deeper meaning – see the content section above.
2. **Emotional** experiential learning through simulations to embed knowledge – this enables participants to 'feel' what the implications of the new knowledge is like or what it is trying to impart. An example is the complexity game outline in Chapter 6.
3. **Behavioural** specific actions back at the office with support to deliver. This is best done using the KISS approach in Chapter 11 with peer group coaching using the GROW approach in Chapter 10. This can also be complemented by on-the-job support by faculty if needed, for example, having a faculty/coach watching an individual during day-to-day work.

The best learning interventions are like a fractal – in other words there is a repeating pattern of how the learning is imparted:

- Participants gain new knowledge which enhances current knowledge (both intellectual and emotional).
- They try stuff out to experience how it feels and so learn on the emotional level.
- They then review what they did to embed the knowledge and required behaviour.

The flow of each of these three components can differ in order, depending on the specific needs.

This pattern is repeated both in the detail of the learning/development interventions (that is, the events that are delivered), as well as within the overall design (that is, the leadership development process which is designed and supported).

A typical workshop event could be:

1. Individuals consider an issue which they need within leadership development and are exposed to more knowledge. The event content would be designed on specific needs – 'just in time' leadership development tools that can be applied quickly are more effective than 'just in case' that could be applied in the future if needed.
2. Experiential learning – this can be a brief simulation or a series of challenges ranging from indoor team challenges to outdoor adventure expeditions. The location can help as well and locations can range from a normal hotel/country club to the more adventurous (for example, alpine mountain hut, Arab Red Sea dhow) to the unusual (for example, SAS training and leadership development area).
3. Behaviours of the simulation/challenge are reviewed and key behavioural actions are undertaken using KISS format (Behaviours to: Keep, Increase, Start and Stop).

This pattern is repeated at a programme level:

1. Knowledge – this would normally be identified through a needs analysis process and can range from an informal chat with participants beforehand to a more formal 360 degree tool.
2. Experiential – after the event participants are supported to put learning into action (where support is necessary through a variety of mechanisms which can be virtual or face-to-face).
3. Review and embed – an event would be followed up by another learning event to embed learning and, if necessary, start the learning cycle again.

This design dynamic formed the core of the LEAD Programme. LEAD stands for:

- **Learn** – participants pick up new knowledge (intellect);
- **Exercise** – they put the knowledge into practice (behaviour);
- **Achieve** – they gain insight in the practice (emotion); and
- **Define** – they define further development and learning needs.

The exercise of new knowledge could be on the day job, within a specifically designed project, or even in a job swap. There are a variety of ways within each of the four areas to achieve the desired effect, and a good leadership development programme will have a mix within each area, including 360 degree feedbacks to help the 'Achieve' and 'Define' parts.

The design of any intervention needs to be based on what result is wanted. Too many firms invest large amounts of money in leadership development, but seldom measure downstream the intended results. A CAL intervention can be broadly delivered at three levels to achieve three differing results:

1. Individual awareness – A half to one day introduction to enable the individual leader too widen their view of leadership. This may result in her/him leading a little differently.
2. Behaviour change – A two to four day programme that enables the individual to indetfiy specific actions and changes of behaviour to move his followers to level 5, and

to devolve more to do more valuable things. Up to one to two days a week of time can be saved by leaders who can manage complexity in more effective ways.

3. Organisational change – A modular programme spread over several months with co-coaching and 'T3Os' (Things To Try Out) which are then reported back in the following module to re-enforce behaviour change and enable wider organisational impact.

Since the publication of the First Edition, and at the time of writing the Second Edition, the CAL network of associates has delivered a variety of such interventions to over 1,000 executives across 30 countries and 20 different industries to good effect. More can be seen at: http://www.complexadaptiveleadership.com/clientsandservices/.

Figure D.3   LEAD: Programme dynamic

Summary

A good Complex Adaptive Leadership development programme will have:

1. For content: a balance of the 'soft' skills (Yin) which are more geared to the 'people' side of the leadership equation and 'hard' skills (Yang) which are more geared to the 'goal' side of the equation.
2. For delivery/process: a good mix of learning approaches ranging from job swaps to master classes/workshop and a dynamic which involves the participant in defining needs.
3. A defined process to take the learning and apply it, thus learning more and further defining learning and development needs.

Bibliography

General Books/Articles on Chaos/Complexity

Aihara, K. (May 2002), 'Chaos Engineering and its Application to Parallel Distributed Processing with Chaotic Neural Networks', *Proceedings of the IEEE*, 90:5.

Anderson, C. and Bartholdi, J.J. III (2000), 'Centralized Versus Decentralized Control in Manufacturing: Lessons from Social Insects', presented at 'Complexity and Complex Systems in Industry', University of Warwick, Georgia Institute of Technology.

Axelrod, R. and Cohen, M.D. (1999), *Harnessing Complexity – Understanding Implications of a Scientific Frontier*, The Free Press.

Banks, J., Brooks, J., Cairns, G., Davis, G. and Stacey, P. (1992), 'On Devaney's Definition of Chaos', *The American Mathematical Monthly*.

Baranger, M. (2000), *Chaos, Complexity, and Entropy: A Physics Talk for Non-Physicists*, Cambridge, MA: New England Complex Systems Institute.

Barnsley, M. (1988), *Fractals Everywhere*, San Diego: Academic Press.

Battram, A. (2002), *Navigating Complexity: The Essential Guide to Complexity Theory in Business and Management*, London: Spiro Press.

Berreby, D. (1996), 'Between Chaos and Order: What Complexity Theory Can Teach Business', *Strategy + Business*, second quarter edition, issue 3.

Broer, H.W. (2000) 'The How and What of Chaos', University of Groenigen paper, *Nieuw Arch. Wisk.* 5th series, 1:1, 34–43.

Byrne, D. (1998), *Complexity Theory and the Social Sciences – An Introduction*, Routledge.

Cilliers, P. (1998), *Complexity and Post-modernism – Understanding Complex Systems*, Routledge

Cohen, J. and Stewart, I. (1995), *The Collapse of Chaos – Discovering Simplicity in a ComplexWorld*, London: Penguin.

Corning, P.A. (2007), 'The Re-emergence of Emergence – A Venerable Concept in Search of a Theory', *Complexity* 7:6, 18–30

Davis, S.M. and Lawrence, P.R. (1978), 'Problems of Matrix Organisations', *Harvard Business Review* May–June.

Davies, P. (2006), *The Goldilocks Enigma: Why is the Universe Right for Life?*, London: Allen Lane.

DeLanda, M. (2006), *A New Philosophy of Society: Assemblage Theory and Social Complexity*, London: Continuum International Publishing Group.

Diacu, F. and Homes, P. (1999), *Celestial Encounters: The Origins of Chaos and Stability*, Princeton, NJ: Princeton University Press.

Dooley, K., Johnson, T. and Bush, D. (1995) 'TQM, Chaos, and Complexity', *Human Systems Management* 14:4, 1–16.

Eigen, M. and Schuster, P. (1979), *The Hypercycle – A Principle of Natural Self-Organisation*, Berlin: Springer-Verlag.

Gell-Mann, M. (1994), *The Quark and the Jaguar – Adventures in the Simple and the Complex*, London: Little Brown Co.

Gillies, D. (2000), *Philosophical Theories of Probability*, New York: Routledge.

Gleick, J. (1987), *Chaos*, London: Cardinal Sphere Books.

Goerner, S.J. (1994), *Chaos and the Evolving Ecological Universe*, Langhorne, PA: Gordon and Breach Science.

Gribbin, J. (2004), *Deep Simplicity – Chaos, Complexity and the Emergence of Life*, London: Penguin.

Gribbin, M. and Gribbin, J. (1999), *Chaos and Uncertainty*, London: Hodder.

Haken, H. (2004), *Synergetics, Introduction and Advanced Topics*, Berlin: Springer.

Holland, J. (1998), *Emergence – From Chaos to Order*, Oxford: Oxford University Press.

Hazy, James K., Goldstein, Jeffrey A. and Lichtenstein, Benyamin B. (2007), *Complex Systems Leadership Theory – New Perspectives from Complexity Science on Social and Organizational Effectiveness*, Mansfield, MA: ISCE Publishing.

IBM Global CEO report (2010), 'Capitalising on Complexity'.

Johnson, N.L. (1998), 'Collective Problem Solving –Functionality Beyond the Individual', Los Alamos Research Paper number: LA-UR-98-2227, Los Alamos National Laboratory, 1998. Work performed under the auspices of the US Department of Energy.

—— (1999), 'Diversity in Decentralized Systems: Enabling Self-organizing Solutions' Los Alamos.

Kauffman, S. (1995), *At Home in the Universe – The Search for the Laws of Self-organisation and Complexity*, Oxford: Oxford University Press.

—— (2008), *Reinventing the Sacred: A New View of Science, Reason and Religion,* Basic Books

Lewin, R. (1993), *Complexity – Life at the Edge of Chaos*, London: J.M. Dent.

Li, T.Y. and Yorke, J. (1975), 'Period Three Implies Chaos', *American Mathematical Monthly* 82:10, 985–92.

Lissack, M. (1996), 'Chaos and Complexity – Knowledge Management?', Leader Values paper.

Lorenz, E. (1963), 'Deterministic Non-periodic Flow', *Journal of Atmospheric Sciences* 20.

—— (1993), *The Essence of Chaos*, Washington: University of Washington Press.

Lovelock, J.E. (1979), *Gaia: A New Look at Life on Earth*, Oxford: Oxford University Press.

Mandelbrot, B. (1967), 'How Long Is the Coast of Britain? Statistical Self-Similarity and Fractional Dimension', *Science*, 156:3775.

—— (1983), *The Fractal Geometry of Nature – Updated and Augmented*, New York: W.H. Freeman & Lay.

Matsushita, R., Figueiredo, G.A. and Da Silva, S. (2006), 'The Chinese Chaos Game', *Physica A*, 378:2, 427–42.

Maturana, H.R. and Varela, F.J. (1992), *The Tree of Knowledge: The Biological Roots of Human Understanding*, Boston, MA: Shambhala Publications.

Maturana, H.R. and Varela, F.J. (1980), *Autopoiesis and Cognition: The Realization of the Living*, Dordrecht: D. Reidal Publishing.

McCulloch, W.S. and Pitts, W. (1943), 'A Logical Calculus of the Ideas Immanent in Nervous Activity', *Bulletin of Mathematical Biophysics* 5.

McMillan, E. (2003), *Complexity, Organisations and Change*, London: Routledge.

Miller, J. and Page, S. (2007), *Complex Adaptive Systems – An Introduction to Computational Models of Social Nature*, Princeton, NJ: Princeton University Press.

Mingers, J. (1994), *Self-producing Systems: Implications and Applications of Autopoiesis*, New York: Springer.

Mitchell, M. (2009), *Complexity – A Guided Tour,* Oxford University Press.

Mlodinow, L. (2008), *The Drunkards Walk – How Randomness Rules Our Lives*, Allen Lane Penguin Books.

Moore, A. (2011), *No Straight Lines – Making Sense of Our Non-linear World*, Bloodstone Books.

Morowitz, H.J. and Singer, J.L. (eds) (1995), *The Mind, The Brain And Complex Adaptive Systems (Santa Fe Institute Studies in the Sciences of Complexity Proceedings)*, Reading MA: Addison-Wesley/Perseus Books.

Nicolis, G. and Prigogine, I. (1989), *Exploring Complexity – An Introduction*, New York: W.H. Freeman.

Pascale, R., Millemann, M. and Gioja, L. (2000), *Surfing on the Edge of Chaos – The Laws of Nature and the New Laws of Business*, New York: Random House.

Peak, D. and Frame, M. (1994), *Chaos Under Control – The Art and Science of Complexity*, New York: W.H. Freeman.

Peters, T. (1987), *Thriving on Chaos – Handbook for a Management Revolution*, Vermont: Pan Books.

Polkinghorne, J. (1994), *Quarks, Chaos and Christianity*, London: Triangle.

Potts, W.K. (1984), 'The Chorus-line Hypothesis of Coordination in Avian Flocks', *Nature*, 309, 344–5.

Prigogine, I. (2003), *Is the Future Given?*, London: World Scientific.

—— (1996), *The End of Certainty – Time, Chaos and the New Laws of Nature*, New York: Free Press.

Rice, T.J. (1994), 'Ulysses, Chaos and Complexity', *James Joyce Quarterly*, 31:2, 41–54.

Remington, K. (2013), *Kairos: Harnessing Time and Emergence in Complex Projects,* ICCPM kindle edition on Amazon

Roberts, P. (1998), 'John Deere Runs on Chaos', *Fast Company* 19.

Sanford, C. and Mang, P. (1982), *A Self-Organizing Leadership View of Paradigms*, InterOctave Development Group Inc.

Sardar, Z. and Abrams, I. (1998), *Introducing Chaos*, London: Icon.

Sargut, G. and Gunter McGrath, R. "Learning to Live with Complexity – How to Make Sense of the Unpredictable and the Undefinable in Todays's Hyperconnected Business World", *Harvard Business Review* (September 2011) series on: 'Focus on Managing Complex Organisations'.

Shan, Y. and Yang, A. (eds) (2008), *Applications of Complex Adaptive Systems*, London: IGI Publishing.

Stacey, R.D. (2001), *Complex Responsive Processes in Organizations: Learning and Knowledge Creation (Complexity and Emergence in Organizations)*, London: Routledge.

—— (2010), *Complexity and Organizational Reality – Uncertainty and the Need to Rethink Management After the Collapse of Capitalism,* 2nd Edition, Routledge

Stewart, I. (1995), *Nature's Numbers*, London: Phoenix.

—— (1997), *Does God Play Dice? The New Mathematics of Chaos*, 2nd edition, London: Penguin.

Strognatz, S. (2004), *Sync – The Emerging Science of Spontaneous Order*, London: Penguin.

Sullivan, T, 'Embracing Complexity – An Interview with Michael J Mauboussin'; *Harvard Business Review* (September 2011) series on 'Focus on Managing Complex Organisations'.

Talib, N. (2007), *Black Swan – The Impact of the Highly Improbable*, London: Allen Lane.

Tullaro, N.B., Abbott, T. and Reilly, J.P. (1992), *An Experimental Approach to Nonlinear Dynamics and Chaos*, New York: Addison-Wesley.

Uhl-Bein, M. and Marion, R. (eds) (2007), *Complexity Leadership: Part 1: Conceptual Foundations (Leadership Horizons)*, Information Age Publishing

Vizinczey, S. (1969), *The Rules of Chaos*, London: Macmillan.

Wilson, G. (1999), 'The Complex World: Nonlinear Dynamical Systems as a Paradigm for International Relations Theory', <http://www.garretwilson.com/essays/internationalrelations/complexworld.html> accessed 9 April 2010.

Yorke, J. and Grebogi, C. (1997), *The Impact of Chaos on Science and Society: Proceedings of 1st UNU International Seminar on the Frontiers of Science and Technology, University of Tokyo, 15–17 April 1991*, Tokyo: United Nations University; illustrated edition

General Scientific Books/Articles

Barrow, J. (1998), *Impossibility – Limits of Science and Science of Limits*, Oxford: Oxford University Press.

Brennan, A., Chugh, J. and Kline, T. (2002), 'Traditional Versus Open Office Design: A Longitudinal Field Study, *Environment & Behaviour* 34:3, 279–99.

Bryson, B. (2003), *A Short History of Nearly Everything*, New York: Doubleday.

Capra, F. (1982), *The Tao of Physics*, 3rd edition, New York: Flamingo, Harper Collins.

—— (1996), *The Web of Life – A New Synthesis of Mind and Matter*, New York: Harper Collins.

Davies, P. (1974), *About Time*, London: Penguin.

—— (1992), *The Mind of God*, London: Penguin.

—— (2002), *How To Make A Time Machine*, London: Penguin.

Dawkins, R. (1996), *Climbing Mount Improbable*, London: Penguin.

Feynman, R. (1998), *QED, Strange Theory of Light and Matter*, London: Penguin.

Funtowicz, S. and Ravetz, J. (1990), *Uncertainty and Quality in Science for Policy*, Dordrecht: Kluwer Academic.

Gribbin, J. (1984), *In Search of Schrodinger's Cat – Quantum Physics and Reality*, New York: Bantam.

—— (1998), *Schrodinger's Kittens*, London: Phoenix.

—— (1998), *In search of SUSY – Supersymmetry and the Theory of Everything*, London: Penguin.

Hafele, J.and Keating, R. (1972), 'Around the World Atomic Clocks: Predicted Relativistic Time Gains', *Science*, 177.

Hawking, S. (1988), *A Brief History of Time*, New York: Bantam.

Mandelbrot, B.B. (1967), 'How Long is the Coast of Britain? Statistical Self-similarity and Fractional Dimension' *Science* 156: 636-38.

McEvoy, J. and Zarate, O. (1996), *Quantum for Beginners*, London: Icon.

Minas, K. and Nadeau, R. (2000), *The Conscious Universe: Parts and Wholes in Physical Reality*, New York: Springer.

Rauch, A.C. (1998), 'Chaos in a Driven, Nonlinear Electrical Oscillator: Determining Feigenbaum's Delta', Ohio: College of Wooster, paper 44691.

Sagan, C., (1981), *Cosmos – The Story of Cosmic Evolution, Science and Civilization*, London: MacDonald & Co.

—— (1997), *The Demon Haunted World – Science as a Candle in the Dark*, London: Headline.

Schwartz, J. and McGuiness, M. (1998), *Einstein*, London: Icon.

Sheldrake, R. (1999), *A New Science of Life: The Hypothesis of Morphic Resonance*, Rochester, VE: Inner Traditions Bear and Company.

Snow, C.P. (1969), *Variety of Men*, London: Penguin

Sokal, A. (1996), 'Transgressing the Boundaries: Towards a Transformative Hermeneutics of Quantum Gravity', *Social Text* (Science Wars issue – spring/summer).

Wolfram, S. (2002), *A New Kind of Science*, Champaign, IL: Wolfram Media.

General Background/Historical/Management Books/Articles

Adair, J. (1988), *The Action Centred Leader*, 2nd edition, London: Spiro Press.

Almond, G.A. and Verba, S. (1963), *The Civic Culture: Political Attitudes and Democracy in Five Nations*, Princeton, NJ: Princeton University Press.

—— (1980), *The Civic Culture Revisited*, London: The Book Service.

Arrow, K.J. (1950), 'A Difficulty in the Concept of Social Welfare', *Journal of Political Economy*, 58:4.

Assagioli, R. (1965), *Psychosynthesis*, New York: Hobbs, Dorman & Co. Republished Penguin Books (1976).

Azemikhah, H. (2006), 'The 21st Century, the Competency Era and Competency Theory', *Open Learning Institute of TAFE.*

Badaracco, J.L. (2002), *Leading Quietly: An Unorthodox Guide to Doing the Right Thing*, Boston, MA: Harvard Business School Press.

Banham, R. (2012), 'Freed From the Budget', September, *CFO Magazine.*

Bass, B.M. and Avolio, B.J. (1994), *Improving Organizational Effectiveness Through Transformational Leadership*, London: Sage Publications.

Beddington-Behrens, S. (2013), *Awakening the Universal Heart – A Guide for Spiritual Activist*, Umbria Press

Belasco, J.A. and Stayer, R.C. (1995), *Flight of the Buffalo: Soaring to Excellence, Learning to Let Employees Lead*, New York: Warner Books.

Bennis, W. (1989), *On Becoming a Leader*, Cambridge, MA: Perseus Books.

Bennis, W., Spreitzer, G.M. and Cummings, T.G. (eds) (2001), *The Future of Leadership – Today's Top Leadership and Thinkers Speak to Tomorrow's Leaders*, San Francisco, CA: Jossey Bass.

Berne, E. (1961), *Transactional Analysis in Psychotherapy: A Systematic Individual and Social Psychiatry*, Concord, MA: Grove Press.

—— (2001), *Transactional Analysis in Psychotherapy: The Classic Handbook to its Principles*, London: Souvenir Press.

Birkinshaw, J. (2010), *Reinventing Management: Smarter Choices for Getting Work Done*, Jossey-Bass.

Birkinshaw, J. and Heywood, S. (2010), 'Putting Complexity in its Place', *McKinsey and Company Quarterly Review.*

Bond, R., Devreux, M.P. and Klemm, A. (2005), 'The Effects of Dividend Taxes on Equity Prices: A Re-examination of the 1997 UK Tax Reform', *IMF Working Paper*, no. 07/204.

Bovet, D. and Martha, J. (2000), *Value Nets: Breaking the Supply Chain To Unlock Hidden Profits*, New York: John Wiley & Sons.

Bohm, D. (2004), *On Dialogue*, 2nd edition, New York: Routledge.

Brohm, R. (2005), *Polycentric Order in Organisations*, Rotterdam: Erasmus Research Institute of Management.

Burns, J.M. (1978), *Leadership*, London: Harper Row.

—— (2004), *Transforming Leadership*, Concord, MA: Grove Press.

Burrows, P. (2004), 'Hewlett & Packard: Architects of the Info Age: The Founding Fathers of Silicon Valley Steered Tech Away From Hierarchy', *Business Week*, 29 March.

Buytendijk, F. (2010), *Dealing with Dilemmas: Redefining Strategy*, September-October Volume 12 Number 5 Balanced Scorecard Report, Harvard Business Publishing.

Campbell, B. and Lack, E. (1985), *A Dictionary of Birds*, Friday Harbor, WA: Harrell Books.

Cerri, L. (2004), 'Why the Emergence of Pension Funds in Europe Does Not Enhance Economic Democracy: The Question of Corporate Ownership and the Structural Contradictions of Liberalism Initiative on Economic Democracy', paper, seminar organised by Transform, GUE/NGL and EURED.

Champy, J. (1996), *Reengineering Management – The Mandate for New Leadership*, London: Harper Collins.

Chomsky, N. (2003), *Hegemony or Survival – America's Quest for Global Dominance*, London: Penguin.

Christensen, C. and Dann, J.B.(1999), 'The Process of Strategy Definition and Implementation'. Harvard Business School case.

Christopher, M. (2004), *Logistics & Supply Chain Management*, 3rd edition, London: Financial Times Books.

Clausewitz, C. von, *Vom Kriege* (3 vols., Berlin: 1832–34).

Collins, J. (1999), 'Turning Goals into Results: The Power of Catalytic Mechanisms', *Harvard Business Review*, July–August.

—— (2001), *Good to Great – Why Some Companies Make the Leap and Others Don't*, New York: Harper Business.

—— (2001), 'Level 5 Leadership: The Triumph of Humility and Resolve', *Harvard Business Review*, January.

—— and Porras, J. (1997), *Built to Last – Successful Habits of Visionary Companies*, New York: Harper Business.

Cooper, R. (2003), *The Breaking of Nations – Order and Chaos in the 21st Century*, London: Atlantic Books.

Coutu, D. (2000), 'Creating the Most Frightening Company on Earth – An Interview With Andy Law of St Luke's', *Harvard Business Review*, September–October.

Covey, R.S. (1994), *The 7 Habits Of Highly Effective People. Powerful Lessons In Personal Change*, London: Simon & Schuster.

Csikszentmihalyi, M. (2002), *Flow: The Classic Work on How to Achieve Happiness*, London: Rider & Co.

Dahl, R. (1971), *Polyarchy – Participation and Opposition*, New Haven: Yale University Press.

—— (2002), *How Democratic is the American Constitution?*, New Haven: Yale University Press.

Darwin, C. (1998), *The Origin of Species*, London: Wordsworth.

Degraefe, Z. and Nicholson, N. (2004), *Risk: How to Make Decisions in an Uncertain World*, London: Format Publishing Ltd.

DeLanda, M. (2000), *A Thousand Years of Non-linear History*, New York: Zone Books

Drucker, P. (1954), *The Practice of Management*, London: Butterworth-Heinemann.

Duggan, W. (2007), 'Strategic Intuition: The Creative Spark in Human Achievement' Columbia Business School.

Euclid, (2002), *Euclid's Elements*, trans. T.L. Heath, Santa Fe, NM: Green Lion Press.

Eisenhardt KM and Sull DN, (2001), 'Strategy as Simple Rules', *Harvard Business Review*, January 2001.

Fisher, R., Ury, W. and Patton, B. (1982), *Getting to Yes – Negotiating Agreement without Giving In*, London: Hutchinson.

Foster, L.G. (1986), *A Company That Cares*, New Brunswick, NJ: Johnson & Johnson.

Gerlach, C. (2005), 'Wu-Wei in Europe. A study of Eurasian Economic Thought'. Working Papers of the Global Economic History Network (GEHN), 12/05

Ghemawat, P. and Nueno, J.L. (2003), 'ZARA: Fast Fashion', Boston, MA: Harvard Business School Case Study 703–497.

Gilpin, D.R. and Murphy, P.J. (2008), *Crisis Management in a Complex World*, Oxford University Press.

Gladwell, M. (2001), *The Tipping Point – How Little Things Can Make a Great Big Difference*, London: Abacus.

—— (2005), *Blink – The Power of Thinking Without Thinking*, London: Penguin.

Goddard, J. and Eccles, T. (2013), *Uncommon Sense, Common Nonsense - Why some organisations consistently outperform others*, Profile Books.

Goldstein et al. (2010), *Complexity and the Nexus of Leadership – Leveraging Non-Linear Science to Create Ecologies of Evolution*, Palgrave Macmillan.

Goleman, D. (2000), 'Leadership That Gets Results', *Harvard Business Review*, March–April.

Goyder, M. (1995), *Living Tomorrow's Company*, Aldershot: Gower Publishing.

Graham, G.L. (2002), 'If You Want Honesty, Break Some Rules', April, *Harvard Business Review*.

Greenleaf, R. (1977), *Servant Leadership: A Journey into the Nature of Legitimate Power & Greatness*, Mahwah, NJ: Paulist Press.

Grey, J. (1998), *False Dawn – The Delusions of Global Capitalism*, London: Granta.

Haeckel, S. (1999), *Adaptive Enterprise – Creating and Leading Sense-and-Respond Organizations*, Boston, MA: HBS Press.

Hamel, G. (2011), 'First Let's Fire All the Managers', *Harvard Business* Review, December.

Hammer, M. (1990), 'Reengineering Work: Don't Automate, Obliterate', *Harvard Business Review*, July.

—— (1996), *Beyond Re-Engineering: How the Process-Centered Organisation is Changing Our Work and Our Lives*, London: Harper Business.

—— (2001), *The Agenda – What Every Business Must Do To Dominate the Decade*, New York: Crown Publishing.

—— and Champy, J. (1993), *Re-engineering the Corporation – A Manifesto for Business Revolution*, London: Allen & Unwin.

Hardy, R. (1977), *Longbow – A Social and Military History*, New York: Arco.

Hassdorf, W. (2005), 'Emperor Without Clothes: Financial Market Sentiment and the Limits of British Currency Machismo in the ERM Crisis', *Journal of International Studies* 33:3, 691–722.

Heifitz, R., Linksy, M. and Grashow, A. (2009), *The Practice of Adaptive Leadership: Tools and Tactics for Changing Your Organization and the World*, Harvard Business Press.

Heller, F., Strauss, G., Pusic, E. and Wilpert, B. (1998), *Organizational Participation: Myth and Reality*, Oxford: Oxford University Press.

Hersey, P. and Blanchard, K.H. (1969), 'Life Cycle Theory of Leadership', *Training and Development Journal* 23, 26–33.

Hesiod (1966), *Theogony*, edited by West, M.L., Oxford: Oxford University Press, academic monograph reprints.

Hirschhorn, L. and Gilmore, T. (1992), 'The New Boundaries of the "Boundaryless" Company', *Harvard Business Review*, May–June.

Höpfl, H.M. (2000), 'Ordered Passions: Commitment and Hierarchy in the Organizational Ideas of Founders', *Management Learning* 31:3, 313–29.

Howell, L. (1969), *Freedom City: The Substance of Things Hoped For*, London: John Knox Press.

Huy, Q.N. (2000), 'In Praise of Middle Managers', *Harvard Business Review*, September.

Kirkland, R.(2004), *Taoism: The Enduring Tradition*, New York and London: Routledge.

Kay, J. (2011), *Obliquity: Why Our Goals are Best Achieved Indirectly*, Profile Books.

Jackson, M. (2004), *Systems Thinking – Creative Holism for Managers*, Wiley.

Jaworski, J. (1996), *Synchronicity – The Inner Path of Leadership*, San Francisco, CA: Berrett-Koehler.

Jomini, Henri (1805), *Traité de grande tactique, ou, Relation de la guerre de sept ans, extraite de Tempelhof, commentée at comparée aux principales opérations de la derniére guerre; avec un recueil des maximes les plus important de l'art militaire, justifiées par ces différents événéments*, Paris: Giguet et Michaud.

Jung, C. (1971), *Psychological Types*, Princeton, NJ: Princeton University.

Keller, S. and Price, C. (2011) *Beyond Performance: How Great Organisations Build Ultimate Competitive Advantage*, John Wiley & Sons.

Landsberg, M. (1997), *The Tao of Coaching*, London: Harper Collins.

La Piana, D. (2008), *The Nonprofit Strategy Revolution: Real-Time Strategic Planning in a Rapid-Response World*, Saint Paul, NM: Fieldstone Alliance.

Laszlo, E. (2006), *The Chaos Point – The World at a Crossroads*, Charlottesville, VA: Hampton Roads Publishing.

Laurent, A. and Boels, A-M. (2000), *Arbeiten in Europa: Ein Insider-Handbuch – Das Geheimnis einer Erfolgreichen Karriere im Ausland*, London: Bene Factum Publishing.

Lewin, K. (1943), 'Defining the "Field at a Given Time"', *Psychological Review* 50, 292–310.

Locke, E.A. (1968), 'Toward a Theory of Task Motivation and Incentives', *Organizational Behavior and Human Performance* 3:2, 157–89.

Lowney, C. (2005), *Heroic Leadership – Best Practices from a 450-Year-Old Company that Changed the World*, Chicago, IL: Loyola Press.

McClelland, D.C. (1961), *The Achieving Society*, Princeton, NJ: D. Van Nostrand Company Inc.

McGovern, G. (2014), 'Lead from the Heart', *Harvard Business Review*, March.

Manz, C.M. and Sims, H.P. (2001), *The New Super Leadership – Leading Others to Lead Themselves*, San Francisco, CA: Berrett-Koehler.

Marlier, D. and Parker, C. (2009), *Engaging Leadership – Three Agendas for Sustaining Achievement*, London: Macmillan.

Maslow, A. (1943), 'A Theory of Human Motivation', *Psychological Review* 50, 370–96.

Matsushita, R., Gleria, I., Figueiredo, A., and Da Silva, S., (2003), 'Fractal structure in the Chinese yuan/US dollar rate', *Economics Bulletin*, 7:2, 1–13.

May M et al (2013) *The Laws of Subtraction – Six Simple Rules for Winning*, McGraw-Hill.

Mintzberg, H. (1983), *Power In and Around Organisations*, Englewood Cliffs, NJ: Prentice Hall,

—— (1994), *The Rise and Fall of Strategic Planning*, New York: The Free Press.

—— (1978), 'Patterns in strategy formulation', *Management Science Journal,* 24:9, May.

—— and Waters, J., (1985), 'Of strategies deliberate and emergent', *Strategic Management Journal,* 6, 257–272.

Mitchell, M. (1989), 'The Impact of External Parties on Brand name Capital: The 1982 Tylenol Poisonings and Subsequent Cases', *Economic Inquiry*, 28.

Morgan C. and Langford, D. (1981), *Facts and Fallacies: A Book of Definitive Mistakes and Misguided Predictions*, London: Webb & Bower.

Morieux, Y. 'Smart Rules – Six Ways to Get People to Solve Problems Without You', *Harvard Business Review* (September 2011) series on: 'Focus on Managing Complex Organisations'.

Newton, I. (1999), *The Principia: Mathematical Principles of Natural Philosophy*. A new translation by B. Cohen, and A. Whitman, Berkeley, CA: University of California Press.

Nickols, F. (1995), 'Feedback about Feedback', *Human Resources Development Quarterly*, Jossey-Bass.

Niemi, G.R. and Weisberg, H.F. (1993), *Controversies in Voting Behavior*, Washington DC: CQ Press.

Nippert-Eng, C. (1996), *Home and Work: Negotiating Boundaries Through Everyday Life*, Chicago, IL: University of Chicago Press.

Nonaka, I. and Takeuchi, H. (1995), *The Knowledge-Creating Company: How Japanese Companies Create the Dynamics of Innovation*, New York: Oxford University Press.

Obolensky, N. (1994), *Practical Business Re-engineering: Tools and Techniques for Achieving Effective Change*, London: Kogan Page.

—— (2013) *Leading Complex Projects – Key Principles and Strategies,* ICCPM Kindle edition, Amazon.

Oncken, Jnr. W. and Wass, D.L. (1999), 'Management Time: Who's Got the Monkey?', *Harvard Business Review* article, November–December. (Reprint of popular original article from *HBR* December 1974).

Owen, H. (1992), *Open Space Technology – A User's Guide*, 2nd edition, San Francisco, CA: Berrett-Koehler Publishers.

Packman, H.M. and Casmir, F.L. (1999), 'Learning from the Euro Disney Experience – A Case Study in International/Intercultural Communication', *International Communication Gazette* 61:6.

Pascale, R. (1990), *Managing on the Edge*, London: Penguin.

Patterson, T.E. (2002), *The Vanishing Voter: Public Involvement in an Age of Uncertainty*, New York: Alfred, A. Knopf.

Patty, W.L. and Johnson, L.S. (1953), *Personality and Adjustment*, New York: McGraw-Hill.

Peters, B.G. (2001), *The Politics of Bureaucracy*, London: Routledge.

Pinchbeck, D. (2006), *2012: The Return of Quetzalcoatl*, London: Penguin.

Pink, D.H. (2009), *Drive – The Surprising Truth About What Motivates Us*, Riverhead Books.

Rackham, N. (1995), *SPIN Selling*, Aldershot: Gower.

Rasiel, E. (1999), *The McKinsey Way* 1st edition, McGraw-Hill.

Reichheld, F.F. and Teal, T. (1996), *The Loyalty Effect – The Hidden Force Beyond Growth, Profits and Lasting Value*, Boston, MA: Harvard Business School Press.

Reeves, M. and Deimler, M. (2011), 'Adaptabtibility: The New Competitive Advantage', *Harvard Business Review,* April–May.

Ryde, R. (2013), *Never Mind the Bosses: Hastening the Death of Deference for Business Success*, John Wiley & Sons.

Samuels, W.J. and Tool, M.R. (1989), *The Economy as a System of Power*, New Brunswick, NJ: Transaction.

Sachitanand, R. (2003), 'Where Employee is King', *Business Today*, 20 November.

Semler, R. (1993), *Maverick – The Success Story Behind the World's Most Unusual Workplace*, New York: Warner.

—— (2000), 'How We Went Digital Without a Strategy', *Harvard Business Review*, September-October.

Senge, P. (1990), *The Fifth Discipline: The Art and Practice of The Learning Organization*, London: Transworld.

Shelton, C.D. and Darling, J.R. (2003), 'From Theory to Practice: Using New Science Concepts to Create Learning Organizations', *The Learning Organization Journal* 10:6.

Snowden, D. and Boone, M. (2007), 'A Leaders Framework for Decision Making', *Harvard Business Review.*

Stack, J. (1992), *The Great Game of Business*, New York: Doubleday.

Stayer, R. (1990), 'How I Learned to Let My Workers Lead', *Harvard Business Review*, November–December.

Stewart, T.A. (1992), *Intellectual Capital: The New Wealth of Organizations*, New York: Doubleday Business.

Strauss, R.E. and Hummel, T. 'The New Industrial Engineering Revisited: Information Technology, Business Process R-engineering and Lean Management in the Self-organising Fractal Company', Paper published for Engineering Management Conference, 1995. Global Engineering Management: Emerging Trends in the Asia Pacific, Proceedings of 1995 IEEE Annual International.

Sullivan, T. (2011), 'Embracing Complexity – An Interview with Michael J Mauboussin', *Harvard Business Review.*

Sull, D.N. and Eisenhardt, K.M. (2012), 'Simple Rules for a Complex World', *Harvard Business Review* September 2012.

Surowiecki, J. (2004), *The Wisdom of Crowds*, New York: Doubleday.

Taylor, F.W. (1911), *The Principles of Scientific Management*, New York: Harper and Row.

Tool, M.R. and Samuel, W.J. (1989), *The Economy as a System of Power*, New Brunswick: Transaction Publishers.

Trist, E.L. (1963), *Organizational Choice: Capabilities of Groups at the Coal Face Under Changing Technologies: The Loss, Re-discovery & Transformation of a Work Tradition*, London: Tavistock Publications.

Tzu, C. (2007), *Zhuangzi*, trans. H. Hochsmann, Y. Guorong and D. Kolak, London: Prentice Hall.

Tzu, L. (1994), *Tao Te Ching*, trans. M. Kwok, eds M. Palmer and J. Ramsay, Shaftesbury: Element Classical Editions.

Tzu, S. (1910), *The Art of War* trans. Lionel Giles, Penguin.

United National Development Programme (UNDP) Human Development Report 2009, 'Overcoming Barriers: Human Mobility and Development', New York: Palgrave Macmillan.

Useem. M. (2001), *Leading Up – Managing Your Boss So You Both Win*, Crown Business.

Vroom, V.H. (1964), *Work and Motivation*, New York: John Wiley & Sons.

—— and Yetton, P. (1973), *Leadership and Decision-Making*, Pittsburgh, PA: University of Pittsburgh Press.

—— and Jago, A.G. (1988), *The New Leadership: Managing Participation in Organizations*, Englewood Cliffs, NJ: Prentice-Hall.

Warnecke, H.J. (1993), *The Fractal Company – A Revolution in Corporate Culture*

Weisbord, M. and Janoff, S. (2000), *Future Search: An Action Guide to Finding Common Ground in Organizations*, San Francisco, CA: Berrett-Koehler.

Wheatley, M. (1996), *A Simpler Way*, San Francisco: Berrett-Koehler.

—— (1999), *Leadership and the New Science – Discovering Order in a Chaotic World*, San Francisco, CA: Berret-Koehler.

White, R.P., Hodgson, P. and Crainer, S. (1996), *The Future of Leadership – Riding the Corporate Rapids into the 21st Century*, Lanham, MD: Pitman.

Wilhelm, R. and Baynes, C.F. (trans.) (2003), *I Ching or Book of Changes*, London: Penguin.

Worthy, C.J. (1986), 'Human Relations Research at Sears, Roebuck in the 1940s: A Memoir', *Academy of Management*.

Yoho, S.K. (2005), 'Toward a Contingency Model of Leadership and Psychological Empowerment: When Should Self-leadership be Encouraged?', *Journal of Leadership & Organizational Studies*, June.

Zamoyski, A. (2005), *1812 – Napoleon's Fatal March on Moscow*, London: Harper Perennial.

Zerubavel, E. (1991), *The Fine Line – Making Distinctions in Everyday Life*, New York: Free Press.

Index